FRAMING FILMS

Critical Perspectives on Film History

Natalie McKnight
Boston University

Kendall Hunt
publishing company

Kendall Hunt
publishing company

www.kendallhunt.com
Send all inquiries to:
4050 Westmark Drive
Dubuque, IA 52004-1840

Copyright © 2009 by Kendall Hunt Publishing Company

Revised Printing 2010

ISBN 978-0-7575-8412-1

Contents

Acknowledgements

The Editors of this book would like to thank the faculty (past and present) of the Humanities Division of the College of General Studies, Boston University for their wisdom and discernment in selecting films, writing film guides and designing film classes and assignments over the years. We would also like to thank Samantha Sawyer and Sarah Knockel of Kendall Hunt Publishing for their expert advice and guidance throughout this project.

Preface to Framing Films

This book has been compiled by professors teaching a freshman-level, Humanities survey course at the College of General Studies at Boston University. The two-semester, required course sequence focuses primarily on literature but also includes art, music and film history. The first semester is entitled "Traditions in the Humanities" and the second "Breaks with Tradition in the Humanities." In the first semester we begin with literature and art of the ancient world and continue to the Renaissance, tracing the development of core traditions in the arts. In the second term we begin with the Enlightenment and continue to the present, exploring noteworthy breaks with traditions in poetry, drama, and fiction that mirror similar developments in art and music. Film history is a subcomponent of the course sequence in both semesters and therefore follows its own historic timeline. We teach five or six films each semester, beginning in the fall with silent films, such as Chaplin's *The Kid or Goldrush* and finishing in the spring with more recent films, such as Jane Campion's *The Piano* and Zhang Yimou's *Hero*. The faculty select the films collaboratively, and we make changes every year. Throughout the year we introduce students to film genres and influential directors that we feel they should know. While we sometimes draw connections between the literature and the films we study, the films are never meant to illustrate literary works but are examined as their own art form. Still, we encourage students to bring the same critical reading skills to bear on films that we expect them to use in analyzing literature and art.

While our students tend to enjoy films in general, and some are true film enthusiasts and major in film studies, others find older films and foreign films hard to appreciate. They find the pace to be slower than in current films, and some don't find black-and-white film to be very stimulating. Over the years we have composed hundreds of film guides to help students see the artistry of the films we choose and to educate them about film genres and directorial styles. This book concludes with 31 film guides, ones for the films that have worked the best in class for us over the years. They are meant to give context for the films and to provide professors and students with questions that can lead to good discussions. We have also included critical essays written by renowned film critics. These also help students to see the artistry of film while demonstrating how critical reading can be applied to the film medium. The care these authors take in their approach to a range of film topics models for students the respect we hope they will cultivate for this newest art form.

Although this book has grown organically from a very specific course sequence at Boston University, we feel that it could be useful to anyone teaching a film history or film appreciation course, or anyone who regularly incorporates film into a cultural studies or humanities course. Getting students to recognize the artistry of films outside their culture or before their time takes some critical framing, and that's what we've set out to do in this book.

Part I

Film Criticism

The Cinematographic Principle and the Ideogram

Sergei Eisenstein

IT IS a weird and wonderful feat to have written a pamphlet on something that in reality does not exist. There is, for example, no such thing as a cinema without cinematography. And yet the author of the pamphlet preceding this essay* has contrived to write a book about the *cinema* of a country that has no *cinematography*. About the cinema of a country that has, in its culture, an infinite number of cinematographic traits, strewn everywhere with the sole exception of—its cinema.

This essay is on the cinematographic traits of Japanese culture that lie outside the Japanese cinema, and is itself as apart from the preceding pamphlet as these traits are apart from the Japanese cinema.

Cinema is: so many corporations, such and such turnovers of capital, so and so many stars, such and such dramas.

Cinematography is, first and foremost, montage.

The Japanese cinema is excellently equipped with corporations, actors, and stories. But the Japanese cinema is completely unaware of montage. Nevertheless the principle of montage can be identified as the basic element of Japanese representational culture.

Writing—for their writing is primarily representational.

The hieroglyph.

The naturalistic image of an object, as portrayed by the skilful Chinese hand of Ts'ang Chieh 2650 years before our era, becomes slightly formalized and, with its 539 fellows, forms the first "contingent" of hieroglyphs. Scratched out with a stylus on a slip of bamboo, the portrait of an object maintained a resemblance to its original in every respect.

But then, by the end of the third century, the brush is invented. In the first century after the "joyous event" (A.D.)— paper. And, lastly, in the year 220—India ink.

A complete upheaval. A revolution in draughtsmanship. And, after having undergone in the course of history no fewer than fourteen different styles of handwriting, the hieroglyph crystallized in its present form. The means of production (brush and India ink) determined the form.

The fourteen reforms had their way. As a result:

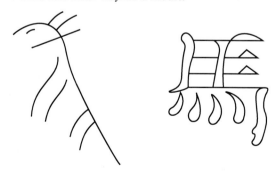

* Eisenstein's essay was originally published as an "afterword" to N. Kaufman's pamphlet, *Japanese Cinema* (Moscow, 1929).

In the fierily cavorting hieroglyph *ma* (a horse) it is already impossible to recognize the features of the dear little horse sagging pathetically in its hindquarters, in the writing style of Ts'ang Chieh, so well-known from ancient Chinese bronzes.

But let it rest in the Lord, this dear little horse, together with the other 607 remaining *hsiang cheng* symbols—the earliest extant category of hieroglyphs.

The real interest begins with the second category of hieroglyphs—the *huei-i*, i.e., "copulative."

The point is that the copulation (perhaps we had better say, the combination) of two hieroglyphs of the simplest series is to be regarded not as their sum, but as their product, i.e., as a value of another dimension, another degree; each, separately, corresponds to an *object*, to a fact, but their combination corresponds to a *concept*. From separate hieroglyphs has been fused—the ideogram. By the combination of two "depictables" is achieved the representation of something that is graphically undepictable.

For example: the picture for water and the picture of an eye signifies "to weep"; the picture of an ear near the drawing of a door = "to listen";

a dog + a mouth = "to bark";
a mouth + a child = "to scream";
a mouth + a bird = "to sing";
a knife + a heart = "sorrow," and so on.
But this is—montage!

Yes. It is exactly what we do in the cinema, combining shots that are *depictive*, single in meaning, neutral in content—into *intellectual* contexts and series.

This is a means and method inevitable in any cinematographic exposition. And, in a condensed and purified form, the starting point for the "intellectual cinema."

For a cinema seeking a maximum laconism for the visual representation of abstract concepts.

And we hail the method of the long-lamented Ts'ang Chieh as a first step along these paths.

We have mentioned laconism. Laconism furnishes us a transition to another point. Japan possesses the most laconic form of poetry: the *haikai* (appearing at the beginning of the thirteenth century and known today as "haiku" or "hokku") and the even earlier *tanka* (mythologically assumed to have been created along with heaven and earth).

Both are little more than hieroglyphs transposed into phrases. So much so that half their quality is appraised by their calligraphy. The method of their resolution is completely analogous to the structure of the ideogram.

As the ideogram provides a means for the laconic imprinting of an abstract concept, the same method, when transposed into literary exposition, gives rise to an identical laconism of pointed imagery.

Applied to the collision of an austere combination of symbols this method results in a dry definition of abstract concepts. The same method, expanded into the luxury of a group of already formed verbal combinations, swells into a splendor of *imagist* effect.

The concept is a bare formula; its adornment (an expansion by additional material) transforms the formula into an image— a finished form.

Exactly, though in reverse, as a primitive thought process— imagist thinking, displaced to a definite degree, becomes transformed to conceptual thinking.

But let us turn to examples.

The *haiku* is a concentrated impressionist sketch:

> A lonely crow
> On leafless bough,
> One autumn eve.
>
> BASHŌ

> What a resplendent moon!
> It casts the shadow of pine boughs
> Upon the mats.
>
> KIKAKU

> An evening breeze blows.
> The water ripples
> Against the blue heron's legs.
>
> BUSON

> It is early dawn.
> The castle is surrounded
> By the cries of wild ducks.
>
> KYOROKU

The earlier *tanka* is slightly longer (by two lines):

> O mountain pheasant
> long are the feathers trail'st thou
> on the wooded hill-side—
> as long the nights seem to me
> on lonely couch sleep seeking.
>
> HITOMARO[?]

From our point of view, these are montage phrases. Shot lists. The simple combination of two or three details of a material kind yields a perfectly finished representation of another kind—psychological.

And if the finely ground edges of the intellectually defined concepts formed by the combined ideograms are blurred in these poems, yet, in *emotional quality*, the concepts have blossomed forth immeasurably. We should observe that the emotion is directed towards the reader, for, as Yone Noguchi has said, "it is the readers who make the *haiku's* imperfection a perfection of art."

It is uncertain in Japanese writing whether its predominating aspect is as a system of characters (denotative), or as an independent creation of graphics (depictive). In any case, born of the dual mating of the depictive by method, and the denotative by purpose, the ideogram continued both these lines (not consecutive historically but consecutive in principle in the minds of those developing the method).

Not only did the denotative line continue into literature, in the *tanka*, as we have shown, but exactly the same method (in its depictive aspect) operates also in the most perfect examples of Japanese pictorial art.

Sharaku-creator of the finest prints of the eighteenth century, and especially of an immortal gallery of actors' portraits. The Japanese Daumier. Despite this, almost unknown to us. The characteristic traits of his work have been analyzed only in our century. One of these critics, Julius Kurth, in discussing the question of the influence on Sharaku of sculpture, draws a parallel between his wood-cut portrait of the actor Nakayama Tomisaburō and an antique mask of the semi-religious Nō theater, the mask of a Rozo.

The faces of both the print and the mask wear an *identical expression*. . . . Features and masses are similarly arranged although the mask represents an old priest, and the print a young woman. This relationship is striking, yet these two works are otherwise totally dissimilar; this in itself is a demonstration of Sharaku's originality. While the carved mask was constructed according to fairly accurate anatomical proportions, the proportions of the portrait print are simply impossible. The space between the eyes comprises a width that makes mock of all good sense. The nose is almost twice as long in relation to the eyes as any normal nose would dare to be, and the chin stands in no sort of relation to the mouth; the brows, the mouth, and every feature—is hopelessly misrelated. *This observation may be made in all the large heads by Sharaku.* That the artist was unaware that all these proportions are false is, of course, out of the question. It was with a full awareness that he repudiated normalcy, and, while the drawing of the separate features depends on severely concentrated naturalism, their proportions have been subordinated to purely intellectual considerations. *He set up the essence of the psychic expression as the norm for the proportions of the single features.*

Is not this process that of the ideogram, combining the independent "mouth" and the dissociated symbol of "child" to form the significance of "scream"?

Is this not exactly what we of the cinema do temporally, just as Sharaku in simultaneity, when we cause a monstrous disproportion of the parts of a normally flowing event, and suddenly dismember the event into "close-up of clutching hands," "medium shots of the struggle," and "extreme close-up of bulging eyes," in making a montage disintegration of the event in various planes? In making an eye twice as large as a man's full figure?! By combining these monstrous incongruities we newly collect the disintegrated event into one whole, but in *our* aspect. According to the treatment of our relation to the event.

The disproportionate depiction of an event is organically natural to us from the beginning. Professor Luriya, of the Psychological Institute in Moscow, has shown me a drawing by a child of "lighting a stove." Everything is represented in passably accurate relationship and with great care. Firewood. Stove. Chimney. But what are those zigzags in that huge central rectangle? They turn out to be—matches. Taking into account the crucial importance of these matches for the depicted process, the child provides a proper scale for them.*

The representation of objects in the actual (absolute) proportions proper to them is, of course, merely a tribute to orthodox formal logic. A subordination to an inviolable order of things.

Both in painting and sculpture there is a periodic and invariable return to periods of the establishment of absolutism. Displacing the expressiveness of archaic disproportion for regulated "stone tables" of officially decreed harmony.

Absolute realism is by no means the correct form of perception. It is simply the function of a certain form of social structure. Following a state monarchy, a state uniformity of thought is implanted. Ideological uniformity of a sort that can be developed pictorially in the ranks of colors and designs of the Guards regiments . . .

Thus we have seen how the principle of the hieroglyph— "denotation by depiction"—split in two: along the line of its purpose (the principle of "denotation"), into the principles of creating literary imagery; along the line of its method of realizing this purpose (the principle of "depiction"), into the striking methods of expressiveness used by Sharaku.*

And, just as the two outspreading wings of a hyperbola meet, as we say, at infinity (though no one has visited so distant a region!), so the principle of hieroglyphics, infinitely splitting into two parts (in accordance with the function of symbols), unexpectedly unites again from this dual estrangement, in yet a fourth sphere—in the theater.

Estranged for so long, they are once again—in the cradle period of the drama— present in a *parallel* form, in a curious dualism.

The *significance* (denotation) of the action is effected by the reciting of the *Jōruri* by a voice behind the stage—the *representation* (depiction) of the action is effected by silent marionettes on the stage. Along with a specific manner of movement this archaism migrated into the early Kabuki theater, as well. To this day it is preserved, as a partial method, in the classical repertory (where certain parts of the action are narrated from behind the stage while the actor mimes).

But this is not the point. The most important fact is that into the technique of acting itself the ideographic (montage) method has been wedged in the most interesting ways.

However, before discussing this, let us be allowed the luxury of a digression—on the matter of the shot, to settle the debated question of its nature, once and for all.

A shot. A single piece of celluloid. A tiny rectangular frame in which there is, organized in some way, a piece of an event.

---

* It is possible to trace this particular tendency from its ancient, almost pre-historical source (". . . in all ideational art, objects are given size according to their importance, the king being twice as large as his subjects, or a tree half the size of a man when it merely informs us that the scene is out-of-doors. Something of this principle of size according to significance persisted in the Chinese tradition. The favorite disciple of Confucius looked like a little boy beside him and the most important figure in any group was usually the largest.") through the highest development of Chinese art, parent of Japanese graphic arts: ". . . natural scale always had to bow to pictorial scale. . . size according to distance never followed the laws of geometric perspective but the needs of the design. Foreground features might be diminished to avoid obstruction and overemphasis, and far distant objects, which were too minute to count pictorially, might be enlarged to act as a counterpoint to the middle distance or foreground."

* It has been left to James Joyce to develop in *literature* the depictive line of the Japanese hieroglyph. Every word of Kurth's analysis of Sharaku may be applied, neatly and easily, to Joyce.

"Cemented together, these shots form montage. When this is done in an appropriate rhythm, of *course!*"

This, roughly, is what is taught by the old, old school of film-making, that sang:

"Screw by screw,
Brick by brick . . ."

Kuleshov, for example, even writes with a brick:

If you have an idea-phrase, a particle of the story, a link in the whole dramatic chain, then that idea is to be expressed and accumulated from shot-ciphers, just like bricks.

"The shot is an element of montage. Montage is an assembly of these elements." This is a most pernicious make-shift analysis.

Here the understanding of the process as a whole (connection, shot-montage) derives only from the external indications of its flow (a piece cemented to another piece). Thus it would be possible, for instance, to arrive at the well-known conclusion that street-cars exist in order to be laid across streets. An entirely logical deduction, if one limits oneself to the external indications of the functions they performed during the street-fighting of February, 1917, here in Russia. But the materialist conception of history interprets it otherwise.

The worst of it is that an approach of this kind does actually lie, like an insurmountable street-car, across the potentialities of formal development. Such an approach overrules dialectical development, and dooms one to mere evolutionary "perfecting," in so far as it gives no bite into the dialectical substance of events.

In the long run, such evolutionizing leads either through refinement to decadence or, on the other hand, to a simple withering away due to stagnation of the blood.

Strange as it may seem, a melodious witness to both these distressing eventualities, simultaneously, is Kuleshov's latest film, *The Gay Canary* [1929].

The shot is by no means an *element* of montage.

The shot is a montage *cell*.

Just as cells in their division form a phenomenon of another order, the organism or embryo, so, on the other side of the dialectical leap from the shot, there is montage.

By what, then, is montage characterized and, consequently, its cell—the shot?

By collision. By the conflict of two pieces in opposition to each other. By conflict. By collision.

In front of me lies a crumpled yellowed sheet of paper. On it is a mysterious note:

"Linkage—P" and "Collision—E."

This is a substantial trace of a heated bout on the subject of montage between P (Pudovkin) and E (myself).

This has become a habit. At regular intervals he visits me late at night and behind closed doors we wrangle over matters of principle. A graduate of the Kuleshov school, he loudly defends an understanding of montage as a *linkage* of pieces. Into a chain. Again, "bricks." Bricks, arranged in series to *expound* an idea.

I confronted him with my viewpoint on montage as a *collision*. A view that from the collision of two given factors *arises* a concept.

From my point of view, linkage is merely a possible *special* case.

Recall what an infinite number of combinations is known in physics to be capable of arising from the impact (collision) of spheres. Depending on whether the spheres be resilient, non-resilient, or mingled. Amongst all these combinations there is one in which the impact is so weak that the collision is degraded to an even movement of both in the same direction.

This is the one combination which would correspond with Pudovkin's view.

Not long ago we had another talk. Today he agrees with my point of view. True, during the interval he took the opportunity to acquaint himself with the series of lectures I gave during that period at the State Cinema Institute. . . .

So, montage is conflict.

As the basis of every art is conflict (an "imagist" transformation of the dialectical principle). The shot appears as the *cell* of montage. Therefore it also must be considered from the viewpoint of *conflict*.

Conflict within the shot is potential montage, in the development of its intensity shattering the quadrilateral cage of the shot and exploding its conflict into montage impulses *between* the montage pieces. As, in a zigzag of mimicry, the *mise-en-scène* splashes out into a spatial zigzag with the *same* shattering. As the slogan, "All obstacles are vain before Russians," bursts out in the multitude of incident of *War and Peace*.

If montage is to be compared with something, then a phalanx of montage pieces, of shots, should be compared to the series of explosions of an internal combustion engine, driving forward its automobile or tractor: for, similarly, the dynamics of montage serve as impulses driving forward the total film.

Conflict within the frame. This can be very varied in character: it even can be a conflict in—the story. As in that "prehistoric" period in films (although there are plenty of instances in the present, as well), when entire scenes would be photographed in a single, uncut shot. This, however, is outside the strict jurisdiction of the film-form.

These are the "cinematographic" conflicts within the frame:

Conflict of graphic directions.

(*Lines—either static or dynamic*)

Conflict of scales.
Conflict of volumes.
Conflict of masses.

(*Volumes filled with various intensities of light*)

Conflict of depths.

And the following conflicts, requiring only one further impulse of intensification before flying into antagonistic pairs of pieces:

Close shots and long shots.

Pieces of graphically varied directions. Pieces resolved in volume, with pieces resolved in area.

Pieces of darkness and pieces of lightness.

And, lastly, there are such unexpected conflicts as:

Conflicts between an object and its dimension—and conflicts between an event and its duration.

These may sound strange, but both are familiar to us. The first is accomplished by an optically distorted lens, and the second by stop-motion or slow-motion.

The compression of all cinematographic factors and properties within a single dialectical formula of conflict is no empty rhetorical diversion.

We are now seeking a unified system for methods of cinematographic expressiveness that shall hold good for all its elements. The assembly of these into series of common indications will solve the task as a whole.

Experience in the separate elements of the cinema cannot be absolutely measured.

Whereas we know a good deal about montage, in the theory of the shot we are still floundering about amidst the most academic attitudes, some vague tentatives, and the sort of harsh radicalism that sets one's teeth on edge.

To regard the frame as a particular, as it were, molecular case of montage makes possible the direct application of montage practice to the theory of the shot.

And similarly with the theory of lighting. To sense this as a collision between a stream of light and an obstacle, like the impact of a stream from a fire-hose striking a concrete object, or of the wind- buffeting a human figure, must result in a usage of light entirely different in comprehension from that employed in playing with various combinations of "gauzes" and "spots."

Thus far we have one such significant principle of conflict: *the principle of optical counterpoint.*

And let us not now forget that soon we shall face another and less simple problem in counterpoint: *the conflict in the sound film of acoustics and optics.*

Let us return to one of the most fascinating of optical conflicts: the conflict between the frame of the shot and the object!

The camera position, as a materialization of the conflict between organizing logic of the director and the inert logic of the object, in collision, reflects the dialectic of the camera-angle.

In this matter we are still impressionistic and lacking in principle to a sickening degree. Nevertheless, a sharpness of principle can be had in the technique of this, too. The dry quadrilateral, plunging into the hazards of nature's diffuseness . . .

And once again we are in Japan! For the cinematographic method is used in teaching drawing in Japanese schools.

What is our method of teaching drawing? Take any piece of white paper with four corners to it. Then cram onto it, usually even without using the edges (mostly greasy from the long drudgery!), some bored caryatid, some conceited Corinthian capital, or, a plaster Dante (not the magician performing at the Moscow Hermitage, but the other one—Alighieri, the comedy writer).

The Japanese approach this from a quite different direction:

Here's the branch of a cherry-tree. And the pupil cuts out from this whole, with a square, and a circle, and a rectangle-compositional units:

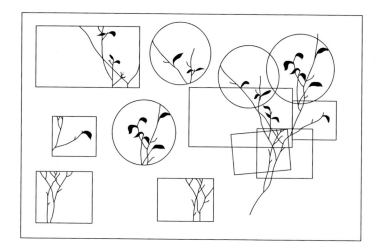

He frames a shot!

These two ways of teaching drawing can characterize the two basic tendencies struggling within the cinema of today. One—the expiring method of artificial spatial organization of an event in front of the lens. From the "direction" of a sequence, to the erection of a Tower of Babel in front of the lens. The other—a "picking-out" by the camera: organization by means of the camera. Hewing out a piece of actuality with the ax of the lens.

However, at the present moment, when the center of attention is finally beginning, in the intellectual cinema, to be transferred from the materials of cinema, as such, to "deductions and conclusions," to "slogans" based on the material, both schools of thought are losing distinction in their differences and can quietly blend into a synthesis.

Several pages back we lost, like an overshoe in a street-car, the question of the theater. Let us turn back to the question of methods of montage in the Japanese theater, particularly in acting.

The first and most striking example, of course, is the purely cinematographic method of "acting without transitions." Along with mimic transitions carried to a limit of refinement, the Japanese actor uses an exactly contrary method as well. At a certain moment of his performance he halts; the black-shrouded *kurogo* obligingly conceals him from the spectators. And lo!—he is resurrected in a new make-up. And in a new wig. Now characterizing another stage (degree) of his emotional state.

Thus, for example, in the Kabuki play *Narukami*, the actor Sadanji must change from drunkenness to madness. This transition is solved by a mechanical cut. And a change in the arsenal of grease-paint colors on his face, emphasizing those streaks whose duty it is to fulfill the expression of a higher intensity than those used in his previous make-up.

This method is organic to the film. The forced introduction into the film, by European acting traditions, of pieces of "emotional transitions" is yet another influence forcing the cinema to mark time. Whereas the method of "cut" acting makes possible the construction of entirely new methods. Replacing one changing face with a whole scale of facial types of varying moods affords a far more acutely expressive result than does the changing surface, too receptive and devoid of organic resistance, of any single professional actor's face.

In our new film [*Old and New*] I have eliminated the intervals between the sharply contrasting polar stages of a face's expression. Thus is achieved a greater sharpness in the "play of doubts" around the new cream separator. Will the milk thicken or no? Trickery? Wealth? Here the psychological process of mingled faith and doubt is broken up into its two extreme states of joy (confidence) and gloom (disillusionment). Furthermore, this is sharply emphasized by light—illumination in no wise conforming to actual light conditions. This brings a distinct strengthening of the tension.

Another remarkable characteristic of the Kabuki theater is the principle of "disintegrated" acting. Shocho, who played the leading female rôles in the Kabuki theater that visited Moscow, in depicting the dying daughter in *Yashaō* (*The Mask-Maker*), performed his rôle in pieces of acting completely detached from each other: Acting with only the right arm. Acting with one leg. Acting with the neck and head only. (The whole process of the death agony was disintegrated into solo performances of each member playing its own rôle: the rôle of the leg, the rôle of the arms, the rôle of the head.) A break-ing-up into shots. With a gradual shortening of these separate, successive pieces of acting as the tragic end approached.

Freed from the yoke of primitive naturalism, the actor is enabled by this method to fully grip the spectator by "rhythms," making not only acceptable, but definitely attractive, a stage built on the most consecutive and detailed flesh and blood of naturalism.

Since we no longer distinguish in principle between questions of shot-content and montage, we may here cite a third example:

The Japanese theater makes use of a slow tempo to a degree unknown to our stage. The famous scene of hara-kiri in *Chushingura* is based on an unprecedented slowing down of all movement—beyond any point we have ever seen. Whereas, in the previous example, we observed a disintegration of the transitions between movements, here we see disintegration of the process of movement, viz., slow-motion. I have heard of only one example of a thorough application of this method, using the technical possibility of the film with a compositionally reasoned plan. It is usually employed with some purely pictorial aim, such as the "submarine kingdom" in *The Thief of Bagdad*, or to represent a dream, as in *Zvenigora*. Or, more often, it is used simply for formalist jackstraws and unmotivated camera mischief as in Vertov's *Man with the Movie-Camera*. The more commendable example appears to be in Jean Epstein's *La chute de la Maison Usher*—at least according to the press reports. In this film, normally acted emotions filmed with a speeded-up camera are said to give unusual emotional pressure by their unrealistic slowness on the screen. If it be borne in mind that the effect of an actor's performance on the audience is based on its identification by each spectator, it will be easy to relate both examples (the Kabuki play and the Epstein film) to an identical causal explanation. The intensity of perception increases as the didactic process of identification proceeds more easily along a disintegrated action.

Even instruction in handling a rifle can be hammered into the tightest motormentality among a group of raw recruits if the instructor uses a "break-down" method.

The most interesting link of the Japanese theater is, of course, its link with the sound film, which can and must learn its fundamentals from the Japanese—the reduction of visual and aural sensations to a common physiological denominator.*

* Discussed in the preceding essay.—EDITOR.

So, it has been possible to establish (cursorily) the permeation of the most varied branches of Japanese culture by a pure cinematographic element—its basic nerve, montage.

And it is only the Japanese cinema that falls into the same error as the "leftward drifting" Kabuki. Instead of learning how to extract the principles and technique of their remarkable acting from the traditional feudal forms of their materials, the most progressive leaders of the Japanese theater throw their energies into an adaptation of the spongy shapelessness of our own "inner" naturalism. The results are tearful and saddening. In its cinema Japan similarly pursues imitations of the most revolting examples of American and European entries in the international commercial film race.

To understand and apply her cultural peculiarities to the cinema, this is the task of Japan! Colleagues of Japan, are you really going to leave this for us to do?

1929

Comedy's Greatest Era

James Agee

In the language of screen comedians four of the main grades of laugh are the titter, the yowl, the belly laugh and the boffo. The titter is just a titter. The yowl is a runaway titter. Anyone who has ever had the pleasure knows all about a belly laugh. The boffo is the laugh that kills. An ideally good gag, perfectly constructed and played, would bring the victim up this ladder of laughs by cruelly controlled degrees to the top rung, and would then proceed to wobble, shake, wave and brandish the ladder until he groaned for mercy. Then, after the shortest possible time out for recuperation, he would feel the first wicked tickling of the comedian's whip once more and start up a *new ladder*.

The reader can get a fair enough idea of the current state of screen comedy by asking himself how long it has been since he has had that treatment. The best of comedies these days hand out plenty of titters and once in a while it is possible to achieve a yowl without overstraining. Even those who have never seen anything better must occasionally have the feeling, as they watch the current run or, rather, trickle of screen comedy, that they are having to make a little cause for laughter go an awfully long way. And anyone who has watched screen comedy over the past ten or fifteen years is bound to realize that it has quietly but steadily deteriorated. As for those happy atavists who remember silent comedy in its heyday and the belly laughs and boffos that went with it, they have something close to an absolute standard by which to measure the deterioration.

When a modern comedian gets hit on the head, for example, the most he is apt to do is look sleepy. When a silent comedian got hit on the head he seldom let it go so flatly. He realized a broad license, and a ruthless discipline within that license. It was his business to be as funny as possible physically, without the help or hindrance of words. So he gave us a figure of speech, or rather of vision, for loss of consciousness. In other words he gave us a poem, a kind of poem, moreover, that everybody understands. The least he might do was to straighten up stiff as a plank and fall over backward with such skill that his whole length seemed to slap the floor at the same instant. Or he might make a cadenza of it—look vague, smile like an angel, roll up his eyes, lace his fingers, thrust his hands palms downward as far as they would go, hunch his shoulders, rise on tiptoe, prance ecstatically in narrowing circles until, with tallow knees, he sank down the vortex of his dizziness to the floor and there signified nirvana by kicking his heels twice, like a swimming frog.

Startled by a cop, this same comedian might grab his hatbrim with both hands and yank it down over his ears, jump high in the air, come to earth in a split violent enough to telescope his spine, spring thence into a coattail-flattening sprint and dwindle at rocket speed to the size of a gnat along the grand, forlorn perspective of some lazy back boulevard.

Those are fine clichés from the language of silent comedy in its infancy. The man who could handle them properly combined several of the more difficult accomplishments of the *acrobat*, the *dancer*, the *clown* and the *mime*. Some very gifted comedians, unforgettably Ben Turpin, had an immense vocabulary of these clichés and were in part so lovable because they were deep conservative classicists and never tried to break away from them. The still more gifted men, of course, simplified and invented, finding out new and much deeper uses for the idiom. They learned to show emotion through it, and comic psychology, more eloquently than most language has ever managed to, and they discovered beauties of comic motion which are hopelessly beyond reach of words.

It is hard to find a theater these days where a comedy is playing; in the days of the silents it was equally hard to find a theater which was not showing one. The laughs today are pitifully few, far between, shallow, quiet, and short. They almost never build, as they used to, into something combining the jabbering frequency of a machine gun with the delirious momentum of a roller coaster. Saddest of all, there are few comedians now below middle age and there are none who seem to learn much from picture to picture, or to try anything new.

To put it unkindly, the only thing wrong with screen comedy today is that it takes place on a screen which talks. Because it talks, the only comedians who ever mastered the screen cannot work, for they cannot combine their comic style with talk. Because there is a screen, talking comedians are trapped into a continual exhibition of their inadequacy as screen comedians on a surface as big as the side of a barn.

At the moment, as for many years, the chances to see silent comedy are rare. There is a smattering of it on television—too often treated as something quaintly archaic, to be laughed at, not with. Some two hundred comedies—long and short—can be rented for home projection. And a lucky minority has access to the comedies in the collection of New York's Museum of Modern Art, which is still incomplete but which is probably the best in the world. In the near future, however, something of this lost art will return to regular theaters. A thick straw in the wind is the big business now being done by a series of revivals of W. C. Field's memorable movies, a kind of comedy more akin to the old silent variety than anything which is being made today. Mack Sennett now is preparing a sort of potpourri variety show called *Down Memory Lane* made up out of his old movies, featuring people like Fields and Bing Crosby when they were movie beginners, but including also interludes from silents. Harold Lloyd has re-released *Movie Crazy*, a talkie, and plans to revive four of his best silent comedies, *Grandma's Boy, Safety Last, Speedy* and *The Freshman*. Buster Keaton hopes to remake at feature length, with a minimum of dialogue, two of the funniest short comedies ever made, one about a porous homemade boat and one about a prefabricated house.

Awaiting these happy events, we will discuss here what has gone wrong with screen comedy and what, if anything, can be done about it. But mainly we will try to suggest what it was like in its glory in the years from 1912 to 1930, as practiced by the employees of Mack Sennett, the father of American screen comedy, and by the four most eminent masters: Charlie Chaplin, Harold Lloyd, the late Harry Langdon and Buster Keaton.

Mack Sennett made two kinds of comedy: parody laced with slapstick, and plain slapstick. The parodies were the unceremonious burial of a century of hamming, including the new hamming in serious movies, and nobody who has missed Ben Turpin in *A Small Town Idol*, or kidding Erich von Stroheim in *Three Foolish Weeks* or as *The Shriek of Araby*, can imagine how rough parody can get and still remain subtle and roaringly funny. The plain slapstick, at its best, was even better: a profusion of hearty young women in disconcerting bathing suits, frisking around with a gaggle of insanely incompetent policemen and of equally certifiable male civilians sporting museum-piece mustaches. All these people zipped and caromed about the pristine world of the screen as jazzily as a convention of water bugs. Words can hardly suggest how energetically they collided and bounced apart, meeting in full gallop around the corner of a house; how hard and how often they fell on their backsides; or with what fantastically adroit clumsiness they got themselves fouled up in folding ladders, garden hoses, tethered animals and each other's headlong cross-purposes. The gestures were ferociously emphatic; not a line or motion of the body was wasted or inarticulate. The reader may remember how splendidly upright wandlike old Ben Turpin could stand for a Renunciation Scene, with his lampshade mustache twittering and his sparrowy chest stuck out and his head flung back like Paderewski assaulting a climax and the long babyish back hair trying to look lionlike, while his Adam's apple, an orange in a Christmas stocking, pumped with noble emotion. Or huge Mack Swain, who looked like a hairy mushroom, rolling his eyes in a manner patented by French romantics and gasping in some dubious ectasy. Or Louise Fazenda, the perennial farmer's daughter and the perfect low-comedy housemaid, primping her spit curl; and how her hair tightened a good-looking face into the incarnation of rampant gullibility. Or snouty James Finlayson, gleefully foreclosing a mortgage, with his look of eternally tasting a spoiled pickle. Or Chester Conklin, a myopic and inebriated little walrus stumbling around in outsize pants. Or Fatty Arbuckle, with his cold eye and his loose, serene smile, his silky manipulation of his bulk and his satanic marksmanship with pies (he was ambidextrous and could simultaneously blind two people in opposite directions).

The intimate tastes and secret hopes of these poor ineligible dunces were ruthlessly exposed whenever a hot stove, an electric fan or a bulldog took a dislike to their outer garments: agonizingly elaborate drawers, worked up on some lonely evening out of some Godforsaken lace curtain; or men's underpants with big round black spots on them. The Sennett sets—delirious wallpaper, megalomaniacally scrolled iron beds, Grand Rapids *in extremis*—outdid even the underwear. It was their business, after all, to kid the squalid braggadocio which infested the domestic interiors of the period, and that was almost beyond parody. These comedies told their stores to the unaided eye, and by every means possible they screamed to it. That is one reason for the India ink silhouettes of the cops, and for convicts and prison bars and their shadows in hard sunlight, and for bare-footed husbands, in tigerish pajamas, reacting like dervishes to stepped-on tacks.

The early silent comedians never strove for or consciously thought of anything which could be called artistic "form," but they achieved it. For Sennett's rival, Hal Roach, Leo McCarey once devoted almost the whole of a Laurel and Hardy two-reeler to pie throwing. The first pies were thrown thoughtfully, almost philosophically.

Then innocent bystanders began to get caught into the vortex. At full pitch it was Armageddon. But everything was calculated so nicely that until late in the picture, when havoc took over, every pie made its special kind of point and piled on its special kind of laugh.

Sennett's comedies were just a shade faster and fizzier than life. According to legend (and according to Sennett) he discovered the tempo proper to screen comedy when a green cameraman, trying to save money, cranked too slow. Realizing the tremendous drumlike power of mere motion to exhilarate, he gave inanimate objects a mischievous life of their own, broke every law of nature the tricked camera would serve him for and made the screen dance like a witches' Sabbath. The thing one is surest of all to remember is how toward the end of nearly every Sennett comedy, a chase (usually called the "rally") built up such a majestic trajectory of pure anarchic motion that bathing girls, cops, comics, dogs, cats, babies, automobiles, locomotives, innocent bystanders, sometimes what seemed like a whole city, an entire civilization, were hauled along head over heels in the wake of that energy like dry leaves following an express train.

"Nice" people, who shunned all movies in the early days, condemned the Sennett comedies as vulgar and naive. But millions of less pretentious people loved their sincerity and sweetness, their wild-animal innocence and glorious vitality. They could not put these feelings into words, but they flocked to the silents. The reader who gets back deep enough into that world will probably even remember the theater: the barefaced honky-tonk and the waltzes by Waldteufel, slammed out on a mechanical piano; the searing redolence of peanuts and demirep perfumery, tobacco and feet and sweat; the laughter of unrespectable people having a hell of a fine time, laughter as violent and steady and deafening as standing under a waterfall.

Sennett wheedled his first financing out of a couple of ex-bookies to whom he was already in debt. He took his comics out of music halls, burlesque, vaudeville, circuses and limbo, and through them he tapped in on that great pipeline of horsing and miming which runs back unbroken through the fairs of the Middle Ages at least to ancient Greece. He added all that he himself had learned about the large and spurious gesture, the late decadence of the Grand Manner, as a stage-struck boy in East Berlin, Connecticut, and as a frustrated opera singer and actor. The only thing he claims to have invented is the pie in the face, and he insists, "Anyone who tells you he has discovered something new is a fool or a liar or both."

The silent-comedy studio was about the best training school the movies have ever known, and the Sennett studio was about as free and easy and as fecund of talent as they came. All the major comedians we will mention worked there, at least briefly. So did some of the major stars of the '20s and since—notably Gloria Swanson, Phyllis Haver, Wallace Beery, Marie Dressier and Carole Lombard. Directors Frank Capra, Leo McCarey and George Stevens also got their start in silent comedy; much that remains most flexible, spontaneous and visually alive in sound movies can be traced, through them and others, to this silent apprenticeship. Everybody did pretty much as he pleased on the Sennett lot, and everybody's ideas were welcome. Sennett posted no rules, and the only thing he strictly forbade was liquor. A Sennett story conference was a most informal affair. During the early years, at least, only the most important scenario might be jotted on the back of an envelope. Mainly Sennett's men thrashed out a few primary ideas and carried them in their heads, sure that better stuff would turn up while they were shooting, in the heat of physical action. This put quite a load on the prop man; he had to have the most improbable apparatus on hand—bombs, trick telephones, what not—to implement whatever idea might suddenly turn up. All kinds of things did—and were recklessly used. Once a low-comedy auto got out of control and killed the cameraman, but he was not visible in the shot, which was thrilling and undamaged; the audience never knew the difference.

Sennett used to hire a "wild man" to sit in on his gag conferences, whose whole job was to think up "wildies." Usually he was an all but brainless, speechless man, scarcely able to communicate his idea; but he had a totally uninhibited imagination. He might say nothing for an hour; then he'd mutter, "You take . . ." and all the relatively rational others would shut up and wait. "You take this cloud . . ." he would get out, sketching vague shapes in the air. Often he could get no further; but thanks to some kind of thought transference, saner men would take this cloud and make something of it. The wild man seems in fact to have functioned as the group's subconscious mind, the source of all creative energy. His ideas were so weird and amorphous that Sennett can no longer remember a one of them, or even how it turned out after rational processing. But a fair equivalent might be one of the best comic sequences in a Laurel and Hardy picture. It is simple enough—simple and real, in fact, as a nightmare. Laurel and Hardy are trying to move a piano across a narrow suspension bridge. The bridge is slung over a sickening chasm, between a couple of Alps. Midway they meet a gorilla.

Had he done nothing else, Sennett would be remembered for giving a start to three of the four comedians who now began to apply their sharp individual talents to this newborn language. The one whom he did not train (he was on the lot briefly but Sennett barely remembers seeing him around) wore glasses, smiled a great deal and looked like the sort of eager young man who might have quit divinity school to hustle brushes. That was Harold Lloyd. The others were grotesque and poetic in their screen characters in degrees which appear to be impossible when the magic of silence is broken. One, who never smiled, carried a face as still and sad as a daguerreotype through some of the most preposterously ingenious and visually satisfying physical comedy ever invented. That was Buster Keaton. One looked like an elderly baby and, at times, a baby dope fiend; he could do more with less than any other comedian. That was Harry Langdon. One looked like Charlie Chaplin, and he was the first man to give the silent language a soul.

When Charlie Chaplin started to work for Sennett he had chiefly to reckon with Ford Sterling, the reigning comedian. Their first picture together amounted to a duel before the assembled professionals. Sterling, by no means untalented, was a big man with a florid Teutonic style which, under this special pressure, he turned on full blast. Chaplin defeated him within a few minutes with a wink of the mustache, a hitch of the trousers, a quirk of the little finger.

With *Tillie's Punctured Romance*, in 1914, he became a major star. Soon after, he left Sennett when Sennett refused to start a landslide among the other comedians by meeting the raise Chaplin demanded. Sennett is understandably wry about it in retrospect, but he still says, "I was right at the time." Of Chaplin he says simply, "Oh well, he's just the greatest artist that ever lived." None of Chaplin's former rivals rates him much lower than that; they speak of him no more jealously than they might of God. We will try here only to suggest the essence of his supremacy. Of all comedians he worked most deeply and most shrewdly within a realization of what a human being is, and is up against. The Tramp is as centrally representative of humanity, as many-sided and as mysterious, as Hamlet, and it seems unlikely that any dancer or actor can ever have excelled him in eloquence, variety or poignancy of motion. As for pure motion, even if he had never gone on to make his magnificent feature-length comedies, Chaplin would have made his period in movies a great one singlehanded even if he had made nothing except *The Cure*, or *One A.M.* In the latter, barring one immobile taxi driver, Chaplin plays alone, as a drunk trying to get upstairs and into bed. It is a sort of inspired elaboration on a soft-shoe dance, involving an angry stuffed wildcat, small rugs on slippery floors, a Lazy Susan table, exquisite footwork on a flight of stairs, a contretemps with a huge, ferocious pendulum and the funniest and most perverse Murphy bed in movie history—and, always made physically lucid, the delicately weird mental processes of a man ethereally sozzled.

A shivering Tramp in *The Gold Rush* (1925). "Of all comedians he worked most deeply and most shrewdly within a realization of what a human being is, and is up against. . . . The finest pantomime, the deepest emotion, the richest and most poignant poetry were in Chaplin's work" (AGEE, pages 542, 544).

© Charles Chaplin / Photofest

Before Chaplin came to pictures people were content with a couple of gags per comedy; he got some kind of laugh every second. The minute he began to work he set standards—and continually forced them higher. Anyone who saw Chaplin eating a boiled shoe like brook trout in *The Gold Rush*, or embarrassed by a swallowed whistle in *City Lights*, has seen perfection. Most of the time, however, Chaplin got his laughter less from the gags, or from milking them in any ordinary sense, than through his genius for what may be called *inflection*—the perfect, changeful shading of his physical and emotional attitudes toward the gag. Funny as his bout with the Murphy bed is, the glances of awe, expostulation and helpless, almost whimpering desire for vengeance which he darts at this infernal machine are even better.

A painful and frequent error among tyros is breaking the comic line with a too-big laugh, then a letdown; or with a laugh which is out of key or irrelevant. The masters could ornament the main line beautifully; they never addled it. In *A Night Out* Chaplin, passed out, is hauled along the sidewalk by the scruff of his coat by staggering Ben Turpin. His toes trail; he is as supine as a sled. Turpin himself is so drunk he can hardly drag him. Chaplin comes quietly to, realizes how well he is being served by his struggling pal, and with a royally delicate gesture plucks and savors a flower.

The finest pantomime, the deepest emotion, the richest and most poignant poetry were in Chaplin's work. He could probably pantomime Bryce's *The American Commonwealth* without ever blurring a syllable and make it paralyzingly funny into the bargain. At the end of *City Lights* the blind girl who has regained her sight, thanks to the Tramp, sees him for the first time. She has imagined and anticipated him as princely, to say the least; and it has never seriously occurred to him that he is inadequate. She recognizes who he must be by his shy, confident, shining joy as he comes silently toward her. And he recognizes himself, for the first time, through the terrible changes in her face. The camera just exchanges a few quiet close-ups of the emotions which shift and intensify in each face. It is enough to shrivel the heart to see, and it is the greatest piece of acting and the highest moment in movies.

Harold Lloyd worked only a little while with Sennett. During most of his career he acted for another major comedy producer, Hal Roach. He tried at first to offset Chaplin's influence and establish his own individuality by playing Chaplin's exact opposite, a character named Lonesome Luke who wore clothes much too small for him and whose gestures were likewise as un-Chaplinesque as possible. But he soon realized that an opposite in itself was a kind of slavishness. He discovered his own comic identify when he saw a movie about a fighting parson: a hero who wore glasses. He began to think about those glasses day and night. He decided on horn rims because they were youthful, ultravisible on the screen and on the verge of becoming fashionable (he was to make them so). Around these large lensless horn rims he began to develop a new character, nothing grotesque or eccentric, but a fresh, believable young man who could fit into a wide variety of stories.

Lloyd depended more on story and situation than any of the other major comedians (he kept the best stable of gagmen in Hollywood, at one time hiring six); but unlike most "story" comedians he was also a very funny man from inside. He had, as he has written, "an unusually large comic vocabulary." More particularly he had an expertly expressive body and even more expressive teeth, and out of this thesaurus of smiles he could at a moment's notice blend prissiness, breeziness and asininity, and still remain tremendously likable. His movies were more extroverted and closer to ordinary life than any others of the best comedies: the vicissitudes of a New York taxi driver; the unaccepted college boy who, by desperate courage and inspired ineptitude, wins the Big Game. He was especially good at putting a very timid, spoiled or brassy young fellow through devastating embarrassments. He went through one of his most uproarious Gethsemanes as a shy country youth courting the nicest girl in town in *Grandma's Boy*. He arrived dressed "strictly up to date for the Spring of 1862," as a subtitle observed, and found that the ancient colored butler wore a similar flowered waistcoat and moldering cut-away. He got one wandering, nervous forefinger dreadfully stuck in a fancy little vase. The girl began cheerfully to try to identify that queer smell which dilated from him; Grandpa's best suit was rife with mothballs. A tenacious litter of kittens feasted off the goose grease on his home-shined shoes.

Lloyd was even better at the comedy of thrills. In *Safety Last*, as a rank amateur, he is forced to substitute for a human fly and to climb a medium-sized skyscraper. Dozens of awful things happen to him. He gets fouled up in a tennis net. Popcorn falls on him from a window above, and the local pigeons treat him like a cross between a lunch wagon and St. Francis of Assisi. A mouse runs up his britches leg, and the crowd below salutes his desperate dance on the window ledge with wild applause of the daredevil. A good deal of this full-length picture hangs thus by its eyelashes along the face of a building. Each new floor is like a new stanza in a poem; and the higher and more horrifying it gets, the funnier it gets.

In this movie Lloyd demonstrates beautifully his ability to do more than merely milk a gag, but to top it. (In an old, simple example of topping, an incredible number of tall men get, one by one, out of a small closed auto. After as many have clambered out as the joke will bear, one more steps out: a midget. That tops the gag. Then the auto collapses. That tops the topper.) In *Safety Last* Lloyd is driven out to the dirty end of a flagpole by a furious dog; the pole breaks and he falls, just managing to grab the minute hand of a huge clock. His weight promptly pulls the hand down from IX to VI. That would be more than enough for any ordinary comedian, but there is further logic in the situation. Now, hideously, the whole clockface pulls loose and slants from its trembling springs above the street. Getting out of difficulty with the clock, he makes still further use of the instrument by getting one foot caught in one of these obstinate springs.

A proper delaying of the ultrapredictable can of course be just as funny as a properly timed explosion of the unexpected. As Lloyd approaches the end of his horrible hegira up the side of the building in *Safety Last*, it becomes clear to the audience, but not to him, that if he raises his head another couple of inches he is going to get murderously conked by one of the four arms of a revolving wind gauge. He delays the evil moment almost interminably, with one distraction and another, and every delay is a suspense-tightening laugh; he also gets his foot nicely entangled in a rope, so that when he does get hit, the payoff of one gag sends him careening head downward through the abyss into another. Lloyd was outstanding even among the master craftsmen at setting up a gag clearly, culminating and getting out of it deftly, and linking it smoothly to the next. Harsh experience also taught him a deep and fundamental rule: Never try to get "above" the audience.

Lloyd tried it in *The Freshman*. He was to wear an unfinished, basted-together tuxedo to a college party, which would gradually fall apart as he danced. Lloyd decided to skip the pants, a low-comedy cliché, and lose just the coat. His gag men warned him. A preview proved how right they were. Lloyd had to reshoot the whole expensive sequence, build it around defective pants and climax it with the inevitable. It was one of the funniest things he ever did.

When Lloyd was still a very young man he lost about half his right hand (and nearly lost his sight) when a comedy bomb exploded prematurely. But in spite of his artificially built-out hand he continued to do his own dirty work, like all of the best comedians. The side of the building he climbed in *Safety Last* did not overhang the street, as it appears to. But the nearest landing place was a roof three floors below him, as he approached the top, and he did everything, of course, the hard way, i.e., the comic way, keeping his bottom stuck well out, his shoulders hunched, his hands and feet skidding over perdition.

If great comedy must involve something beyond laughter, Lloyd was not a great comedian. If plain laughter is any criterion—and it is a healthy counterbalance to the other—few people have equaled him, and nobody has ever beaten him.

Chaplin and Keaton and Lloyd were all more like each other, in one important way, than Harry Langdon was like any of them. Whatever else the others might be doing, they all used more or less elaborate physical comedy; Langdon showed how little of that one might use and still be a great silent-screen comedian. In his screen character he symbolized something as deeply and centrally human, though by no means as rangily so, as the Tramp. There was, of course, an immense difference in inventiveness and range of virtuosity. It seemed as if Chaplin could do literally anything, on any instrument in the orchestra. Langdon had one queerly toned, unique little reed. But out of it he could get incredible melodies.

Like Chaplin, Langdon wore a coat which buttoned on his wishbone and swung out wide below, but the effect was very different: he seemed like an outsized baby who had begun to outgrow his clothes. The crown of his hat was rounded and the brim was turned up all around, like a little boy's hat, and he looked as if he wore diapers under his pants. His walk was that of a child which has just got sure on its feet, and his body

Harold Lloyd in trouble in *Safety Last* (1923). "Lloyd was outstanding . . . at setting up a gag clearly, culminating and getting out of it deftly, and linking it smoothly to the next" (AGEE, pages 546–48).

© Pathe Exchange / Photofest

A childish Harry Langdon (complete with bicycle) tips his hat to a gun moll in *Long Pants* (1927). "Langdon's magic was in his innocence . . . [he] looked like an elderly baby and, at times, a baby dope fiend . . ." (AGEE, pages 542, 551).

© First National Pictures / Photofest.

and hands fitted that age. His face was kept pale to show off, with the simplicity of a nursery school drawing, the bright, ignorant, gentle eyes and the little twirling mouth. He had big moon cheeks, with dimples, and a Napoleonic forelock of mousy hair; the round, docile head seemed large in ratio to the cream-puff body. Twitchings of his face were signals of tiny discomforts too slowly registered by a tinier brain; quick, squirty little smiles showed his almost prehuman pleasures, his incurably premature trustfulness. He was a virtuoso of hesitations and of delicately indecisive motions, and he was particularly fine in a high wind, rounding a corner with a kind of skittering toddle, both hands nursing his hatbrim.

He was as remarkable a master as Chaplin of subtle emotional and mental process and operated much more at leisure. He once got a good three hundred feet of continuously bigger laughs out of rubbing his chest, in a crowded vehicle, with Limburger cheese, under the misapprehension that it was a cold salve. In another long scene, watching a brazen show girl change her clothes, he sat motionless, back to the camera, and registered the whole lexicon of lost innocence, shock, disapproval and disgust, with the back of his neck. His scenes with women were nearly always something special. Once a lady spy did everything in her power (under the Hays Office) to seduce him. Harry was polite, willing, even flirtatious in his little way. The only trouble was that he couldn't imagine what in the world she was leering and pawing at him for, and that he was terribly ticklish. The Mata Hari wound up foaming at the mouth.

There was also a sinister flicker of depravity about the Langdon character, all the more disturbing because babies are premoral. He had an instinct for bringing his actual adulthood and figurative babyishness into frictions as crawly as a fingernail on a slate blackboard, and he wandered into areas of strangeness which were beyond the other comedians. In a nightmare in one movie he was forced to fight a large, muscular young man; the girl Harry loved was the prize. The young man was a good boxer; Harry could scarcely lift his gloves. The contest took place in a fiercely lighted prize ring, in a prodigious pitch-dark arena. The only spectator was the girl, and she was rooting against Harry. As the fight went on, her eyes glittered ever more brightly with blood lust and, with glittering teeth, she tore her big straw hat to shreds.

Langdon came to Sennett from a vaudeville act in which he had fought a losing battle with a recalcitrant automobile. The minute Frank Capra saw him he begged Sennett to let him work with him. Langdon was almost as childlike as the character he played. He had only a vague idea of his story or even of each scene as he played it; each time he went before the camera Capra would brief him on the general situation and then, as this finest of intuitive improvisers once tried to explain his work, "I'd go into my routine." The whole tragedy of the coming of dialogue as far as these comedians were concerned—and one reason for the increasing rigidity of comedy ever since—can be epitomized in the mere thought of Harry Langdon confronted with a script.

Langdon's magic was in his innocence, and Capra took beautiful care not to meddle with it. The key to the proper use of Langdon, Capra always knew, was "the principle of the brick." "If there was a rule for writing Langdon material," he explains, "it was this: His only ally was God. Langdon might be saved by the brick falling on the cop, but it was *verboten* that he in any way motivate the brick's fall." Langdon became quickly and fantastically popular with three pictures, *Tramp, Tramp, Tramp, The Strong Man* and *Long Pants;* from then on he went downhill even faster. "The trouble was," Capra says, "that high-brow critics came around to explain his art to him. Also he developed an interest in dames. It was a pretty high life for such a little fellow." Langdon made two more pictures with highbrow writers, one of which (*Three's a Crowd*) had some wonderful passages in it, including the prize-ring nightmare; then First National canceled his contract. He was reduced to mediocre roles and two-reelers which were more rehashes of his old gags; this time around they no longer seemed funny. "He never did really understand what hit him," says Capra. "He died broke [in 1944]. And he died of a broken heart. He was the most tragic figure I ever came across in show business."

Buster Keaton started work at the age of three and a half with his parents in one of the roughest acts in vaudeville ("The Three Keatons"); Harry Houdini gave the child the name Buster in admiration for a fall he took down a flight of stairs. In his first movies Keaton teamed with Fatty Arbuckle under Sennett. He went on to become one of Metro's biggest stars and earners; a Keaton feature cost about $200,000 to make and reliably grossed $2 million. Very early in his movie career friends asked him why he never smiled on the screen. He didn't realize he didn't. He had got the deadpan habit in variety; on the screen he had merely been so hard at work it had never occurred to him there was anything to smile about. Now he tried it just once and never again. He was by his whole style and nature so much the most deeply "silent" of the silent comedians that even a smile was as deafeningly out of key as a yell. In a way his pictures are like a transcendent juggling act in which it seems that the whole universe is in exquisite flying motion and the one point of repose is the juggler's effortless, uninterested face.

Keaton's face ranked almost with Lincoln's as an early American archetype; it was haunting, handsome, almost beautiful, yet it was irreducibly funny; he improved matters by topping it off with a deadly horizontal hat, as flat and thin as a phonograph record. One can never forget Keaton wearing it, standing erect at the prow as his little boat is being launched. The boat goes grandly down the skids and, just as grandly, straight on to the bottom. Keaton never budges. The last you see of him, the water lifts the hat off the stoic head and it floats away.

21

Buster Keaton surveying the situation in _The General_ (1926). "He was by his whole style and nature so much the most deeply 'silent' of the silent comedians that even a smile was as deafeningly out of key as a yell" (AGEE, page 552).

© United Artists / Photofest.

No other comedian could do as much with the deadpan. He used this great, sad, motionless face to suggest various related things: a one-track mind near the track's end of pure insanity; mulish imperturbability under the wildest of circumstances; how dead a human being can get and still be alive; an awe-inspiring sort of patience and power to endure, proper to granite but uncanny in flesh and blood. Everything that he was and did bore out this rigid face and played laughs against it. When he moved his eyes, it was like seeing them move in a statue. His short-legged body was all sudden, machinelike angles, governed by a daft aplomb. When he swept a semaphorelike arm to point, you could almost hear the electrical impulse in the signal block. When he ran from a cop his transitions from accelerating walk to easy jog trot to brisk canter to headlong gallop to flogged-piston sprint-always floating, above this frenzy, the untroubled, untouchable face—were as distinct and as soberly in order as an automatic gearshift.

Keaton was a wonderfully resourceful inventor of mechanistic gags (he still spends much of his time fooling with Erector sets); as he ran afoul of locomotives, steamships, prefabricated and over-electrified houses, he put himself through some of the hardest and cleverest punishment ever designed for laughs. In _Sherlock Jr._, boiling along on the handlebars of a motorcycle quite unaware that he has lost his driver, Keaton whips through city traffic, breaks up a tug-of-war, gets a shovelful of dirt in the face from each of a long line of Rockette-timed ditchdiggers, approaches at high speed a log which is hinged open by dynamite precisely soon enough to let him through and, hitting an obstruction, leaves the handlebars like an arrow leaving a bow, whams through the window of a shack in which the heroine is about to be violated, and hits the heavy feet first, knocking him through the opposite wall. The whole sequence is as clean in motion as the trajectory of a bullet.

Much of the charm and edge of Keaton's comedy, however, lay in the subtle leverages of expression he could work against his nominal deadpan. Trapped in the side wheel of a ferryboat, saving himself from drowning only by walking, then desperately running, inside the accelerating wheel like a squirrel in a cage, his only real concern was, obviously, to keep his hat on. Confronted by Love, he was not as deadpan as he was cracked up to be, either; there was an odd, abrupt motion of his head which suggested a horse nipping after a sugar lump.

Keaton worked strictly for laughs, but his work came from so far inside a curious and original spirit that he achieved a great deal besides, especially in his feature-length comedies. (For plain hard laughter his nineteen short comedies—the negatives of which have been lost—were even better.) He was the only major comedian who kept sentiment almost entirely out of his work, and he brought pure physical comedy to its greatest heights. Beneath his lack of emotion he was also uninsistently sardonic; deep below that, giving a disturbing tension and grandeur to the foolishness, for those who sensed it, there was in his comedy a freezing whisper not of pathos but of melancholia. With the humor, the craftsmanship and the action there was often, besides, a fine, still and sometimes dreamlike beauty. Much of his Civil War picture *The General* is within hailing distance of Mathew Brady. And there is a ghostly, unforgettable moment in *The Navigator* when, on a deserted, softly, rolling ship, all the pale doors along a deck swing open as one behind Keaton and, as one, slam shut, in a hair-raising illusion of noise.

Perhaps because "dry" comedy is so much more rare and odd than "dry" wit, there are people who never much cared for Keaton. Those who do cannot care mildly.

As soon as the screen began to talk, silent comedy was pretty well finished. The hardy and prolific Mack Sennett made the transfer; he was the first man to put Bing Crosby and W. C. Fields on the screen. But he was essentially a silent-picture man, and by the time the Academy awarded him a special Oscar for his "lasting contribution to the comedy technique of the screen" (in 1938), he was no longer active. As for the comedians we have spoken of in particular, they were as badly off as fine dancers suddenly required to appear in plays.

Harold Lloyd, whose work was most nearly realistic, naturally coped least unhappily with the added realism of speech; he made several talking comedies. But good as the best were, they were not so good as his silent work, and by the late '30s he quit acting. A few years ago he returned to play the lead (and play it beautifully) in Preston Sturges' *The Sin of Harold Diddlebock*, but this exceptional picture—which opened, brilliantly, with the closing reel of Lloyd's *The Freshman*—has not yet been generally released.

Like Chaplin, Lloyd was careful of his money; he is still rich and active. Last June, in the presence of President Truman, he became Imperial Potentate of the A.A.O.N.M.S. (Shriners). Harry Langdon, as we have said, was a broken man when sound came in.

Up to the middle '30s Buster Keaton made several feature-length pictures (with such players as Jimmy Durante, Wallace Beery and Robert Montgomery); he also made a couple of dozen talking shorts. Now and again he managed to get loose into motion, without having to talk, and for a moment or so the screen would start singing again. But his dark, dead voice, though it was in keeping with the visual character, tore his intensely silent style to bits and destroyed the illusion within which he worked. He gallantly and correctly refuses to regard himself as "retired." Besides occasional bits, spots and minor roles in Hollywood pictures, he has worked on summer stages, made talking comedies in France and Mexico and clowned in a French circus. This summer he has played the straw hats in *Three Men on a Horse*. He is planning a television program. He also has a working agreement with Metro. One of his jobs there is to construct comedy sequences for Red Skelton.

The only man who really survived the flood was Chaplin, the only one who was rich, proud and popular enough to afford to stay silent. He brought out two of his greatest nontalking comedies, *City Lights* and *Modern Times*, in the middle of an avalanche of talk, spoke gibberish and, in the closing moments, plain English in *The Great Dictator*, and at last made an all-talking picture, *Monsieur Verdoux*, creating for that purpose an entirely new character who might properly talk a blue streak. *Verdoux* is the greatest of talking comedies though so cold and savage that it had to find its public in grimly experienced Europe.

Good comedy, and some that was better than good, outlived silence, but there has been less and less of it. The talkies brought one great comedian, the late, majestically lethargic W. C. Fields, who could not possibly have worked as well in silence; he was the toughest and the most warmly human of all screen comedians, and *It's a Gift* and *The Bank Dick*, fiendishly funny and incisive white-collar comedies, rank high among the best comedies (and best movies) ever made. Laurel and Hardy, the only comedians who managed to preserve much of the large, low style of silence and who began to explore the comedy of sound, have made nothing since 1945. Walt Disney, at his best an inspired comic inventor and teller of fairy stories, lost his stride during the war and has since regained it only at moments. Preston Sturges has made brilliant, satirical comedies, but his pictures are smart, nervous comedy-dramas merely italicized with slapstick. The Marx Brothers were sidesplitters but they made their best comedies years ago. Jimmy Durante is mainly a night-club genius; Abbott and Costello are semiskilled laborers, at best; Bob Hope is a good radio comedian with a pleasing presence, but not much more, on the screen.

There is no hope that screen comedy will get much better than it is without new, gifted young comedians who really belong in movies, and without freedom for their experiments. For everyone who may appear we have one last, invidious comparison to offer as a guidepost.

One of the most popular recent comedies is Bob Hope's *The Paleface*. We take no pleasure in blackening *The Paleface;* we single it out, rather, because it is as good as we've got. Anything that is said of it here could be said, with interest, of other comedies of our time. Most of the laughs in *The Paleface* are verbal. Bob Hope is very adroit with his lines and now and then, when the words don't get in the way, he makes a good beginning as a visual comedian. But only the beginning, never the middle or the end. He is funny, for instance, reacting to a shot of violent whisky. But he does not know how to get still funnier (i.e., how to build and milk) or how to be funniest last (i.e., how to top or cap his gag). The camera has to fade out on the same old face he started with.

One sequence is promisingly set up for visual comedy. In it, Hope and a lethal local boy stalk each other all over a cow town through streets which have been emptied in fear of their duel. The gag here is that through accident and stupidity they keep just failing to find each other. Some of it is quite funny. But the fun slackens between laughs like a weak clothesline, and by all the logic of humor (which is ruthlessly logical) the biggest laugh should come at the moment, and through the way, they finally spot each other. The sequence is so weakly thought out that at that crucial moment the camera can't afford to watch them; it switches to Jane Russell.

Now we turn to a masterpiece. In *The Navigator* Buster Keaton works with practically the same gag as Hope's duel. Adrift on a ship which he believes is otherwise empty, he drops a lighted cigarette. A girl finds it. She calls out and he hears her; each then tries to find the other. First each walks purposefully down the long, vacant starboard deck, the girl, then Keaton, turning the corner just in time not to see each other. Next time around each of them is trotting briskly, very much in earnest; going at the same pace, they miss each other just the same. Next time around each of them is going like a bat out of hell. Again they miss. Then the camera withdraws to a point of vantage at the stern, leans its chin in its hand and just watches the whole intricate superstructure of the ship as the protagonists stroll, steal and scuttle from level to level, up, down and sidewise, always managing to miss each other by hairbreadths, in an enchantingly neat and elaborate piece of timing. There are no subsidiary gags to get laughs in this sequence and there is little loud laughter; merely a quiet and steadily increasing kind of delight. When Keaton has got all he can out of this fine modification of the movie chase he invents a fine device to bring the two together: the girl, thoroughly winded, sits down for a breather, indoors, on a plank which workmen have left across sawhorses. Keaton pauses on an upper deck, equally winded and puzzled. What follows happens in a couple of seconds at most: Air suction whips his silk topper backward down a ventilator; grabbing frantically for it, he backs against the lip of the ventilator, jackknifes and falls in backward. Instantly the camera cuts back to the girl. A topper falls through the ceiling and lands tidily, right side up, on the plank beside her. Before she can look more than startled, its owner follows, head between his knees, crushes the topper, breaks the plank with the point of his spine and proceeds to the floor. The breaking of the plank smacks Boy and Girl together.

It is only fair to remember that the silent comedians would have as hard a time playing a talking scene as Hope has playing his visual ones, and that writing and directing are as accountable for the failure as Hope himself. But not even the humblest journeyman of the silent years would have let themselves off so easily. Like the masters, they knew, and sweated to obey, the laws of their craft.

1949

The One and Only . . .

Luc Sante

The Third Man (1949) is one of that handful of motion pictures (*Rashomon, Casablanca, The Searchers*) that have become archetypes—not merely a movie that would go on to influence myriad other movies but a construct that would lodge itself deep in the unconscious of an enormous number of people, including people who've never even seen the picture. The first time you see it, your experience is dotted with tiny shocks of recognition—lines and scenes and moments whose echoes have already made their way to you from intermediary sources. If you have already seen it, even a dozen or more times, the experience is like hearing a favorite piece of music—you can, as it were, sing along.

It had its origin in a sort of Ultimate Fiction Challenge gambit. "I had paid my last farewell to Harry a week ago, when his coffin was lowered into the frozen February ground, so that it was with incredulity that I saw him pass by, without a sign of recognition, among the host of strangers in the Strand," Graham Greene had written, without any idea how he would resolve the conundrum. Thus the picture seems to have been destined from the first to be a dizzying mechanical contraption, like a pinball machine.

Holly Martins (Joseph Cotten) rolls along the alleys, down the holes, up the ladders, apparently a plaything of circumstance, but one who seems to land more often than not on his feet. Oddly, World War II and its fallout seem to have had this same effect on a number of cinematic protagonists: Joel McCrea's Johnny Jones in Alfred Hitchcock's *Foreign Correspondent* (1940) and Ray Milland's Stephen Neale in Fritz Lang's *The Ministry of Fear* (1944) both follow this capricious course of constant motion and surprise, and only the latter was also written by Greene.

Although both Greene and director Carol Reed were British, and the film was partly subsidized by the British government, *The Third Man's* viewpoint seems particularly American, a fact that is only partly explained by the presence of Cotten and Orson Welles. Vienna after the war represents the ruins of Europe. It is filled, of course, with literal ruins, but the variously sinuous and palatial architecture of its more viable buildings seems ruined by irrelevance, like so many monuments to Ozymandias. Likewise, most of the Europeans on display are music-hall types—memorably played by a troupe of Austrian and German character actors—who conform magnificently to the mingled fears and derision of the untraveled American. The American is straightforward, the European circumambient, and their courses alternate between collision and side step, almost as if secondary cultural characteristics constituted a natural law.

Welles is, of course, the ghost in the machine here, for all that his actual screen time is brief. His character is alluded to in every scene, as well as the title, and he wrote the single most memorable speech in the script (Italy and the Borgias, Switzerland and cuckoo clocks). Furthermore, his exchanges with Cotten, a frequent player in his own movies, bear Welles's characteristic rhythmic stamp: undertone overlapping with overtone, lines stepping on lines in a continual roundelay of alternating currents. So it is that uninformed film buffs have sometimes suspected that he had a hand in the direction as well—all that chiaroscuro, the tilted compositions, the breathless moving-camera adventures.

In this they underestimate Carol Reed, a director far too little known in the United States, who made superb pictures both before (*Odd Man Out*, *The Fallen Idol*) and after (*Outcast of the Islands*, *Our Man in Havana*) this one. Reed was sufficiently flexible to provide a significant challenge to the auteur theory. *The Third Man* is true to his best form, engineering a tight drama with sharply drawn characters, in a setting so delineated it might also be counted as one of the cast. It is anomalous in having received a great deal of attention worldwide, becoming in effect a "big" movie; when he purposely set about making big movies later in his career, the quality and distinctiveness fell off precipitously.

The Third Man presents such a nonstop visual experience that it is easy to miss what a small, seat-of-the-pants picture it essentially was. Consider, for example, that Anton Karas, without whose score the movie would be substantially different, was found on location, playing in a restaurant. That sort of chance discovery, in the course of production, of a fundamental element of a film would have been difficult if not unthinkable in Hollywood even then. *The Third Man* is in fact a brilliant succession of dice throws, a borderline counterintuitive combination of disparate elements that somehow come together as if they had been destined to do so. It is a singular object, a fluke, a well-oiled machine, a time-capsule item, a novelty hit. There has never been another movie quite like it.

2007

The Evolution of the Language of Cinema

André Bazin

From *What is Cinema?*

By 1928 the silent film had reached its artistic peak. The despair of its elite as they witnessed the dismantling of this ideal city, while it may not have been justified, is at least understandable. As they followed their chosen aesthetic path it seemed to them that the cinema had developed into an art most perfectly accommodated to the "exquisite embarrassment" of silence and that the realism that sound would bring could only mean a surrender to chaos.

In point of fact, now that sound has given proof that it came not to destroy but to fulfill the Old Testament of the cinema, we may most properly ask if *the technical revolution created by the sound track* was in any sense *an aesthetic revolution*. In other words, did the years from 1928 to 1930 actually witness the birth of a new cinema? Certainly, as regards editing, history does not actually show as wide a breach as might be expected between the silent and the sound film. On the contrary there is discernible evidence of a close relationship between certain directors of 1925 and 1935 and especially of the 1940's through the 1950's. Compare for example Erich von Stroheim and Jean Renoir or Orson Welles, or again Carl Theodore Dreyer and Robert Bresson. These more or less clear-cut affinities demonstrate first of all that the gap separating the 1920's and the 1930's can be bridged, and secondly that certain cinematic values actually carry over from the silent of the sound film and, above all, that it is less a matter of setting silence over against sound than of contrasting certain families of styles, certain basically different concepts of cinematographic expression.

Aware as I am that the limitations imposed on this study restrict me to a simplified and to that extent enfeebled presentation of my argument, and holding it to be less an objective statement than a working hypothesis, I will distinguish, in the cinema between 1920 and 1940, between two broad and opposing trends: those *directors who put their faith in the image* and those who put *their faith in reality*. By "*image*" I here mean, very broadly speaking, *everything that the representation on the screen adds to the object there represented*. This is a complex inheritance but it can be reduced essentially to two categories: those that *relate to the plastics of the image* and those that *relate to the resources of montage*, which after all, is simply the ordering of images in time.

Under the heading "plastics" must be included the style of the sets, of the make-up, and, up to a point, even of the performance, to which we naturally add the lighting and, finally, the framing of the shot which gives us its composition. As regards montage, derived initially as we all know from the masterpieces of Griffith, we have the statement of *Malraux* in his *Psychologie du cinéma* that it was *montage* that *gave birth to film as an art*, setting it apart from mere animated photography, in short, *creating a language*.

The use of *montage* can be "*invisible*" and this was generally the case in the prewar classics of the American screen. Scenes were broken down just for one purpose, namely, to analyze an episode according to the material or dramatic logic of the scene.

It is this logic which conceals the fact of the analysis, the mind of the spectator quite naturally accepting the viewpoints of the director which are justified by the geography of the action or the shifting emphasis of dramatic interest.

But the neutral quality of this "invisible" editing fails to make use of the full potential of montage. On the other hand these potentialities are clearly evident from the three processes generally known as *parallel montage, accelerated montage, montage by attraction*. In creating parallel montage, Griffith succeeded in conveying a sense of the simultaneity of two actions taking place at a geographical distance by means of alternating shots from each. In *La Roue* Abel Gance created the illusion of the steadily increasing speed of a locomotive without actually using any images of speed (indeed the wheel could have been turning on one spot) simply by a multiplicity of shots of ever-decreasing length.

Finally there is "montage by attraction," the creation of S. M. Eisenstein, and not so easily described as the others, but which may be roughly defined as the reenforcing of the meaning of one image by association with another image not necessarily part of the same episode—for example the fireworks display in *The General Line* following the image of the bull. In this extreme form, montage by attraction was rarely used even by its creator but one may consider as very near to it in principle the more commonly used ellipsis, comparison, or metaphor, examples of which are the throwing of stockings onto a chair at the foot of a bed, or the milk overflowing in H.G. Clouzot's *Quai des orfèvres*. There are of course a variety of possible combinations of these three processes.

Whatever these may be, one can say that they share that trait in common which constitutes the *very definition of montage*, namely, *the creation of a sense or meaning not proper to the images themselves but derived exclusively from their juxtaposition*. The well-known experiment of Kuleshov with the shot of Mozhukhin in which a smile was seen to change its significance according to the image that preceded it, sums up perfectly the properties of montage.

Montage as used by Kuleshov, Eisenstein, or Gance did not give us the event; it alluded to it. Undoubtedly they derived at least the greater part of the constituent elements from the reality they were describing but the final significance of the film was found to reside in the ordering of these elements much more than in their objective content.

The matter under recital, whatever the realism of the individual image, is born essentially from these relationships—Mozhukhin plus dead child equal pity—that is to say an abstract result, none of the concrete elements of which are to be found in the premises; maidens plus appletrees in bloom equal hope. The combinations are infinite. But the only thing they have in common is the fact that they suggest an idea by means of a metaphor or by an association of ideas. Thus between the scenario properly so-called, the ultimate object of the recital, and the image pure and simple, there is a relay station, a sort of aesthetic "transformer." The meaning is not in the image, it is in the shadow of the image projected by montage onto the field of consciousness of the spectator.

Let us sum up. Through the contents of the image and the resources of montage, the cinema has at its disposal a whole arsenal of means whereby to impose its interpretation of an event on the spectator. By the end of the silent film we can consider this arsenal to have been full. On the one side the Soviet cinema carried to its ultimate consequences the theory and practice of montage while the German school did every kind of violence to the plastics of the image by way of sets and lighting. Other cinemas count too besides the Russian and German, but whether in France or Sweden or the United States, it does not appear that the language of cinema was at a loss for ways of saying what it wanted to say.

McTeague (Gibson Gowland) confronting Marcus Schouler (Jean Hersholt) in the wastes of Death Valley in *Greed* (1923); Nanook building his igloo in *Nanook of the North* (1922). Von Stroheim and Flaherty were two of "those who put their faith in reality" (BAZIN, page 124).

© MGM / Photofest

© Pathe Exchange / Photofest

If the art of cinema consists in everything that plastics and montage can add to a given reality, the silent film was an art on its own. Sound could only play at best a subordinate and supplementary role: a counterpoint to the visual image. But this possible enhancement—at best only a minor one—is likely not to weigh much in comparison with the additional bargain-rate reality introduced at the same time by sound.

Thus far we have put forward the view that expressionism of montage and image constitute the essence of cinema. And it is precisely on this generally accepted notion that directors from silent days, such as *Erich von Stroheim*, F.W. *Murnau*, and Robert *Flaherty*, have by implication cast a doubt. In their films, montage plays no part, unless it be the negative one of inevitable elimination where reality superabounds. The camera cannot see everything at once but it makes sure not to lose any part of what it chooses to see. What matters to Flaherty, confronted with Nanook hunting the seal, is the relation between Nanook and the animal; the actual length of the waiting period. Montage could suggest the time involved. Flaherty however confines himself to showing the actual waiting period; the length of the hunt is the very substance of the image, its true object. Thus in the film this episode requires one set-up. Will anyone deny that it is thereby much more moving than a montage by attraction?

Murnau is interested not so much in time as in the reality of dramatic space. Montage plays no more of a decisive part in *Nosferatu* than in *Sunrise*. One might be inclined to think that the plastics of his image are impressionistic. But this would be a superficial view. The composition of his image is in no sense pictorial. It adds nothing to the reality, it does not deform it, it forces it to reveal its structural depth, to bring out the preexisting relations which become constitutive of the drama. For example, in *Tabu*, the arrival of a ship from left screen gives an immediate sense of destiny at work so that Murnau has no need to cheat in any way on the uncompromising realism of a film whose settings are completely natural.

But it is most of all *Stroheim* who rejects photographic expressionism and the tricks of montage. In his films reality lays itself bare like a suspect confessing under the relentless examination of the commissioner of police. He has one simple rule for direction. Take a close look at the world, keep on doing so, and in the end it will lay bare for you all its cruelty and its ugliness. One could easily imagine as a matter of fact a film by Stroheim composed of a single shot as long-lasting and as close-up as you like. These three directors do not exhaust the possibilities. We would undoubtedly find scattered among the works of others elements of nonexpressionistic cinema in which montage plays no part—even including Griffith. But these examples suffice to reveal, at the very heart of the silent film, a cinematographic art the very opposite of that which has been identified as "*cinéma par excellence*," a language the semantic and syntactical unit of which is in no sense the Shot; in which the image is evaluated not according to what it adds to reality but what it reveals of it. In the latter art the silence of the screen was a drawback, that is to say, it deprived reality of one of its elements. *Greed*, like Dreyer's *Jeanne d'Arc*, is already virtually a talking film. The moment that you cease to maintain that montage and the plastic composition of the image are the very essence of the language of cinema, sound is no longer the aesthetic crevasse dividing two radically different aspects of the seventh art. The cinema that is believed to have died of the soundtrack is in no sense "*the* cinema." The real dividing line is elsewhere. It was operative in the past and continues to be through thirty-five years of the history of the language of the film.

Having challenged the aesthetic unity of the silent film and divided it off into two opposing tendencies, now let us take a look at the history of the last twenty years.

From 1930 to 1940 there seems to have grown up in the world, originating largely in the United States, a common form of cinematic language. It was the triumph in Hollywood, during that time, of five or six major kinds of film that gave it its overwhelming superiority: (1) American comedy (*Mr. Smith Goes to Washington*, 1936); (2) The burlesque film (The Marx Brothers); (3) The dance and vaudeville film (Fred Astaire and Ginger Rogers and the Ziegfield Follies); (4) The crime and gangster film (*Scarface, I Am a Fugitive from a Chain Gang, The Informer*); (5) Psychological and social dramas (*Back Street, Jezebel*); (6) Horror or fantasy films (*Dr. Jekyll and Mr. Hyde, The Invisible Man, Frankenstein*); (7) The western (*Stagecoach*, 1939). During that time the French cinema undoubtedly ranked next. Its superiority was gradually manifested by way of a trend towards what might be roughly called *stark somber realism*, or poetic realism, in which four names stand out: Jacques *Feyder*, Jean *Renoir*, Marcel *Carné*, and Julien *Duyivier*. My intention not being to draw up a list of prize-winners, there is little use in dwelling on the Soviet, British, German, or Italian films for which these years were less significant than the ten that were to follow. In any case, American and French production sufficiently clearly indicate that the sound film, prior to World War II, had reached a well-balanced stage of maturity.

First as to *content*: Major varieties with clearly defined rules capable of pleasing a worldwide public, as well as a cultured elite, provided it was not inherently hostile to the cinema.

Secondly as to *form*: well-defined styles of photography and editing perfectly adapted to their subject matter; a complete harmony of image and sound. In seeing again today such films as *Jezebel* by William Wyler, *Stagecoach* by John Ford, or *Le Jour se lève* by Marcel Carné, one has the feeling that in them an art has found its perfect balance, its ideal form of expression, and reciprocally one admires them for dramatic and moral themes to which the cinema, while it may not have created them, has given a grandeur, an artistic effectiveness, that they would not otherwise have had. In short, here are all the characteristics of the ripeness of a classical art.

I am quite aware that one can justifiably argue that the originality of the postwar cinema as compared with that of 1938 derives from the growth of certain national schools, in particular the dazzling display of the Italian cinema and of a native English cinema freed from the influence of Hollywood. From this one might conclude that the really important phenomenon of the years 1940-1950 is the introduction of new blood, of hitherto unexplored themes. That is to say, the real revolution took place more on the level of subject matter than of style. Is not neorealism primarily a kind of humanism and only secondarily a style of film-making? Then as to the style itself, is it not essentially a form of self-effacement before reality?

Our intention is certainly not to preach the glory of form over content. Art for art's sake is just as heretical in cinema as elsewhere, probably more so. On the other hand, a new subject matter demands new form, and as good a way as *any towards understanding what a film is trying to say to us is to know how it is saying it*.

Thus by 1938 or 1939 the talking film, particularly in France and in the United States, had reached a level of classical perfection as a result, on the one hand, of the maturing of different kinds of drama developed in part over the past ten years and in part inherited from the silent film, and, on the other, of the stabilization of technical progress. The 1930's were the years, at once, of sound and of panchromatic film. Undoubtedly studio equipment had continued to improve but only in matters of detail, none of them opening up new, radical possibilities for direction. The only changes in this situation since 1940 have been in photography, thanks to the increased sensitivity of the film stock. Panchromatic stock turned visual values upside down, ultrasensitive emulsions have made a modification in their structure possible. Free to shoot in the studio with a much smaller aperture, the operator could, when necessary, eliminate the *soft-focus background* once considered essential. Still there are a number of examples of the prior use of deep focus, for example in the work of Jean Renoir. This had always been possible on exteriors, and given a measure of skill, even in the studios. Anyone could do it who really wanted to. So that it is less a question basically of a technical problem, the solution of which has admittedly been made easier, than of a search after a style—a point to which we will come back. In short, with panchromatic stock in common use, with an understanding of the potentials of the microphone, and with the crane as standard studio equipment, one can really say that since 1930 all the technical requirements for the art of cinema have been available.

Since the determining technical factors were practically eliminated, we must look elsewhere for the signs and principles of the evolution of film language, that is to say by *challenging the subject matter* and *as a consequence the styles necessary for its expression.*

By 1939 the cinema had arrived at what geographers call the equilibrium-profile of a river. By this is meant that ideal mathematical curve which results from the requisite amount of erosion. Having reached this equilibrium-profile, the river flows effortlessly from its source to its mouth without further deepening of its bed. But if any geological movement occurs which raises the erosion level and modifies the height of the source, the water sets to work again, seeps into the surrounding land, goes deeper, burrowing and digging. Sometimes when it is a chalk bed, a new pattern is dug across the plain, almost invisible but found to be complex and winding, if one follows the flow of the water.

The Evolution of Editing since the Advent of Sound

In 1938 there was an almost universal standard pattern of editing. If, somewhat conventionally, we call the kind of silent films based on the plastics of the image and the artifices of montage, "expressionist" or "symbolistic," we can describe the new form of storytelling "analytic" and "dramatic." Let us suppose, by way of reviewing one of the elements of the experiment of Kuleshov, that we have a table covered with food and a hungry tramp. One can imagine that in 1936 it would have been edited as follows:

(1) Full shot of the actor and the table.

(2) Camera moves forward into a close-up of a face expressing a mixture of amazement and longing.

(3) Series of close-ups of food.

(4) Back to full shot of person who starts slowly towards the camera.

(5) Camera pulls slowly back to a three-quarter shot of the actor seizing a chicken wing.

Whatever variants one could think of for this scene, they would all have certain points in common:

(1) The verisimilitude of space in which the position of the actor is always determined, even when a close-up eliminates the decor.

(2) The purpose and the effects of the cutting are exclusively dramatic or psychological.

In other words, if the scene were played on a stage and seen from a seat in the orchestra, it would have the same meaning, the episode would continue to exist objectively. The changes of point of view provided by the camera would add nothing. They would present the reality a little more forcefully, first by allowing a better view and then by putting the emphasis where it belongs.

It is true that the stage director like the film director has at his disposal a margin within which he is free to vary the interpretation of the action but it is only a margin and allows for no modification of the inner logic of the event. Now, by way of contrast, let us take the montage of the stone lions in *The End of St. Petersburg.* By skillful juxtaposition a group of sculptured lions are made to look like a single lion getting to its feet, a symbol of the aroused masses. This clever device would be unthinkable in any film after 1932. As late as 1935 Fritz Lang, in *Fury,* followed a series of shots of women dancing the can-can with shots of clucking chickens in a farmyard. This relic of associative montage came as a shock even at the time, and today seems entirely out of keeping with the rest of the film. However decisive the art of Marcel Carné, for example, in our estimate of the respective values of *Quai des Brumes* or of *Le Jour se lève his editing remains on the level of the reality he is analyzing.* There is only one proper way of looking at it. That is why we are witnessing the almost complete disappearance of optical effects such as superimpositions, and even, especially in the United States, of the close-up, the too violent impact of which would make the audience conscious of the cutting. *In the typical American comedy* the director returns as often as he can to a shot of the characters from the knees up, which is said to be best suited to catch the spontaneous attention of the viewer—the natural point of balance of his mental adjustment.

Actually this use of montage originated with the silent movies. This is more or less the part it plays in Griffith's films, for example in *Broken Blossoms,* because with *Intolerance* he had already introduced that synthetic concept of montage which the Soviet cinema was to carry to its ultimate conclusion and which is to be found again, although less exclusively, at the end of the silent era. It is understandable, as a matter of fact, that the sound image, far less flexible than the visual image, would carry montage in the direction of realism, increasingly eliminating both plastic impressionism and the symbolic relation between images.

Thus around 1938 films were edited, almost without exception, according to the same principle. The story was unfolded in a series of set-ups numbering as a rule about 600. The characteristic procedure was by *shot-reverse-shot,* that is to say, in a dialogue scene, the camera followed the order of the text, alternating the character shown with each speech.

It was this fashion of editing, so admirably suitable for the best films made between 1930 and 1939, that was challenged by the *shot in depth introduced, by Orson Welles and William Wyler. Citizen Kane* can never be too highly praised. Thanks to the depth of field, whole scenes are covered in one take, the camera remaining motionless. Dramatic effects for which we had formerly relied on montage were created out of the movements of the actors within a fixed framework. Of course Welles did not invent the in-depth shot any more than Griffith invented the close-up. All the pioneers used it and for a very good reason. Soft focus only appeared with montage. It was not only a technical must consequent upon the use of images in juxtaposition, it was a logical consequence of montage, its plastic equivalent. If at a given moment in the action the director, as in the scene imagined above, goes to a close-up of a bowl of fruit, it follows naturally that he also isolates it in space through the focusing of the lens. The soft

The shot-in-depth from *Citizen Kane* (1941). (Note the perfect focus of the image on all three planes—the three faces extremely close to the camera, the face in the middle distance, and the letters on the sign in the far distance.) "Thanks to the depth of field, whole scenes are covered in one take, the camera remaining motionless. . . . Director and cameraman have converted the screen into a dramatic checkerboard, planned down to the last detail" (BAZIN, pages 133, 135).

© RKO Radio Pictures Inc. / Photofest

focus of the background confirms therefore the effect of montage, that is to say, while it is of the essence of the storytelling, it is only an accessory of the style of the photography. Jean Renoir had already clearly understood this, as we see from a statement of his made in 1938 just after he had made *La Bête humaine* and *La Grande illusion* and just prior to *La Règle du jeu:* "The more I learn about my trade the more I incline to direction in depth relative to the screen. The better it works, the less I use the kind of set-up that shows two actors facing the camera, like two well-behaved subjects posing for a still portrait." The truth of the matter is, that if you are looking for the precursor of Orson Welles, it is not Louis Lumière or Zecca, but rather Jean Renoir. In his films, the search after composition in depth is, in effect, a partial replacement of montage by frequent panning shots and entrances. It is based on a respect for the continuity of dramatic space and, of course, of its duration.

To anybody with eyes in his head, it is quite evident that the sequence of shots used by Welles in *The Magnificent Ambersons* is in no sense the purely passive recording of an action shot within the same framing. On the contrary, his refusal to break up the action, to analyze the dramatic field in time, is a positive action the results of which are far superior to anything that could be achieved by the classical "cut."

All you need to do is compare two frames shot in depth, one from 1910, the other from a film by Wyler or Welles, to understand just by looking at the image, even apart from the context of the film, how different their functions are. The framing in the 1910 film is intended, to all intents and purposes, as a substitute for the missing fourth wall of the theatrical stage, or at least in exterior shots, for the best vantage point to view the action, whereas in the second case the setting, the lighting, and the camera angles give an entirely different reading. Between them, director and cameraman have converted the screen into a dramatic checkerboard, planned down to the last detail. The clearest if not the most original examples of this are to be found in *The Little Foxes* where the *mise-en-scène* takes on the severity of a working drawing. Welles' pictures are more difficult to analyze because of his over-fondness for the baroque. Objects and characters are related in such a fashion that it is impossible for the spectator to miss the significance of the scene. To get the same results by way of montage would have necessitated a detailed succession of shots.

What we are saying then is that the sequence of shots "in depth" of the contemporary director does not exclude the use of montage—how could he, without reverting to a primitive babbling?—he makes it an integral part of his "plastic." The storytelling of Welles or Wyler is no less explicit that John Ford's but theirs has the advantage over his that it does not sacrifice the specific effects that can be derived from unity of image in space and time. Whether an episode is analyzed bit by bit or presented in its physical entirety cannot surely remain a matter of indifference, at least in a work with some pretensions to style. It would obviously be absurd to deny that montage has added considerably to the progress of film language, but this has happened at the cost of other values, no less definitely cinematic.

This is why *depth of field* is not just a stock in trade of the cameraman like the use of a series of filters or of such-and-such a style of lighting, it is a capital gain in the field of direction—a dialectical step forward in the history of film language.

Nor is it just a formal step forward. Well used shooting in depth is not just a more economical, a simpler, and at the same time a more subtle way of getting the most out of a scene. In addition to affecting the structure of film language, it also affects the relationships of the minds of the spectators to the image, and in consequence it influences the interpretation of the spectacle.

It would lie outside the scope of this article to analyze the psychological modalities of these relations, as also their aesthetic consequences, but it might be enough here to note, in general terms:

(1) That *depth of focus brings the spectator into a relation with the image closer to that which he enjoys with reality*. Therefore it is correct to say that independently of the contents of the image, its structure is more realistic;

(2) That it implies, consequently, both a *more active mental attitude on the part of the spectator* and *a more positive contribution on his part to the action in progress*. While *analytical montage* only calls for him to follow his guide, to let his attention follow along smoothly with that of the director who will choose what he should see, here he is called upon to exercise at least a minimum of personal choice. It is from his attention and his will that the meaning of the image in part derives.

(3) From the two preceding propositions, which belong to the realm of psychology, there follows a third which may be described as metaphysical. In analyzing reality, montage presupposes of its very nature the unity of meaning of the dramatic event. Some other form of analysis is undoubtedly possible but then it would be another film. In short, *montage by its very nature rules out ambiguity of expression*. Kulelshov's experiment proves this *per absurdum* in giving on each occasion a precise meaning to the expression on a face, the ambiguity of which alone makes the three successively exclusive expressions possible.

On the other hand, *depth of focus reintroduced ambiguity into the structure of the image* if not of necessity—Wyler's films are never ambiguous—at least as a possibility. Hence it is no exaggeration to say that *Citizen Kane* is unthinkable shot in any other way but in depth. The uncertainty in which we find ourselves as to the spiritual key or the interpretation we should put on the film is built into the very design of the image.

It is not that Welles denies himself any recourse whatsoever to the expressionistic procedures of montage, but just that their use from time to time in between sequences of shots in depth gives them a new meaning. Formerly montage was the very stuff of cinema, the texture of the scenario. In *Citizen Kane* a series of superimpositions is contrasted with a scene presented in a single take, constituting another and deliberately abstract mode of story-telling. Accelerated montage played tricks with time and space while that of Welles, on the other hand, is not trying to deceive us; it offers us a contrast, condensing time, and hence is the equivalent for example of the French imperfect or the English frequentative tense. Like accelerated montage and montage of attractions these superimpositions, which the talking film had not used for ten years, rediscovered a possible use related to temporal realism in a film without montage.

If we have dwelt at some length on Orson Welles it is because the date of his appearance in the filmic firmament (1941) marks more or less the beginning of a new period and also because his case is the most spectacular and, by virtue of his very excesses, the most significant.

Yet *Citizen Kane* is part of a general movement, of a vast stirring of the geological bed of cinema, confirming that everywhere up to a point there had been a revolution in the language of the screen.

I could show the same to be true, although by different methods, of the Italian cinema. In Roberto Rossellini's *Paisà* and *Allemania Anno Zero* and Vittorio de Sica's *Ladri de Biciclette,* Italian neo-realism contrasts with previous forms of film realism in its stripping away of all expressionism and in particular in the total absence of the effects of montage. As in the films of Welles and in spite of conflicts of style, neorealism tends to give back to the cinema a sense of the ambiguity of reality. The preoccupation of Rossellini when dealing with the face of the child in *Allemania Anno Zero* is the exact opposite of that of Kuleshov with the close-up of Mozhukhin. Rossellini is concerned to preserve its mystery. We should not be misled by the fact that the evolution of neorealism is not manifest, as in the United States, in any form of revolution in editing. They are both aiming at the same results by different methods. The means used by Rossellini and de Sica are less spectacular but they are no less determined to do away with montage and to transfer to the screen the *continuum* of reality. The dream of Zavattini is just to make a ninety-minute film of the life of a man to whom nothing ever happens. The most "aesthetic" of the neorealists, Luchino Visconti, gives just as clear a picture as Welles of the basic aim of his directorial art in *La Terra Trema,* a film almost entirely composed of one-shot sequences, thus clearly showing his concern to cover the entire action in interminable deep-focus panning shots.

However we cannot pass in review all the films that have shared in this revolution in film language since 1940. Now is the moment to attempt a synthesis of our reflections on the subject.

It seems to us that the decade from 1940 to 1950 marks a decisive step forward in the development of the language of the film. If we have appeared since 1930 to have lost sight of the trend of the silent film as illustrated particularly by Stroheim, F. W. Murnau, Robert Flaherty, and Dreyer, it is for a purpose. It is not that this trend seems to us to have been halted by the talking film. On the contrary, we believe that it represented the richest vein of the so-called silent film and, precisely because it was not aesthetically tied to montage, but was indeed the only tendency that looked to the realism of sound as a natural development. On the other hand it is a fact that the talking film between 1930 and 1940 owes it virtually nothing save for the glorious and retrospectively prophetic exception of Jean Renoir. He alone in his searchings as a director prior to *La Règle du jeu* forced himself to look back beyond the resources provided by montage and so uncovered the secret of a film form that would permit everything to be said without chopping the world up into little fragments, that would reveal the hidden meanings in people and things without disturbing the unity natural to them.

It is not a question of thereby belittling the films of 1930 to 1940, a criticism that would not stand up in the face of the number of masterpieces, it is simply an attempt to establish the notion of a dialectic progress, the highest expression of which was found in the films of the 1940's. Undoubtedly, the talkie sounded the knell of a certain aesthetic of the language of film, but only wherever it had turned its back on its vocation in the service of realism. The sound film nevertheless did preserve the essentials of montage, namely discontinuous description and the dramatic analysis of action. What it turned its back on was metaphor and symbol in exchange for the illusion of objective presentation. The expressionism of montage has virtually disappeared but the relative realism of the kind of cutting that flourished around 1937 implied a congenital limitation which escaped us so long as it was perfectly suited to its subject matter. Thus American comedy reached its peak within the framework of a form of editing in which the realism of the time played no part. Dependent on logic for its effects, like vaudeville and plays on words, entirely conventional in its moral and sociological content, American comedy had everything to gain, in strict line-by-line progression, from the rhythmic resources of classical editing.

Undoubtedly it is primarily with the Stroheim-Murnau trend—almost totally eclipsed from 1930 to 1940—that the cinema has more or less consciously linked up once more over the last ten years. But it has no intention of limiting itself simply to keeping this trend alive. It draws from it the secret of the regeneration of realism in storytelling and thus of becoming capable once more of bringing together real time, in which things exist, along with the duration of the action, for which classical editing had insidiously substituted mental and abstract time. On the other hand, so far from wiping out once and for all the conquests of montage, this reborn realism gives them a body of reference and a meaning. It is only an increased realism of the image that can support the abstraction of montage. The stylistic repertory of a director such as Hitchcock, for example, ranged from the power inherent in the basic document as such, to superimpositions, to large close-ups. But the close-ups of Hitchcock are not the same as those of C. B. de Mille in *The Cheat* [1915]. They are just one type of figure, among others, of his style. In other words, *in the silent days, montage evoked what the director wanted to say; in the editing of 1938, it described it.* Today we can say that at last the director writes in film. The image—its plastic composition and the way it is set in time, because it is founded on a much higher degree of realism—has at its disposal more means of manipulating reality and of modifying it from within. The film-maker is no longer the competitor of the painter and the playwright, he is, at last, the equal of the novelist.

1950—55

Bicycle Thieves

André Bazin

... With *Bicycle Thieves*, De Sica has managed to escape from the impasse, to reaffirm anew the entire aesthetic of neorealism.

Bicycle Thieves [1948] certainly is neorealist, by all the principles one can deduce from the best Italian films since 1946. The story is from the lower classes, almost populist: an incident in the daily life of a worker. But the film shows no extraordinary events, such as those that befell the fated workers in Gabin films. There are no crimes of passion, none of those grandiose coincidences common in detective stories, which simply transfer to a realm of proletarian exoticism the great tragic debates once reserved for the dwellers on Olympus. Truly an insignificant, even a banal, incident: a workman spends a whole day looking in vain in the streets of Rome for the bicycle someone has stolen from him. This bicycle has been the tool of his trade, and if he doesn't find it he will again be unemployed. Late in the day, after hours of fruitless wandering, he, too, tries to steal a bicycle. Apprehended and then released, he is as poor as ever, but now he feels the shame of having sunk to the level of the thief.

Plainly there is not enough material here even for a news item; the whole story would not deserve two lines in a stray-dog column. One must take care not to confuse it with realist tragedy in the Prévert or James Cain manner, where the initial news item is a diabolic trap placed by the gods amid the cobblestones of the street. In itself the event contains no proper dramatic valence. It takes on meaning only because of the social (and not psychological or aesthetic) position of the victim. Without the haunting specter of unemployment, which places the event in Italian society of 1948, it would be an utterly banal misadventure. Likewise, the choice of a bicycle as the key object in the drama is characteristic both of Italian urban life and of a period when mechanical means of transportation were still rare and expensive. There is no need to insist on the hundreds of other meaningful details that multiply the vital links between the scenario and actuality, situating the event in political and social history, in a given place, at a given time.

The techniques employed in the mise-en-scène likewise meet the most exacting specifications of Italian neorealism. Not one scene shot in a studio. Everything was filmed in the streets. As for the actors, none had the slightest experience in theater or film. The workman came from the Breda factory, the child was found hanging around in the street, the wife was a journalist.

These, then, are the facts of the case. It is clear that they do not appear to recall in any sense the neorealism of *Quattro passi fra le nuvole* [1942], *Vivere in pace* [1947], or *Shoeshine*. On the face of it, then, one should have special reasons for being wary. The sordid side of the tale tends toward that most debatable aspect of Italian stories: indulgence in the wretched, a systematic search for squalid detail.

If *Bicycle Thieves* is a true masterpiece, comparable in rigor to *Paisà* [1946], it is for certain precise reasons, none of which emerge either from a simple outline of the scenario or from a superficial disquisition on the technique of the mise-en-scène.

The scenario is diabolically clever in its construction: beginning with the alibi of a current event, it makes good use of a number of systems of dramatic coordinates radiating in all directions. *Bicycle Thieves* is certainly the only valid Communist film of

© Arthur Mayer & Joseph Burstyn Inc. / Photofest

© Arthur Mayer & Joseph Burstyn Inc. / Photofest

the whole past decade, precisely because it still has meaning even when you have abstracted its social significance. Its social message is not detached, it remains immanent in the event, but it is so clear that nobody can overlook it, still less take exception to it, since it is never made explicitly a message. The thesis implied is wondrously, outrageously simple: in the world where this workman lives, the poor must steal from each other in order to survive. But this thesis is never stated as such; it is just that events are so linked together that they have the appearance of a formal truth while retaining an anecdotal quality. Basically, the workman might have found his bicycle in the middle of the film; only then there would have been no film. (Sorry to have bothered you, the director might say, we really did think he would never find it, hut since he has, all is well, good for him, the performance is over, you can turn up the lights.) In other words, a propaganda film would try to prove that the workman could not find his bicycle, and that he is inevitably trapped in the vicious circle of poverty. De Sica limits himself to showing that the workman cannot find his bicycle and that as a result he doubtless will be unemployed again. No one can fail to see that it is the accidental nature of the script that gives the thesis its quality of necessity; the slightest doubt cast on the necessity of the events in the scenario of a propaganda film renders the argument hypothetical.

Although on the basis of the workman's misfortune we have no alternative but to condemn a certain kind of relation between a man and his work, the film never makes the events or the people part of an economic or political Manichaeism. It takes care not to cheat on reality, not only by contriving to give the succession of events the appearance of an accidental and, as it were, anecdotal chronology but in treating each of them according to its phenomenological integrity. In the middle of the chase, the little boy suddenly needs to piss. So he does. A downpour forces the father and son to shelter in a carriageway, so like them we have to forgo the chase and wait till the storm is over. The events are not necessarily signs of something, of a truth of which we are to be convinced; they all carry their own weight, their complete uniqueness, that ambiguity that characterizes any fact. So, if you do not have the eyes to see, you are free to attribute what happens to bad luck or to chance. The same applies to the people in the film. The worker is just as deprived and isolated among his fellow trade unionists as he is walking along the street or even in that ineffable scene of the Catholic "Quakers," into whose company he will shortly stray, because the trade union does not exist to find lost bikes but to transform a world in which losing his bike condemns a man to poverty. Nor does the worker come to lodge a complaint with the trade union but to find comrades who will be able to help him discover the stolen object. So here you have a collection of proletarian members of a union who behave no differently than a group of paternalistic bourgeois toward an unfortunate workman. In his private misfortune, the poster hanger is just as alone in his union as in church (buddies apart, that is—but then, who your buddies are is your own affair). But this parallel is extremely useful, because it points up a striking contrast. The indifference of the trade union is normal and justified because a trade union is striving for justice, not for charity. But the cumbersome paternalism of the Catholic Quakers is unbearable, because their eyes are closed to his personal tragedy while they in fact actually do nothing to change the world that is the cause of it. On this score, the most success-ful scene is that in the storm, under the porch, when a flock of Austrian seminarians crowd around the worker and his son. We have no valid reason to blame them for chattering so much and still less for talking German. But it would be difficult to create a more *objectively* anticlerical scene.

Clearly, and I could find twenty more examples, events and people are never introduced in support of a social thesis—but the thesis emerges fully armed and all the more irrefutable because it is presented to us as something thrown into the bargain. It is our intelligence that discerns and shapes it, not the film. De Sica wins every play on the board without ever having made a bet.

This technique is not entirely new in Italian films, and we have elsewhere stressed its value at length, both apropos of *Paisa* and of *Germany Year Zero* [1948], but these two films were based on themes from either the Resistance or the war. *Bicycle Thieves* is the first decisive example of the possibility of the conversion of this kind of objectivity to other, similar subjects. De Sica and Zavattini have transferred neorealism from the Resistance to the Revolution.

Thus the thesis of the film is hidden behind an objective social reality that in turn moves into the background of the moral and psychological drama, which could of itself justify the film. The idea of the boy is a stroke of genius, and one does not know definitely whether it came from the script or in the process of directing, so little does this distinction mean anymore. It is the child who gives to the workman's adventure its ethical dimension and fashions, from an individual moral standpoint, a drama that might well have been only social. Remove the boy, and the story remains much the same. The proof: a résumé of it would not differ in detail. In fact, the boy's part is confined to trotting along beside his father. But he is the intimate witness of the tragedy, its private chorus. It is supremely clever to have virtually eliminated the role of the wife in order to give flesh and blood to the private character of the tragedy in the person of the child. The complicity between father and son is so subtle that it reaches down to the foundations of the moral life. It is the admiration the child feels for his father and the father's awareness of it that gives its tragic stature to the ending. The public shame of the worker, exposed and clouted in the open street, is of little account compared with the fact that his son witnessed it. When he feels tempted to steal the bike, the silent presence of the little child, who guesses what his father is thinking, is cruel to the verge of obscenity. Trying to get rid of him by sending him to take the streetcar is like telling a child in some cramped apartment to go and wait on the landing outside for an hour. Only in the best Chaplin films are there situations of an equally overwhelming conscience.

In this connection, the final gesture of the little boy, in giving his hand to his father, has been frequently misinterpreted. It would be unworthy of the film to see here a concession to the feelings of the audience. If De Sica gives them this satisfaction it is because it is a logical part, of the drama. This experience marks henceforth a definite stage in the relations between father and son, rather like reaching puberty. Up to that moment the man has been like a god to his son; their relations came under the heading of admiration. By his action the father has now compromised them. The tears they shed as they walk side by side, arms swinging, signify their despair over a paradise lost. But the son returns to a father who has fallen from grace. He will love him henceforth as a human being, shame and all. The hand that slips into his is neither a symbol of forgiveness nor of a childish act of consolation. It is rather the most solemn gesture that could ever mark the relations between a father and a son: one that makes them equals.

It would take too long to enumerate the multiple secondary functions of the boy in the film, both as to the story structure and as to the mise-en-scène itself. However, one should at least pay attention to the change of tone (almost in the musical sense of the term) that his presence introduces into the middle of the film. As we slowly wander back and forth between the little boy and the workman, we are taken from the social and economic plane to that of their private lives, and the supposed death by drowning of the child, in making the father suddenly realize the relative insignificance of his misfortune, creates a dramatic oasis (the restaurant scene) at the heart of the story. It is, however, an illusory one, because the reality of this intimate happiness in the long run depends on the precious bike. Thus the child provides a dramatic reverse that, as the occasion arises, serves as a counterpoint, as an accompaniment, or moves, on the contrary, into the foreground of the melodic structure. This function in the story is, furthermore, clearly observable in the orchestration of the steps of the child and of the grown-up. Before choosing this particular child, De Sica did not ask him to perform, just to walk. He wanted to play off the striding gait of the man against the short trotting steps of the child, the harmony of this discord being for him of capital importance for the understanding of the film as a whole. It would be no exaggeration to say that *Bicycle Thieves* is the story of a walk through Rome by a father and his son. Whether the child is ahead, behind, alongside—or when, sulking after having his ears boxed, he is dawdling behind in a gesture of revenge—what he is doing is never without meaning. On the contrary, it is the phenomenology of the script.

It is difficult, after the success of this pairing of a workman and his son, to imagine De Sica having recourse to established actors. The absence of professional actors is nothing new. But here again *Bicycle Thieves* goes further than previous films. Henceforth the cinematic purity of the actors does not derive from skill, luck, or a happy combination of a subject, a period, and a people. Probably too much importance has been attached to the ethnic factor. Admittedly, the Italians, like the Russians, are the most naturally theatrical of people. In Italy any little street urchin is the equal of a Jackie Coogan, and life is a perpetual commedia dell'arte. However, it seems to me unlikely that these acting talents are shared equally by the Milanese, the Neapolitans, the peasants of the Po, or the fishermen of Sicily. Racial difference apart, the contrasts in their history, language, and economic and social condition would suffice to cast doubt on a thesis that sought to attribute the natural acting ability of the Italian people simply to an ethnic quality. It is inconceivable that films as different as *Paisà, Bicycle Thieves, La terra trema* [1948J, and even *Cielo sulla palude* [1949] could share in common such a superbly high level of acting. One could conceive that the urban Italian has a special gift for spontaneous histrionics, but the peasants in *Cielo sulla palude* are absolute cavemen beside the farmers of *Farrebique* [1946]. Merely to recall [Georges] Rouquier's film in connection with [Augusto] Genina's is enough at least in this respect to relegate the experiment of the French director to the level of a touchingly patronizing effort. Half the dialogue in Farrebique is spoken offstage, because Rouquier could never get the peasants not to laugh during a speech of any length. Genina in *Cielo sulla palude*, Visconti in *La terra trema*, both handling peasants or fishermen by the dozen, gave them complicated roles and got them to recite long speeches in scenes in which the camera concentrated on their faces as pitilessly as in an American studio. It is an understatement to say that these temporary actors are good or even perfect. In these films the very concept of actor, performance, character has no longer any meaning. An actorless cinema? Undoubtedly. But the original meaning of the formula is now outdated, and we should talk today of cinema without acting, of a cinema of which we no longer ask whether the character gives a good performance or not, since here man and the character he portrays are so completely one.

We have not strayed as far as it might seem from *Bicycle Thieves*. De Sica hunted for his cast for a long time and selected them for specific characteristics. Natural nobility, that purity of countenance and bearing that the common people have . . . He hesitated for months between this person and that, took a hundred tests only to decide finally, in a flash and by intuition, on the basis of a silhouette suddenly come upon at the bend of a road. But there is nothing miraculous about that. It is not the unique excellence of this workman and this child that guarantees the quality of their performance, but the whole aesthetic scheme into which they are fitted. When De Sica was looking for a producer to finance his film, he finally found one, but on condition that the workman was played by Cary Grant. The mere statement of the problem in these terms shows the absurdity of it. Actually, Cary Grant plays this kind of part extremely well, but it is obvious that the question here is not one of playing a part but of getting

© Arthur Mayer & Joseph Burstyn Inc. / Photofest

© Arthur Mayer & Joseph Burstyn Inc. / Photofest

away from the very notion of doing any such thing. The worker had to be at once as perfect and as anonymous and as objective as his bicycle.

This concept of the actor is no less "artistic" than the other. The performance of this workman implies as many gifts of body and of mind and as much capacity to take direction as any established actor has at his command. Hitherto films that have been made either totally or in part without actors, such as *Tabú* [1931], *Thunder over Mexico* [1933], and *Mother* [1926], have seemingly boon successes that are either out of the ordinary or limited to a certain genre. There is nothing, on the other hand, unless it be sound prudence, to prevent De Sica from making fifty films like *Bicycle Thieves*. From now on we know that the absence of professional actors in no way limits the choice of subject. The film without names has finally established its own aesthetic existence. This in no sense means that the cinema of the future will no longer use actors; De Sica, who is one of the world's finest actors, would be the first to deny this. All it means is that some subjects handled in a certain style can no longer be made with professional actors and that the Italian cinema has definitely imposed these working conditions, just as naturally as it imposed authentic settings. It is this transition from an admirable tour de force, precarious as this maybe, into an exact and infallible technique that marks a decisive stage in the growth of Italian neorealism.

With the disappearance of the concept of the actor into a transparency seemingly as natural as life itself comes the disappearance of the set. Let us understand one another, however. De Sica's film took a long time to prepare, and everything was as minutely planned as for a studio superproduction, which as a matter of fact allows for last-minute improvisations, but 1'cannot remember a single shot in which a dramatic effect is born of the shooting script properly so called, which seems as neutral as in a Chaplin film. All the same, the numbering and titling of shots does not noticeably distinguish *Bicycle Thieves* from any ordinary film. But their selection has been made with a view to raising the limpidity of the event to a maximum, while keeping the index of refraction from the style to a minimum.

This objectivity is rather different from Rossellini's in *Paisà*, but it belongs to the same school of aesthetics. One may criticize it on the same grounds that Gide and Martin du Garde criticized romantic prose—that it must tend in the direction of the most neutral kind of transparency. Just as the disappearance of the actor is the result of transcending a style of performance, the disappearance of the mise-en-scène is likewise the fruit of a dialectical progress in the style of the narrative. If the event is sufficient unto itself without the direction having to shed any further light on it by means of camera angles, purposely chosen camera positions, it is because it has reached that stage of perfect luminosity that makes it possible for an art to unmask a nature that in the end resembles it. That is why the impression made on us by *Bicycle Thieves* is unfailingly that of truth.

If this supreme naturalness, the sense of events observed haphazardly as the hours roll by, is the result of an ever-present although invisible system of aesthetics, it is definitely the prior conception of the scenario that allows this to happen. Disappearance of the actor, disappearance of mise-en-scène? Unquestionably, but because the very principle of *Bicycle Thieves* is the disappearance of a story.

The term is equivocal. I know of course that there is a story but of a different kind from those we ordinarily see on the screen. This is even the reason why De Sica could not find a producer to back him. When Roger Leenhardt, in a prophetic critical statement, asked years ago "if the cinema is a spectacle," he was contrasting the dramatic cinema with the novel-like structure of the cinematic narrative. The former borrows from the theater its hidden springs. Its plot, conceived as it may be specifically for the screen, is still the alibi for an action identical in essence with the action of the classical theater. On this score, the film is a spectacle like a play. But on the other hand, because of its realism and the equal treatment it gives to man and to nature, the cinema is related, aesthetically speaking, to the novel.

Without going too far into a theory of the novel—a debatable subject—let us say that the narrative form of the novel or that which derives from it differs by and large from the theater in the primacy given to events over action, to succession over causality, to mind over will. The conjunction belonging to the theater is *therefore*, the particle belonging to the novel is *then*. This scandalously rough definition is correct to the extent that it characterizes the two different movements of the mind in thinking, namely that of the reader and that of the onlooker. Proust can lose us in a madeleine, but a playwright fails in his task if every reply does not link our interest to the reply that is to follow. That is why a novel may be laid down and then picked up again. A play cannot be cut into pieces. The total unity of a spectacle is of its essence. To the extent that it can realize the physical requirements of a spectacle, the cinema cannot apparently escape the spectacle's psychological laws, but it has also at its disposal all the resources of the novel. For that reason, doubtless, the cinema is congenitally a hybrid. It conceals a contradiction. Besides, clearly, the progression of the cinema is toward increasingly its novel-like potential. Not that we are against filmed theater, but if the screen can in some conditions develop and give a new dimension to the theater, it is of necessity at the expense of certain scenic values—the first of which is the physical presence of the actor. Contrariwise, the novel at least ideally need surrender nothing to the cinema. One may think of the film as a supernovel of which the written form is a feeble and provisional version.

This much briefly said, how much of it can be found in the present condition of the cinematographic spectacle? It is impossible to overlook the spectacular and theatrical needs demanded of the screen. What remains to be decided is how to reconcile the contradiction.

The Italian cinema of today is the first anywhere in the world to have enough courage to cast aside the imperatives of the spectacular. *La terra trema* and *Cielo sulla palude* are films without "action," in the unfolding of which, somewhat after the style of the epic novel, no concession is made to dramatic tension. Things happen in them, each at its appointed hour, one after the other, but each carries an equal weight. If some are fuller of meaning than others, it is only in retrospect. We are free to use either *therefore* or *then*. *La terra trema*, especially, is a film destined to be virtually a commercial failure, unexploitable without cuts that would leave it unrecognizable.

That is the virtue of De Sica and Zavattini. Their *Bicycle Thieves* is solidly structured in the mold of tragedy. There is not one frame that is not charged with an intense dramatic power, yet there is not one either that we cannot fail to find interesting, its dramatic continuity apart.

The film unfolds on the level of pure accident: the rain, the seminarians, the Catholic Quakers, the restaurant—all these are seemingly interchangeable, no one seems to have arranged them in order on a dramatic spectrum. The scene in the thieves' quarter is significant. We are not sure that the man who was chased by the workman is actually the bicycle thief, and we shall never know if the epileptic fit was a pretense or genuine. As an "action" this episode would be meaningless had not its novel-like interest, its value as a fact, given it a dramatic meaning to boot.

It is in fact on its reverse side, and by parallels, that the action is assembled—less in terms of "tension" than of a "summation" of the events. Yes it is a spectacle, and what a spectacle! *Bicycle Thieves*, however, does not depend on the mathematical elements of drama; the action does not exist beforehand as if it were an "essence." It follows from the preexistence of the narrative, it is the "integral" of reality. De Sica's supreme achievement, which others have so far only approached with a varying degree of success or failure, is to have succeeded in discovering the cinematographic dialectic capable of transcending the contradiction between the action of a "spectacle" and of an event. For this reason, *Bicycle Thieves* is one of the first examples of pure cinema. No more actors, no more story, no more sets, which is to say that in the perfect aesthetic illusion of reality, there is no more cinema.

Renowned French film critic André Bazin wrote this essay in 1949, several years after he first championed Italian neorealism. It was a time when many critics were beginning to argue that neorealism's moment had passed, that its signature components—lower-class characters, socially minded stories, location shooting—were being co-opted in more mainstream film "spectacles" and melodramas, and that neorealism proper, grounded in a very specific postwar moment and embodied in such works as Roberto Rossellini's *Rome, Open City* (1945) and Vittorio De Sica's *Shoeshine* (1946), had run its course. The piece, excerpted here, is Bazin's impassioned case for neorealism's adaptability and continued relevance—as seen in De Sica's *Bicycle Thieves*.

Notes on the Auteur Theory in 1962

Andrew Sarris

> *I call these sketches Shadowgraphs, partly by the designation to remind you at once that they derive from the darker side of life, partly because, like other shadowgraphs, they are not directly visible. When I take a shadowgraph in my hand, it makes no impression on me, and gives me no clear conception of it. Only when I hold it up opposite the wall, and now look not directly at it, but at that which appears on the wall, am I able to see it. So also with the picture I wish to show here, an inward picture that does not become perceptible until I see it through the external. This external is perhaps not quite unobtrusive, but, not until I look through it, do I discover that inner picture that I desire to show you, an inner picture too delicately drawn to be outwardly visible, woven as it is of the tenderest moods of the soul.*
>
> SØREN KIERKEGAARD, in *Either/Or*

An exhibitor once asked me if an old film I had recommended was *really* good or good only according to the *auteur* theory. I appreciate the distinction. Like the alchemists of old, *auteur* critics are notorious for rationalizing leaden clinkers into golden nuggets. Their judgments are seldom vindicated, because few spectators are conditioned to perceive in individual works the organic unity of a director's career. On a given evening, a film by John Ford must take its chances as if it were a film by Henry King. Am I implying that the weakest Ford is superior to the strongest King? Yes! This kind of unqualified affirmation seems to reduce the *auteur* theory to a game of aesthetic solitaire with all the cards turned face up. By *auteur* rules, the Fords will come up aces as invariably as the Kings will come up deuces. Presumably, we can all go home as soon as the directorial signature is flashed on the screen. To those who linger, *The Gunfighter* (King 1950) may appear worthier than *Flesh* (Ford 1932). (And how deeply one must burrow to undermine Ford!) No matter. The *auteur* theory is unyielding. If, by definition, Ford is invariably superior to King, any evidence to the contrary is merely an optical illusion. Now what could be sillier than this inflexible attitude? Let us abandon the absurdities of the *auteur* theory so that we may return to the chaos of common sense.

My labored performance as devil's advocate notwithstanding, I intend to praise the *auteur* theory, not to bury it. At the very least, I would like to grant the condemned system a hearing before its execution. The trial has dragged on for years, I know, and everyone is now bored by the abstract reasoning involved. I have little in the way of new evidence or new arguments, but I would like to change some of my previous testimony. What follows is, consequently, less a manifesto than a credo, a somewhat disorganized credo, to be sure, expressed in formless notes rather than in formal brief.

I. AIMEZ-VOUS BRAHMS?

> *Goethe? Shakespeare? Everything signed with their names is considered good, and one wracks one's brains to find beauty in their stupidities and failures, thus distorting the general taste. All these great talents, the Goethes, the Shakespeares, the Beethovens, the Michelangelos, created, side by side with their masterpieces, works not merely mediocre, but quite simply frightful.*
>
> —Leo Tolstoy, *Journal*, 1895–99

The preceding quotation prefaces the late André Bazin's famous critique of "*la politique des auteurs*," which appeared in the *Cahiers du Cinéma* of April, 1957. Because no comparably lucid statement opposing the *politique* has appeared since that time, I would like to discuss some of Bazin's arguments with reference to the current situation. (I except, of course, Richard Roud's penetrating article "The French Line," which dealt mainly with the post-*Nouvelle Vague* situation when the *politique* had degenerated into McMahonism.)

As Tolstoy's observation indicates, *la politique des auteurs* antedates the cinema. For centuries, the Elizabethan *politique* has decreed the reading of every Shakespearean play before any encounter with the Jonsonian repertory. At some point between *Timon of Athens* and *Volpone*, this procedure is patently unfair to Jonson's reputation. But not really. On the most superficial level of artistic reputations, the *auteur* theory is merely a figure of speech. If the man in the street could not invoke Shakespeare's name as an identifiable cultural reference, he would probably have less contact with all things artistic. The Shakespearean scholar, by contrast, will always be driven to explore the surrounding terrain, with the result that all the Elizabethan dramatists gain more rather than less recognition through the pre-eminence of one of their number. Therefore, on balance, the *politique*, as a figure of speech, does more good than harm.

Occasionally, some iconoclast will attempt to demonstrate the fallacy of this figure of speech. We will be solemnly informed that *The Gambler* was a potboiler for Dostoyevsky in the most literal sense of the word. In Jacques Rivette's *Paris Nous Appartient*, Jean-Claude Brialy asks Betty Schneider if she would still admire *Pericles* if it were not signed by Shakespeare. Zealous musicologists have played *Wellington's Victory* so often as an example of inferior Beethoven that I have grown fond of the piece, atrocious as it is. The trouble with such iconoclasm is that it presupposes an encyclopedic awareness of the *auteur* in question. If one is familiar with every Beethoven composition, *Wellington's Victory*, in itself, will hardly tip the scale toward Mozart, Bach, or Schubert. Yet that is the issue raised by the *auteur* theory. If not Beethoven, who? And why? Let us say that the *politique* for composers went Mozart, Beethoven, Bach, and Schubert. Each composer would represent a task force of compositions, arrayed by type and quality with the mighty battleships and aircraft carriers flanked by flotillas of cruisers, destroyers, and mine sweepers. When the Mozart task force collides with the Beethoven task force, symphonies roar against symphonies, quartets maneuver against quartets, and it is simply no contest with the operas. As a single force, Beethoven's nine symphonies, outgun any nine of Mozart's forty-one symphonies, both sets of quartets are almost on a par with Schubert's, but *The Magic Flute*, *The Marriage of Figaro*, and *Don Giovanni* will blow poor *Fidelio* out of the water. Then, of course, there is Bach with an entirely different deployment of composition and instrumentation. The Haydn and Handel cultists are moored in their inlets ready to join the fray, and the moderns with their nuclear noises are still mobilizing their forces.

It can be argued that any exact ranking of artists is arbitrary and pointless. Arbitrary up to a point, perhaps, but pointless, no. Even Bazin concedes the polemical value of the *politique*. Many film critics would rather not commit themselves to specific rankings ostensibly because every film should be judged on its own merits. In many instances, this reticence masks the critic's condescension to the medium. Because it has not been firmly established that the cinema is an art at all, it requires cultural audacity to establish a pantheon for film directors. Without such audacity, I see little point in being a film critic. Anyway, is it possible to honor a work of art without honoring the artist involved? I think not. Of course, any idiot can erect a pantheon out of hearsay and gossip. Without specifying any work, the Saganesque seducer will ask quite cynically, "Aimez-vous Brahms?" The fact that Brahms is included in the pantheon of high-brow pickups does not invalidate the industrious criticism that justifies the composer as a figure of speech.

Unfortunately, some critics have embraced the *auteur* theory as a short-cut to film scholarship. With a "you-see-it-or-you-don't" attitude toward the reader, the particularly lazy *auteur* critic can save himself the drudgery of communication and explanation. Indeed, at their worst, *auteur* critiques are less meaningful than the straight-forward plot reviews that pass for criticism in America. Without the necessary research and analysis, the *auteur* theory can degenerate into the kind of snobbish racket that is associated with the merchandising of paintings.

It was largely against the inadequate theoretical formulation of *la politique des auteurs* that Bazin was reacting in his friendly critique. (Henceforth, I will abbreviate *la politique des auteurs* as the *auteur* theory to avoid confusion.) Bazin introduces his arguments within the context of a family quarrel over the editorial policies of *Cahiers*. He fears that, by assigning reviews to admirers of given directors, notably Alfred Hitchcock, Jean Renoir, Roberto Rossellini, Fritz Lang, Howard Hawks, and Nicholas Ray, every work, major and minor, of these exalted figures is made to radiate the same beauties of style and meaning. Specifically, Bazin notes a distortion when the kindly indulgence accorded the imperfect work of a Minnelli is coldly withheld from the imperfect work of Huston. The inherent bias of the *auteur* theory magnifies the gap between the two films.

I would make two points here. First, Bazin's greatness as a critic, (and I believe strongly that he was the greatest film critic who ever lived) rested in his disinterested conception of the cinema as a universal entity. It follows that he would react against a theory that cultivated what he felt were inaccurate judgments for the sake of dramatic paradoxes. He was, if anything, generous to a fault, seeking in every film some vestige of the cinematic art. That he would seek justice for Huston vis-à-vis Minnelli on even the secondary levels of creation indicates the scrupulousness of his critical personality.

However, my second point would seem to contradict my first. Bazin was wrong in this instance, insofar as any critic can be said to be wrong in retrospect. We are dealing here with Minnelli in his *Lust for Life* period and Huston in his *Moby Dick* period. Both films can be considered failures on almost any level. The miscasting alone is disastrous. The snarling force of Kirk Douglas as the tormented Van Gogh, the brutish insensibility of Anthony Quinn as Gauguin, and the nervously scraping tension between these two absurdly limited actors, deface Minnelli's meticulously objective decor, itself inappropriate for the mood of its subject. The director's presentation of the paintings themselves is singularly unperceptive in the repeated failure to maintain the proper optical distance from canvases that arouse the spectator less by their detailed draughtsmanship than by the shock of a *gestalt* wholeness. As for *Moby Dick*, Gregory Peck's Ahab deliberates long enough to let all the demons flee the Pequod, taking Melville's Lear-like fantasies with them. Huston's epic technique with its casually shifting camera viewpoint then drifts on an intellectually becalmed sea toward a fitting rendezvous with a rubber whale. These two films are neither the best nor the worst of their time. The question is: Which deserves the harder review? And there's the rub. At the time, Huston's stock in America was higher than Minnelli's. Most critics expected Huston to do "big" things, and, if they thought about it at all, expected Minnelli to stick to "small" things like musicals. Although neither film was a critical failure, audiences stayed away in large enough numbers to make the cultural respectability of the projects suspect. On the whole, *Lust for Life* was more successful with the audiences it did reach than was *Moby Dick*.

In retrospect, *Moby Dick* represents the turning downward of Huston as a director to be taken seriously. By contrast, *Lust for Life* is simply an isolated episode in the erratic career of an interesting stylist. The exact size of Minnelli's talent may inspire controversy, but he does represent something in the cinema today. Huston is virtually a forgotten man with a few actors' classics behind him surviving as the ruins of a once-promising career. Both Eric Rohmer, who denigrated Huston in 1957, and Jean Domarchi, who was kind to Minnelli that same year, somehow saw the future more clearly on an *auteur* level than did Bazin. As Santayana has remarked: "It is a great advantage for a system of philosophy to be substantially true." If the *auteur* critics of the 1950's had not scored so many coups of clairvoyance, the *auteur* theory would not be worth discussing in the 1960's. I must add that, at the time, I would have agreed with Bazin on this and every other objection to the *auteur* theory, but subsequent history, that history about which Bazin was always so mystical, has substantially confirmed most of the principles of the *auteur* theory–ironically, most of the original supporters of the *auteur* theory have now abandoned it. Some have discovered more useful *politiques* as directors and would-be directors. Others have succumbed to a European-oriented pragmatism where intention is now more nearly equal to talent in critical relevance. Luc Moullet's belated discovery that Samuel Fuller was, in fact, fifty years old, signaled a reorientation of *Cahiers* away from the American cinema. (The handwriting was already on the wall when Truffaut remarked recently that, whereas he and his colleagues had "discovered" *auteurs*, his successors have "invented" them.)

Bazin then explores the implications of Giraudoux's epigram: "There are no works; there are only authors." Truffaut has seized upon this paradox as the battle cry of *la politique des auteurs*. Bazin casually demonstrates how the contrary can be argued with equal probability of truth or error. He subsequently dredges up the equivalents of *Wellington's Victory* for Voltaire, Beaumarchais, Flaubert, and Gide to document his point. Bazin then yields some ground to Rohmer's argument that the history of art does not confirm the decline with age of authentic geniuses like Titian, Rembrandt, Beethoven, or nearer to us, Bonnard, Matisse, and Stravinsky. Bazin agrees with Rohmer that it is inconsistent to attribute senility only to aging film directors while, at the same time, honoring the gnarled austerity of Rembrandt's later style. This is one of the crucial propositions of the *auteur* theory, because it refutes the popular theory of decline for aging giants like Renoir and Chaplin and asserts, instead, that, as a director grows older, he is likely to become more profoundly personal than most audiences and critics can appreciate. However, Bazin immediately retrieves his lost ground by arguing that, whereas the senility of directors is no longer at issue, the evolution of an art form is. Where directors fail and fall is in the realm not of psychology but of history. If a director fails to keep pace with the development of his medium, his work will become obsolescent. What seems like senility is, in reality, a disharmony between the subjective inspiration of the director and the objective evolution of the medium. By making this distinction between the subjective capability of ah *auteur* and the objective value of a work in film history, Bazin reinforces the popular impression that the Griffith of *Birth of a Nation* is superior to the Griffith of *Abraham Lincoln* in the perspective of timing, which similarly distinguishes the Eisenstein of *Potemkin* from the Eisenstein of *Ivan the Terrible*, the Renoir of *La Grande Illusion* from the Renoir of *Picnic in the Grass*, and the Welles of *Citizen Kane* from the Welles of *Mr. Arkadin*.

I have embroidered Bazin's actual examples for the sake of greater contact with the American scene. In fact, Bazin implicitly denies a decline in the later works of Chaplin and Renoir and never mentions Griffith. He suggests circuitously that Hawks's *Scarface* is clearly superior to Hawks's *Gentlemen Prefer Blondes*, although the *auteur* critics would argue the contrary. Bazin is particularly critical of Rivette's circular reasoning on *Monkey Business* as the proof of Hawks's genius. "One sees the danger," Bazin warns, "which is an aesthetic cult of personality."

Bazin's taste, it should be noted, was far more discriminating than that of American film historians. Films Bazin cites as unquestionable classics are still quite debatable here in America. After all, *Citizen Kane* was originally panned by James Agee, Richard Griffith, and Bosley Crowther, and *Scarface* has never been regarded as one of the landmarks of the American cinema by native critics. I would say that the American public has been ahead of its critics on both *Kane* and *Scarface*. Thus, to argue against the *auteur* theory in America is to assume that we have anyone of Bazin's sensibility and dedication to provide an alternative, and we simply don't.

Bazin, finally, concentrates on the American cinema, which invariably serves as the decisive battleground of the *auteur* theory, whether over *Monkey Business* or *Party Girl*. Unlike most "serious" American critics, Bazin likes Hollywood films, but not solely because of the talent of this or that director. For Bazin, the distinctively American comedy, western, and gangster genres have their own mystiques apart from the personalities of the directors concerned. How can one review an Anthony Mann western, Bazin asks, as if it were not an expression of the genre's conventions. Not that Bazin dislikes Anthony Mann's westerns. He is more concerned with otherwise admirable westerns that the *auteur* theory rejects because their directors happen to be unfashionable. Again, Bazin's critical generosity comes to the fore against the negative aspects of the *auteur* theory.

Some of Bazin's arguments tend to overlap each other as if to counter rebuttals from any direction. He argues, in turn, that the cinema is less individualistic an art than painting or literature, that Hollywood is less individualistic than other cinemas, and that, even so, the *auteur* theory never really applies anywhere. In upholding historical determinism, Bazin goes so far as to speculate that, if Racine had lived in Voltaire's century, it is unlikely that Racine's tragedies would have been any more inspired than Voltaire's. Presumably, the Age of Reason would have stifled Racine's neoclassical impulses. Perhaps. Perhaps not. Bazin's hypothesis can hardly be argued to a verifiable conclusion, but I suspect somewhat greater reciprocity between an artist and his *Zeitgeist* than Bazin would allow. He mentions, more than once and in other contexts, capitalism's influence on the cinema. Without denying this influence, I still find it impossible to attribute X directors and Y films to any particular system or culture. Why should the Italian cinema be superior to the German cinema after one war, when the reverse was true after the previous one? As for artists conforming to the spirit of their age, that spirit is often expressed in contradictions, whether between Stravinsky and Sibelius, Fielding and Richardson, Picasso and Matisse, Chateaubriand and Stendhal. Even if the artist does not spring from the idealized head of Zeus, free of the embryonic stains of history, history itself is profoundly affected by his arrival. If we cannot imagine Griffith's *October* or Eisenstein's *Birth of a Nation* because we find it difficult to transpose one artist's unifying conceptions of Lee and Lincoln to the other's dialectical conceptions of Lenin and Kerensky, we are, nevertheless, compelled to recognize other differences in the personalities of these two pioneers beyond their respective cultural complexes. It is with these latter differences that the *auteur* theory is most deeply concerned. If directors and other artists cannot be wrenched from their historical environments, aesthetics is reduced to a subordinate branch of ethnography.

I have not done full justice to the subtlety of Bazin's reasoning and to the civilized skepticism with which he propounds his own arguments as slight probabilities rather than absolute certainties. Contemporary opponents of the *auteur* theory may feel that Bazin himself is suspect as a member of the *Cahiers* family. After all, Bazin does express qualified approval of the *auteur* theory as a relatively objective method of evaluating films apart from the subjective perils of impressionistic and ideological criticism. Better to analyze the director's personality than the critic's nerve centers or politics. Nevertheless, Bazin makes his stand clear by concluding: "This is not to deny the role of the author, but to restore to him the preposition without which the noun is only a limp concept. 'Author,' undoubtedly, but of what?"

Bazin's syntactical flourish raises an interesting problem in English usage. The French preposition "de" serves many functions, but among others, those of possession and authorship. In English, the preposition "by" once created a scandal in the American film industry when Otto Preminger had the temerity to advertise *The Man With the Golden Arm* as a film "by Otto Preminger." Novelist Nelson Algren and the Screenwriters' Guild raised such an outcry that the offending preposition was deleted. Even the noun "author" (which I cunningly mask as "*auteur*") has a literary connotation in English. In general conversation, an "author" is invariably taken to be a writer. Since "by" is a preposition of authorship and not of ownership like the ambiguous "de," the fact that Preminger both produced and directed *The Man with the Golden Arm* did not entitle him in America to the preposition "by." No one would have objected to the possessive form: "Otto Preminger's *The Man with the Golden Arm*." But, even in this case, a novelist of sufficient reputation is usually honored with the possessive designation. Now, this is hardly the case in France, where *The Red and the Black* is advertised as "un film de Claude Autant-Lara." In America, "directed by" is all the director can claim, when he is not also a well-known producer like Alfred Hitchcock or Cecil B. de Mille.

Since most American film critics are oriented toward literature or journalism, rather than toward future film-making, most American film criticism is directed toward the script instead of toward the screen. The writer-hero in *Sunset Boulevard* complains that people don't realize that someone "writes a picture; they think the actors make it up as they go along." It would never occur to this writer or most of his colleagues that people are even less aware of the director's function.

Of course, the much-abused man in the street has a good excuse not to be aware of the *auteur* theory even as a figure of speech. Even on the so-called classic level, he is not encouraged to ask "Aimez-vous Griffith?" or "Aimez-vous Eisenstein?" Instead, it is which Griffith or which Eisenstein? As for less acclaimed directors, he is lucky to find their names in the fourth paragraph of the typical review. I doubt that most American film critics really believe that an indifferently directed film is comparable to an indifferently written book. However, there is little point in wailing at the Philistines on this issue, particularly when some progress is being made in telling one director from another, at least when the film comes from abroad. The Fellini, Bergman, Kurosawa, and Antonioni promotions have helped push more directors up to the first paragraph of a review, even ahead of the plot synopsis. So, we mustn't complain.

Where I wish to redirect the argument is toward the relative position of the American cinema as opposed to the foreign cinema. Some critics have advised me that the *auteur* theory only applies to a small number of artists who make personal films, not to the run-of-the-mill Hollywood director who takes whatever assignment is available. Like most Americans who take films seriously, I have always felt a cultural inferiority complex about Hollywood. Just a few years ago, I would have thought it unthinkable to speak in the same breath of a "commercial" director like Hitchcock and a "pure" director like Bresson. Even today, *Sight and Sound* uses different type sizes for Bresson and Hitchcock films. After years of tortured revaluation, I am now prepared to stake my critical reputation, such as it is, on the proposition that Alfred Hitchcock is artistically superior to Robert Bresson by every criterion of excellence and, further, that, film for film, director for director, the American cinema has been consistently superior to that of the rest of the world from 1915 through 1962. Consequently, I now regard the *auteur* theory primarily as a critical device for recording the history of the American cinema, the only cinema in the world worth exploring in depth beneath the frosting of a few great directors at the top.

These propositions remain to be proven and, I hope, debated. The proof will be difficult because direction in the cinema is a nebulous force in literary terms. In addition to its own jargon, the director's craft often pulls in the related jargon of music, painting, sculpture, dance, literature, theatre, architecture, all in a generally futile attempt to describe the indescribable. What is it the old jazz man says of his art? If you gotta ask what it is, it ain't? Well, the cinema is like that. Criticism can only attempt an approximation, a reasonable preponderance of accuracy over inaccuracy. I know the exceptions to the *auteur* theory as well as anyone. I can feel the human attraction of an audience going one way when I am going the other. The temptations of cynicism, common sense, and facile culture-mongering are always very strong, but, somehow, I feel that the *auteur* theory is the only hope for extending the appreciation of personal qualities in the cinema. By grouping and evaluating films according to directors, the critic can rescue individual achievements from an unjustifiable anonymity. If medieval architects and African sculptors are anonymous today, it is not because they deserved to be. When Ingmar Bergman bemoans the alienation of the modern artist from the collective spirit that rebuilt the cathedral at Chartres, he is only dramatizing his own individuality for an age that has rewarded him handsomely for the travail of his alienation. There is no justification for penalizing Hollywood directors for the sake of collective mythology. So, inactive aside, "Aimez-vous Cukor?"

II. WHAT IS THE *AUTEUR* THEORY?

As far as I know, there is no definition of the *auteur* theory in the English language, that is, by any American or British critic. Truffaut has recently gone to great pains to emphasize that the *auteur* theory was merely a polemical weapon for a given time and a given place, and I am willing to take him at his word. But, lest I be accused of misappropriating a theory no one wants anymore, I will give, the *Cahiers* critics full credit for the original formulation of an idea that reshaped my thinking on the cinema. First of all, how does the *auteur* theory differ from a straightforward theory of directors. Ian Cameron's article "Films, Directors, and Critics," in *Movie* of September, 1962, makes an interesting comment on this issue: "The assumption that underlies all the writing in *Movie* is that the director is the author of a film, the person who gives it any distinctive quality. There are quite large exceptions, with which I shall deal later." So far, so good, at least for the *auteur* theory, which even allows for exceptions. However, Cameron continues: "On the whole, we accept the cinema of directors, although without going to the farthest-out extremes of the *la politique des auteurs*, which makes it difficult to think of a bad director making a good film and almost impossible to think of a good director making a bad one." We are back to Bazin again, although Cameron naturally uses different examples. That three otherwise divergent critics like Bazin, Roud, and Cameron make essentially the same point about the *auteur* theory suggests a common fear of its abuses. I believe there is a misunderstanding here about what the *auteur* theory actually claims, particularly since the theory itself is so vague at the present time.

First of all, the *auteur* theory, at least as I understand it and now intend to express it, claims neither the gift of prophecy nor the option of extracinematic perception. Directors, even *auteurs*, do not always run true to form, and the critic can never assume that a bad director will always make a bad film. No, not always, but almost always, and that is the point. What is a bad director, but a director who has made many bad films? What is the problem then? Simply this: The badness of a director is not necessarily considered the badness of a film. If Joseph Pevney directed Garbo, Cherkassov, Olivier, Belmondo, and Harriet Andersson in *The Cherry Orchard*, the resulting spectacle might not be entirely devoid of merit with so many subsidiary *auteurs* to cover up for Joe. In fact with this cast and this literary property, a Lumet might be safer than a Welles. The realities of casting apply to directors as well as to actors, but the *auteur* theory would demand the gamble with Welles, if he were willing.

Marlon Brando has shown us that a film can be made without a director. Indeed, *One-Eyed Jacks* is more entertaining than many films with directors. A director-conscious critic would find it difficult to say anything good or bad about direction that is nonexistent. One can talk here about photography, editing, acting, but not direction. The film even has personality, but, like *The Longest Day* and *Mutiny* on the *Bounty*, it is a cipher directorially. Obviously, the *auteur* theory cannot possibly cover every vagrant charm of the cinema. Nevertheless, the first premise of the *auteur* theory is the technical competence of a director as a criterion of value. A badly directed or an undirected film has no importance in a critical scale of values, but one can make interesting conversation about the subject, the script, the acting, the color, the photography, the editing, the music, the costumes, the decor, and so forth. That is the nature of the medium. You always get more for your money than mere art. Now, by the *auteur* theory, if a director has no technical competence, no elementary flair for the cinema, he is automatically cast out from the pantheon of directors. A great director has to be at least a good director. This is true in any art. What constitutes directorial talent is more difficult to define abstractly. There is less disagreement, however, on this first level of the *auteur* theory than there will be later.

The second premise of the *auteur* theory is the distinguishable personality of the director as a criterion of value. Over a group of films, a director must exhibit certain recurring characteristics of style, which serve as his signature. The way a film looks and moves should have some relationship to the way a director thinks and feels. This is an area where American directors are generally superior to foreign directors. Because so much of the American cinema is commissioned, a director is forced to express his personality through the visual treatment of material rather than through the literary content of the material. A Cukor, who works with all sorts of projects, has a more developed abstract style than a Bergman, who is free to develop his own scripts. Not that Bergman lacks personality, but his work has declined with the depletion of his ideas largely because his technique never equaled his sensibility. Joseph L. Mankiewicz and Billy Wilder are other examples of writer-directors without adequate technical mastery. By contrast, Douglas Sirk and Otto Preminger have moved up the scale because their miscellaneous projects reveal a stylistic consistency.

The third and ultimate premise of the *auteur* theory is concerned with interior meaning, the ultimate glory of the cinema as an art. Interior meaning is extrapolated from the tension between a director's personality and his material. This conception of interior meaning comes close to what Astruc defines as *mise en scène*, but not quite. It is not quite the vision of the world a director projects nor quite his attitude toward life. It is ambiguous, in any literary sense, because part of it is imbedded in the stuff of the cinema and cannot be rendered in noncinematic terms. Truffaut has called it the temperature of the director on the set, and that is a close approximation of its professional aspect. Dare I come out and say what I think it to be is an *élan* of the soul?

Lest I seem unduly mystical, let me hasten to add that all I mean by "soul" is that intangible difference between one personality and another, all other things being equal. Sometimes, this difference is expressed by no more than a beat's hesitation in the rhythm of a film. In one sequence of *La Règie du Jeu*, Renoir gallops up the stairs, turns to his right with a lurching movement, stops in hoplike uncertainty when his name is called by a coquettish maid, and, then, with marvelous postreflex continuity, resumes his bearishly shambling journey to the heroine's boudoir. If I could describe the musical grace note of that momentary suspension, and I can't, I might be able to provide a more precise definition of the *auteur* theory. As it is, all I can do is point at the specific beauties of interior meaning on the screen and, later, catalogue the moments of recognition.

The three premises of the *auteur* theory may be visualized as three concentric circles: the outer circle as technique; the middle circle, personal style; and the inner circle, interior meaning. The corresponding roles of the director may be designated as those of a technician, a stylist, and an *auteur*. There is no prescribed course by which a director passes through the three circles. Godard once remarked that Visconti had evolved from a *metteur en scène* to an *auteur,* whereas Rossellini had evolved from an *auteur* to a *metteur en scène*. From opposite directions, they emerged with comparable status. Minnelli began and remained in the second circle as a stylist; Buñuel was an *auteur* even before he had assembled the technique of the first circle. Technique is simply the ability to put a film together with some clarity and coherence. Nowadays, it is possible to become a director without knowing too much about the technical side, even the crucial functions of photography and editing. An expert production crew could probably cover up for a chimpanzee in the director's chair. How do you tell the genuine director from the quasi chimpanzee? After a given number of films, a pattern is established.

In fact, the *auteur* theory itself is a pattern theory in constant flux. I would never endorse a Ptolemaic constellation of directors in a fixed orbit. At the moment, my list of *auteurs* runs something like this through the first twenty: Ophuls, Renoir, Mizoguchi, Hitchcock, Chaplin Ford, Welles, Dreyer, Rossellini, Murnau, Griffith, Sternberg, Eisenstein, von Stroheim, Buñuel, Bresson, Hawks, Lang, Flaherty, Vigo. This list is somewhat weighted toward seniority and established reputations. In time, some of these *auteurs* will rise, some will fall, and some will be displaced either by new directors or rediscovered ancients. Again, the exact order is less important than the specific definitions of these and as many as two hundred other potential *auteurs*. I would hardly expect any other critic in the world fully to endorse this list, especially on faith. Only after thousands of films have been revaluated, will any personal pantheon have a reasonably objective validity. The task of validating the *auteur* theory is an enormous one, and the end will never be in sight. Meanwhile, the *auteur* habit of collecting random films in directorial bundles will serve posterity with at least a tentative classification.

Although the *auteur* theory emphasizes the body of a director's work rather than isolated masterpieces, it is expected of great directors that they make great films every so often. The only possible exception to his rule I can think of is Abel Gance, whose greatness is largely a function of his aspiration. Even with Gance, *La Roue* is as close to being a great film as any single work of Flaherty's. Not that single works matter that much. As Renoir has observed, a director spends his life on variations of the same film.

Two recent films—*Boccaccio '70* and *The Seven Capital Sins*—unwittingly reinforced the *auteur* theory by confirming the relative standing of the many directors involved. If I had not seen either film, I would have anticipated that the order of merit in *Boccaccio '70* would be Visconti, Fellini, and De Sica, and in *The Seven Capital Sins* Godard, Chabrol, Demy, Vadim, De Broca, Molinaro. (Dhomme, Ionesco's stage director and an unknown quantity in advance, turned out to be the worst of the lot.) There might be some argument about the relative badness of De Broca and Molinaro, but, otherwise, the directors ran true to form by almost any objective criterion of value. However, the main point here is that even in these frothy, ultracommercial servings of entertainment, the contribution of each director had less in common stylistically with the work of other directors on the project than with his own previous work.

Sometimes, a great deal of corn must be husked to yield a few kernels of internal meaning. I recently saw *Every Night at Eight*, one of the many maddeningly routine films Raoul Walsh has directed in his long career. This 1935 effort featured George Raft, Alice Faye, Frances Langford, and Patsy Kelly in one of those familiar plots about radio shows of the period. The film keeps moving along in the pleasantly unpretentious manner one would expect of Walsh until one incongruously intense scene with George Raft thrashing about in his sleep, revealing his inner fears in mumbling dream-talk. The girl he loves comes into the room in the midst of his unconscious avowals of feeling and listens sympathetically. This unusual scene was later amplified in *High Sierra* with Humphrey Bogart and Ida Lupino. The point is that one of the screen's most virile directors employed an essentially feminine narrative device to dramatize the emotional vulnerability of his heroes. If I had not been aware of Walsh in *Every Night at Eight*, the crucial link to *High Sierra* would have passed unnoticed. Such are the joys of the *auteur* theory.

1962

Psychoanalysis

Laura Mulvey, 'Visual Pleasure and Narrative Cinema'*

Pleasure in Looking/Fascination with the Human Form

A.   The cinema offers a number of possible pleasures. One is scopophilia (pleasure in look-ing). There are circumstances in which looking itself is a source of pleasure, just as, in the reverse formation, there is pleasure in being looked at. Originally, in his *Three Essays on Sexuality*, Freud isolated scopophilia as one of the component instincts of sexuality which exist as drives quite independently of the erotogenic zones. At this point he associated sco-pophilia with taking other people as objects, subjecting them to a controlling and curious gaze. His particular examples centre on the voyeuristic activities of children, their desire to see and make sure of the private and forbidden (curiosity about other people's genital and bodily functions, about the presence or absence of the penis and retrospectively, about the primal scene). In this analysis scopophilia is essentially active. (Later, in 'Instincts and Their Vicissitudes', Freud developed his theory of scopophilia further, attaching it initially to pre-genital auto-eroticism, after which, by analogy, the pleasure of the look is transferred to others. There is a close working here of the relationship between the active instinct and its further development in a narcissistic form.) Although the instinct is modified by other factors, in particular the constitution of the ego, it continues to exist as the erotic basis for pleasure in looking at another person as object. At the extreme, it can become fixated into a perversion, producing obsessive voyeurs and Peeping Toms whose only sexual satisfaction can come from watching, in an active controlling sense, an objectified other.

At first glance, the cinema would seem to be remote from the undercover world of the surreptitious observation of an unknowing and unwilling victim. What is seen on the screen is so manifestly shown. But the mass of mainstream film, and the conventions within which it has consciously evolved, portray a hermetically sealed world which unwinds magically, indifferent to the presence of the audience, producing for them a sense of separation and playing on their voyeuristic fantasy. Moreover, the extreme contrast between the darkness in the auditorium (which also isolates the spectators from one to another) and the brilliance of the shifting patterns of light and shade on the screen helps to promote the illusion of voyeuristic separation. Although the film is really being shown, is there to be seen, conditions of screening and narrative conventions give the spectator an illusion of looking in on a private world. Among other things, the position of the spectators in the cinema is blatantly one of repression of their exhibitionism and projection of the repressed desire onto the performer.

B.   The cinema satisfies a primordial wish for pleasurable looking, but it also goes fur-ther, developing scopophilia in its narcissistic aspect. The conventions of mainstream film focus on the human form. Scale, space, stories are all anthropomorphic. Here, curiosity and the wish to look intermingle with a fascination with likeness and recognition: the human face, the human body, the relationship between the human form and its surround-ings, the visible presence of the person in the world. Jacques Lacan has described how the moment when a child recognises its own image in the mirror is crucial for the constitution

Screen, 16(3) (1975), reprinted in A. Easthope (ed.), *Contemporary Film Theory* (London and New York: Longman, 1996), pp. 113–19.

†Part II is divided into thematic sections in which each text is relevant to every other text in the section. Therefore, the cross-referencing in Part II does not list texts in the same section as the referencing appears.

of the ego. Several aspects of this analysis are relevant here. The mirror phase occurs at a time when children's physical ambitions outstrip their motor capacity, with the result that their recognition of themselves is joyous in that they imagine their mirror image to be more complete, more perfect than they experience in their own body. Recognition is thus overlaid with misrecognition: the image recognised is conceived as the reflected body of the self, but its misrecognition as superior projects this body outside itself as an ideal ego, the alienated subject which, reintrojected as an ego ideal, prepares the way for *identification* with others in the future. This mirror moment predates language for the child.

Important for this article is the fact that it is an image that constitutes the matrix of the imaginary, of recognition/misrecognition and identification, and hence of the first articulation of the I, of subjectivity. This is a moment when an older fascination with looking (at the mother's face, for an obvious example) collides with the initial inklings of self-awareness. Hence it is the birth of the long love affair/despair between image and self-image which has found such intensity of expression in film and such joyous recognition in the cinema audience. Quite apart from the extraneous similarities between screen and mirror (the framing of the human form in its surroundings, for instance), the cinema has structures of fascination strong enough to allow temporary loss of ego while simultaneously reinforcing it. The sense of forgetting the world as the ego has come to perceive it (I forgot who I am and where I was) is nostalgically reminiscent of that pre-subjective moment of image recognition. While at the same time, the cinema has distinguished itself in the production of ego ideals, through the star system for instance. Stars provide a focus or centre both to screen space and screen story where they act out a complex process of likeness and difference (the glamorous impersonates the ordinary).

C. Sections A and B have set out two contradictory aspects of the pleasurable structures of looking in the conventional cinematic situation. The first, scopophilic, arises from pleasure in using another person as an object of sexual stimulation through sight. The second, developed through narcissism and the constitution of the ego, comes from identification with the image seen. Thus, in film terms, one implies a separation of the erotic identity of the subject from the object on the screen (active scopophilia), the other demands identification of the ego with the object on the screen through the spectator's fascination with and recognition of his like. The first is a function of the sexual instincts, the second of ego libido. This dichotomy was crucial for Freud. Although he saw the two as interacting and overlaying each other, the tension between instinctual drives and self-preservation polarises in terms of pleasure. But both are formative structures, mechanisms without intrinsic meaning. In themselves they have no signification, unless attached to an idealisation. Both pursue aims in indifference to perceptual reality, and motivate eroticised phantasmagoria that affect the subject's perception of the world to make a mockery of empirical objectivity.

During its history, the cinema seems to have evolved a particular illusion of reality in which this contradiction between libido and ego has found a beautifully complementary fantasy world. In *reality* the fantasy world of the screen is subject to the law which produces it. Sexual instincts and identification processes have a meaning within, the symbolic order which articulates desire. Desire, born with language, allows the possibility of transcending the instinctual and the imaginary, but its point of reference continually returns to the traumatic moment of its birth: the castration complex. Hence the look, pleasurable in form, can be threatening in content, and it is woman as representation/image that crystallises this paradox.

Woman as Image, Man as Bearer of the Look

A. In a world ordered by sexual imbalance, pleasure in looking has been split between active/male and passive/female. The determining male gaze projects its fantasy on to the female figure, which is styled accordingly. In their traditional exhibitionist role, women are simultaneously looked at and displayed, with their appearance coded for strong visual and erotic impact so that they can be said to connote *to-be-looked-at-ness*. Woman displayed as sexual object is the *leitmotif* of erotic spectacle: from pin-ups to strip-tease, from Ziegfeld to Busby Berkeley, she holds the look, and plays to and signifies male desire. Mainstream film neatly combines spectacle and narrative. (Note, however, how in the musical song-and-dance numbers interrupt the flow of the diegesis.) The presence of woman is an indispensable element of spectacle in normal narrative film, yet her visual presence tends to work against the development of a story-line, to freeze the flow of action in moments of erotic contemplation. This alien presence then has to be integrated into cohesion with the narrative. As Budd Boetticher has put it:

> What counts is what the heroine provokes, or rather what she represents. She is the one, or rather the love or fear she inspires in the hero, or else the concern he feels for her, who makes him act the way he does. In herself the woman has not the slightest importance.

(A recent tendency in narrative film has been to dispense with this problem altogether; hence the development of what Molly Haskell has called the 'buddy movie', in which the active homosexual eroticism of the central male figures can carry the story without distraction.) Traditionally, the woman displayed has functioned on two levels: as erotic object for the characters within the screen story, and as erotic object for the spectator within the auditorium, with a shifting tension between the looks on either side of the screen. For instance, the device of the show-girl allows the two looks to be unified technically without any apparent break in the diegesis. A woman performs within the narrative; the gaze of the spectator and that of the male characters in the film are neatly combined without breaking narrative verisimilitude. For a moment the sexual impact of the performing woman takes the film into-a no man's land outside its own time and space. Thus Marilyn Monroe's first appearance in *The River of No Return* and Lauren Bacall's songs in *To Have and Have Not*. Similarly, conventional close-ups of leg (Dietrich, for instance) or a face (Garbo) integrate into the narrative a different mode of eroticism. One part of a fragmented body destroys the Renaissance space, the illusion of depth demanded by the narrative; it gives flatness, the quality of cut-out or icon, rather than verisimilitude, to the screen.

B.   An active/passive heterosexual division of labour has similarly controlled narrative structure. According to the principles of the ruling ideology and the psychical structures that back it up, the male figure cannot bear the burden of sexual objectification. Man is reluctant to gaze at his exhibitionist like. Hence the split between spectacle and narrative supports the man's role as the active one of advancing the story, making things happen. The man controls the film fantasy and also emerges as the representative of power in a further sense: as the bearer of the look of the spectator, transferring it behind the screen to neutralise the extra-diegetic tendencies represented by woman as spectacle. This is made possible through the processes set in motion by structuring the film around a main controlling figure with whom the spectator can identify. As the spectator identifies with the main male protagonist, he projects his look on to that of his like, his screen surrogate, so that the power of the male protagonist as he controls events coincides with the active power of the erotic look, both giving a satisfying sense of omnipotence. A male movie star's glamorous characteristics are thus not those of the erotic object of the gaze, but those of the more perfect, more complete, more powerful ideal ego conceived in the original moment of recognition in front of the mirror. The character in the story can make things happen and control events better than the subject/spectator, just as the image in the mirror was more in control of motor co-ordination.

In contrast to woman as icon, the active male figure (the ego ideal of the identification process) demands a three-dimensional space corresponding to that of the mirror recognition, in which the alienated subject internalised his own representation of his imaginary existence. He is a figure in a landscape. Here the function of film is to reproduce as accurately as possible the so-called natural conditions of human perception. Camera technology (as exemplified by deep focus in particular) and camera movements (determined by the action of the protagonist), combined with invisible editing (demanded by realism), all tend to blur the limits of screen space. The male protagonist is free to command the stage, a stage of spatial illusion in which he articulates the look and creates the action. (There are films with a woman as main protagonist, of course. To analyse this phenomenon seriously here would take me too far afield. Pam Cook and Claire Johnston's study of *The Revolt of Mamie Stover* in Phil Hardy (ed.), *Raoul Walsh* (Edinburgh, 1974), shows in a striking case how the strength of this female protagonist is more apparent than real.)

C.   Sections III A and B have set out a tension between a mode of representation of woman in film and conventions surrounding the diegesis. Each is associated with a look: that of the spectator in direct scopophilic contact with the female form displayed for his enjoyment (connoting male fantasy) and that of the spectator fascinated with the image of his like set in an illusion of natural space, and through him *gaining* control and possession of the woman within the diegesis. (This tension and the shift from one pole, to the other can structure a single text. Thus both in *Only Angels Have Wings* and *To Have and Have Not*, the film opens with the woman as object of the combined gaze of spectator and all the male protagonists in the film. She is isolated, glamorous, on display, sexualised. But as the narrative progresses she falls in love with the main male protagonist and becomes his property, losing her outward glamorous characteristics, her generalised sexuality, her show-girl connotations; her eroticism is subjected to the male star alone. By means of identification with him, through participation in his power, the spectator can indirectly possess her too.)

But in psychoanalytic terms, the female figure poses a deeper problem. She also connotes something that the look continually circles around but disavows: her lack of a penis, implying a threat of castration and hence unpleasure. Ultimately, the meaning of woman is sexual difference, the visually ascertainable absence of the penis, the material evidence on which is based the castration complex essential for the organisation of entrance to the symbolic order and the law of the father. Thus the woman as icon, displayed for the gaze and enjoyment of men, the active controllers of the look, always threatens to evoke the anxiety it originally signified. The male unconscious has two avenues of escape from this castration anxiety: preoccupation with the re-enactment of the original trauma (investigating the woman, demystifying her mystery), counterbalanced by the devaluation, punishment or saving of the guilty object (an avenue typified by the concerns of the *film noir*); or else complete disavowal of castration by the' substitution of a fetish object or turning the represented figure itself into a fetish so that it becomes reassuring rather than dangerous (hence overvaluation, the cult of the female star).

This second avenue, fetishistic scopophilia, builds up the physical beauty of the object, transforming it into something satisfying in itself. The first avenue, voyeurism, on the contrary, has associations with sadism: pleasure lies in ascertaining guilt (immediately associated with castration), asserting control and subjugating the guilty person through punishment or forgiveness. This sadistic side fits in well with narrative. Sadism demands a story, depends on making something happen, forcing a change in another person, a battle of will and strength, victory/defeat, all occurring in a linear time with a beginning and an end. Fetishistic scopophilia, on the other hand, can exist outside linear time as the erotic instinct is focused on the look alone. These contradictions and ambiguities can be illustrated more simply by using works by Hitchcock and Sternberg, both of whom take the look almost as the content or subject matter of many of their films. Hitchcock is the more complex, as he uses both mechanisms. Steinberg's work, on the other hand, provides many pure examples of fetishistic scopophilia.

Narrative Space*

Stephen Heath

Those terms, as they have been described here, are the terms of a constant welding together: screen and frame, ground and background, surface and depth, the whole setting of movements and transitions, the implication of space and spectator in the taking place of film as narrative. The classical *economy* of film is its organization thus as organic unity and the *form* of that economy is narrative, the *narrativization* of film. Narrative, as it were, determines the film which is contained in its process in that determination, this 'bind' being itself a process – precisely the narrativization. The narration is to be held on the narrated, the enunciation on the enounced; filmic procedures are to be held as narrative instances (very much as 'cues'), exhaustively, without gap or contradiction. What is sometimes vaguely referred to as 'transparency' has its meaning in this narrativization: the proposal of a discourse that disavows its operations and positions in the name of a signified that it proposes as its pre-existent justification. 'Transparency', moreover, is entirely misleading in so far as it implies that narrativization has necessarily to do with some simple 'invisibility' (anyway impossible – no one has yet seen a signified without a signifier). The narration may well be given as visible in its filmic procedures; what is crucial is that it be given as visible *for the narrated* and that the spectator be caught up in the play of *that* process, that the *address* of the film be clear (does anyone who has watched, say, *The Big Sleep* seriously believe that a central part of Hollywood films, differently defined from genre to genre, was not the address of a process with a movement of play and that that was not a central part of their pleasure?).

Within this narrativization of film, the role of the character-look has been fundamental for the welding of a spatial unity of narrative implication. In so many senses, every film is a veritable drama of vision and this drama has thematically and symptomatically 'returned' in film since the very beginning: from the fascination of the magnifying glass in *Grandma's Reading Glass* to Lina's short-sightedness in *Suspicion* to the windscreen and rear-view mirror of *Taxi Driver*, from the keyhole of *A Search for Evidence* to the images that flicker reflected over Brody's glasses in *Jaws* as he turns the pages of the book on sharks, finding the images of the film to come and which he will close as he closes the book; not to mention the extended dramatizations such as *Rear Window* or *Peeping Tom*. How to make sense in film if not through vision, film with its founding ideology of vision as truth? The drama of vision in the film returns the drama of vision of the film: the spectator will be bound to the film as spectacle as

*Screen, 17(3), (Autumn 1976), pp. 68–112. Reprinted in A. Easthope (ed.), *Contemporary Film Theory* (London and New York: Longman, 1996), pp. 81–94.

the world of the film is itself revealed as spectacle on the basis of a narrative organization of look and point of view that moves space into place through the image-flow; the character, figure of the look, is a kind of perspective within the perspective system, regulating the world, orientating space, providing directions – and for the spectator.

Film works at a loss, the loss of the divisions, the discontinuities, the absences that structure it – as, for example, the 'outside' of the frame, off-screen space, the *hors-champ*. Such absence is the final tragedy of a Bazin, who wants to believe in cinema as a global consciousness of reality, an illimitation of picture frame and theatre scene –

> The screen is not a frame like that of a picture, but a mask which allows us to see a part of the event only. When a person leaves the field of the camera, we recognize that he or she is out of the field of vision, though continuing to exist identically in another part of the scene which is hidden from us. The screen has no wings . . .[1]

– but who can only inspect the damage of 'camera angles or prejudices',[2] acknowledge none the less the frame, the scene, the mask, the hidden, the absent. The sequence-shot-with-deep-focus long take functions as a Utopia in this context – the ideal of a kind of 'full angle', without prejudices, but hence too without cinema; the ideal recognized in *Bicycle Thieves*, 'plus de cinema.'

Burch writes that 'off-screen space has only an intermittent or, rather, *fluctuating* existence during any film, and structuring this fluctuation can become a powerful tool in a film-maker's hands'.[4] The term 'fluctuation' is excellent, yet it must be seen that the work of classical continuity is not to hide or ignore off-screen space but, on the contrary, to contain it, to regularize its fluctuation in a constant movement of reappropriation. It is this movement that defines the rules of continuity and the fiction of space they serve to construct, the whole functioning according to a kind of metonymic lock in which off-screen space becomes on-screen space and is replaced in turn by the space it holds off, each joining over the next. The join is conventional and ruthlessly selective (it generally leaves out of account, for example, the space that might be supposed to be masked at the top and bottom of the frame, concentrating much more on the space at the sides of the frame or on that 'in front', 'behind the camera', as in variations of field/reverse field), and demands that the off-screen space recaptured must be 'called for', must be 'logically consequential', must arrive as 'answer', 'fulfilment of promise' or whatever (and not as difference or contradiction) – must be narrativized. Classical continuity, in other words, is an order of the pregnancy of space in frame; one of the narrative acts of a film is the creation of space[5] but what gives the moving space its coherence in time, decides the metonymy as a 'taking place', is here 'the narrative itself', and above all as it crystallizes round character as look and point of view. The fundamental role of these is exactly their pivotal use as a mode of organization and organicization, the joining of a film's constructions, the stitching together of the overlaying metonymies.

'If in the left of the frame an actor in close-up is looking off right, he has an empty space in front of him; if the following shot shows an empty space to the left and an object situated to the right, then the actor's look appears to cross an orientated, rectilinear, thus logical space: it seems to bear with precision on the object. One has an eye-line match.'[6] The look, that is, joins form of expression – the composition of the images and their disposition in relation to one another – and form of content – the definition of the action of the film in the movement of looks, exchanges, objects seen, and so on. Point of view develops on the basis of this joining operation of the look, the camera taking the position of a character in order to show the spectator what he or she sees.[7] Playing on the assumption of point of view, a film has an evident means of placing its space, of giving it immediate and holding significance; Burch talks of the establishment of an organization founded on the 'traditional dichotomy between the "subjective camera" (which "places the spectator in the position of a character") and the "objective camera" (which makes the spectator the ideal, immaterial "voyeur" of a pro-filmic pseudo-reality)'.[8]

This account, however, requires clarification. The point-of-view shot is 'subjective' in that it assumes the position of a subject-character but to refer to that assumption in terms of 'subjective camera' or 'subjective image' can lead to misunderstanding with regard to the functioning of point of view. Subjective images can be many things; Mitry, for example, classifies them into five major categories:

> the purely mental image (more or less impracticable in the cinema); the truly subjective or analytical image (i.e. what is looked at without the person looking), which is practicable in small doses; the semi-subjective or associated image (i.e. the person looking + what is looked at, which is in fact looked at from the viewpoint of the person looking), the most generalizable formula; the complete sequence given over to the imaginary, which does not raise special problems; and finally the memory image, which is in principle simply a variety of the mental image but, when presented in the form of a flash-back with commentary, allows for a specific filmic treatment which is far more successful than in the case of other mental images.[9]

The point-of-view shot includes 'the semi-subjective or associated image' (its general mode) and 'the truly subjective or analytical image (its pure mode, as it were) in that classification but not necessarily any of the other categories (a memory sequence, for instance, need not contain any point-of-view shots); what is 'subjective' in the point-of-view shot is its spatial positioning (its place), not the image or the camera.

To stress this is to stress a crucial factor in the exploitation of the film image and its relation to point-of-view organization. Within the terms of that organization, a true subjective image would effectively need to mark its subjectivity *in the image itself*. Examples are common: the blurred image of Gutman in *The Maltese Falcon* is the subjective image of the drugged Spade; the blurring of focus marks the subjectivity of the image, exclusively Spade's, and the spectator is set not simply *with* Spade but *as* Spade. They are also limited, since they depend exactly on some recognizable – marking – distortion of the 'normal' image, a narratively motivated aberration of vision of some kind or another (the character is drugged, intoxicated, short-sighted, terrified . . . down to he or she running, with hand-held effects of the image 'jogging', or even walking, with regular speed of camera movement forward matched on a shot that effectively establishes the character as in the process of walking; the latter represents the lowest limit on the scale since the camera movement is there a weak subjective marking of the image which itself remains more or less 'normal' – except, of course, and hence this limit position of the banal action of walking, that the normal image is precisely static, that movement in a central perspective system can quickly become a problem of vision). The implication of this, of course, is then the strength of the unmarked image as a constant third person – the vision of picture and scene, the Quattrocento view, Burch's 'voyeur' position – *which is generally continued within point-of-view shots themselves*; the point-of-view shot is marked as subjective in its emplacement but the resulting image is still finally (or rather firstly) objective, the objective sight of what is seen from the subject position assumed. Indicatively enough, the general mode of the point-of-view shot is the shot which shows both what is looked at and the person looking. Instances of the pure shot, showing what is looked at without the person looking, however, are equally conclusive. Take the shot in *Suspicion* of the telegram that Lina receives from Johnnie to tell her of his intention to attend the Hunt Ball: the telegram is clearly shown from Lina's reading position and the end of the shot – the end of the reading – is marked by her putting down her glasses on to the telegram lying on a table, the glasses thus coming down into frame; the position of the shot is marked as subjective with Lina but the image nevertheless continues to be objective, 'the real case' for the narrative.

Point of view, that is, depends on an overlaying of first and third person modes. There is no radical dichotomy between subjective point-of-view shots and objective non-point-of-view shots; the latter mode is the continual basis over which the former can run in its particular organization of space, its disposition of the images. The structure of the photographic image – with its vision, its scene, its distance, its normality – is to the film somewhat as language is to the novel: the grounds of its representations, which representations can include the creation of an acknowledged movement of point of view. This is the sense of the spectator identification with the camera that is so often remarked upon (Benjamin: 'the audience's identification with the actor is really an identification with the camera'; Metz: 'the spectator can do no other than identify with the camera'). The spectator must *see* and this structuring vision is the condition of the possibility of the disposition of the images via the relay of character look and viewpoint which pulls together vision and narrative. Emphasis was laid earlier on the structures of the structuring vision that founds cinema; what is emphasized now is the dependence of our very notion of point of view on those structures; dependence at once in so far as the whole Quattrocento system is built on the establishment of point of view, the central position of the eye, and in so far as the mode of representation thus defined brings with it fixity and movement in a systematic complicity of interaction – brings with it, that is, the 'objective' and the 'subjective', the 'third person' and the 'first person', the view and its partial points, and finds this drama of vision as the resolving action of its narratives.

Identification with the camera, seeing, the 'ideal picture' of the scene: 'the usual scene in a classical film is narrated as if from the point of view of an observer capable of moving about the room.'[12] Such movement may be given in editing or by camera movement within a shot, and the importance accruing to some master view that will define the space of the mobility has been noted. Movement, in fact, will be treated as a supplement to produce precisely the 'ideal *picture*' (going to the movies is going to the pictures): on the basis of the vision of the photographic image, that is, it will provide the 'total' point of view of an observer capable of moving about the room without changing anything of the terms of that vision, the scene laid out for the central observer (and spectator); every shot or refraining adds a difference, but that difference is always the same image, with the organization – the continuity, the rules, the matches, the pyramid structures – constantly doing the sum of the *scene*.

That said, it remains no less true, as has again been noted and as will become important later on, that movement represents a potentially radical disturbance of the smooth stability of the scenographic vision (hence the need for a systematic organization to contain it). Such a disturbance, however, is not as simple as is sometimes suggested and it is necessary briefly to consider at this stage two instances of disturbance as they are conventionally described; both bear on the mobility of the camera.

The first is that of what Branigan characterizes as the impossible place: 'To the extent that the camera is located in an "impossible" place, the narration questions its own origin, that is, suggests a shift in narration.'[13] 'Impossible', of course, is here decided in respect of the 'possible' positions of the observer moving about, the disturbance involved seen as a disjunction of the unity of narration and narrated, enunciation and enounced.

Thus defined, impossible places are certainly utilized in classical narrative cinema, with examples ranging from the relatively weak to the relatively strong. At one end of the range, the weak examples would be any high or low angles that are not motivated as the point of view of a character; or, indeed, any high or low angles that, while so motivated, are nevertheless sufficiently divergent from the assumed normal upright observing position as to be experienced as in some sense 'impossible' in their peculiarity (the most celebrated – and complex – example is the dead-man-in-the-coffin point of view in *Vampyr*).[14] At the other end, the strong examples – those intended by Branigan – can be illustrated by a description of two shots from *Killer's Kiss*: (1) as Davey, the boxer-hero, is seen stooping to feed his goldfish, there is a cut to a shot through the bowl, from the other side, of his face peering in as the feed drops down; since the bowl is on a table against a wall, the place taken by the camera is not possible; (2) Rappello, the dance-hall owner, furious at being left by the heroine, is drinking in a back-room, its walls covered with posters and prints; a close-up of a print showing two men leering from a window is followed by a shot of Rappello who throws his drink at the camera ('at the screen'!); a crack appears as the drink runs down a plate of glass; impossibly, the shot was from 'in' the print. The second – and related – instance of disturbance is that of the development of camera movement as a kind of autonomous figure; what Burch calls 'the camera designated as an "omnipotent and omniscient" (i.e. manipulative and pre-cognitive) presence'.[15] This presence too is utilized in classical narrative cinema and weak and strong examples can once more be indicated. In *Taxi Driver*, Travis Bickle is seen phoning Betsy after the porno-film fiasco; as he stands talking into the pay-phone, fixed on a wall inside a building, the camera tracks right and stops to frame a long empty corridor leading out to the street; when Travis finishes his call, he walks into frame and exits via the corridor. The tracking movement designates the camera with a certain autonomy – there is an effect of a casual decision to go somewhere else, off to the side of the narrative – but the example is ultimately weak: the corridor is eventually brought into the action with Travis's exit and, more importantly, it has its rhyming and thematic resonances – the corridors in the rooming-house used by Iris, the marked existential atmosphere of isolation, nothingness, etc. Stronger examples are provided in the work of an Ophuls or a ²Welles – the spectacular tracking shot at the start of *Touch of Evil* or the intense mobility in many of the shots at the end of that same film.

These two instances of disturbance have been characterized here in their existence in established cinema simply to make one or two points directly in the context of the present account. Thus, the examples given of autonomy of camera movement are all clearly operating in terms of 'style' (Welles, Ophuls, the tics of a new American commercial cinema that has learnt a consciousness of style). The crucial factor is not the valuation of camera movement, be it autonomous, but the point at which a certain work on the camera in movement produces the normality of the third person objective basis as itself a construction, gives it as role or fiction and breaks the balance of the point-of-view system. Similarly, the examples of the impossible place from *Killer's Kiss*, which also have their reality as stylistic marking in the film, are without critically disruptive extension in themselves, are simply *tricks* (in the sense of spatial prestidigitations): the impossible place is entirely possible if held within a system that defines it *as such*, that confirms in its signified exceptionality. The felt element of trick, moreover, raises the general point of the realization of film as process. It is too readily assumed that the operation – the determination, the effect, the pleasure of – classical cinema lies in the attempt at an invisibility of process, the intended transparency of a kind of absolute 'realism' from which all signs of production have been *effaced*. The actual case is much more complex and subtle, and much more telling. Classical cinema does not efface the signs of production, it *contains* them, according to the narrativization described above. It is that process that is the action of the film for the spectator – what counts is as much the representation as the represented, is as much the production as the product. Nor is there anything surprising in this: film is not a static and isolated object but a series of relations with the spectator it imagines, plays and sets as subject in its movement. The process of film is then perfectly available to certain terms of excess – those of that movement in its subject openings, its energetic controls. 'Style' is one area of such controlled excess, as again, more powerfully, are genres in their specific version of process. The musical is an obvious and extreme example with its systematic 'freedom' of space – crane choreography – and its shifting balances of narrative and spectacle; but an example that should not be allowed to mask the fundamental importance of the experience of process in other genres and in the basic order of classical cinema on which the various genres are grounded. Which is to say, finally, that radical disturbance is not to be linked to the mere autonomization of a formal element such as camera movement; on the contrary, it can only be effectively grasped as a work that operates at the expense of the classical suppositions of 'form' and 'content' in cinema, posing not autonomies but contradictions in the process of film and its narrative-subject binding.

The construction of space as a term of that binding in classical cinema is its implication for the spectator in the taking place of film as narrative; implication-process of constant refinding – space regulated, orientated, continued, reconstituted. The use of look and point-of-view structures – exemplarily, the field/reverse field figure (not necessarily dependent, of course, on point-of-view shots)[16] – is fundamental to this process that has been described in terms of suture, a stitching or tying as in the surgical joining of the lips of a wound.[17] In its movement, its framings, its cuts, its intermittences, the film ceaselessly poses an absence, a lack, which is ceaselessly recaptured for – one needs to be able to say 'forin' – the film, that process binding the spectator as subject in the realization of the film's space.

In psychoanalysis, 'suture' refers to the relation of the individual as subject to the chain of its discourse where it figures missing in the guise of a stand-in; the subject is an effect of the signifier in which it is represented, stood in for, taken place (the signifier is the narration of the subject).[18] Ideological representation turns on – supports itself from – this 'initial' production of the subject in the symbolic order (hence the crucial role of psychoanalysis, as potential science of the construction of the subject, with historical materialism), directs it as a set of images and fixed positions, metonymy stopped into fictions of coherence. What must be emphasized, however, is that stopping – the functioning of suture in image, frame, narrative, etc. – is exactly a process: it counters a productivity, an excess, that it states and restates in the very moment of containing in the interests of coherence – thus the film frame, for example, exceeded from within by the outside it delimits and poses and has ceaselessly to recapture (with post-Quattrocento painting itself, images are multiplied and the conditions are laid for a certain mechanical reproduction that the photograph will fulfil, the multiplication now massive, with image machines a normal appendage of the subject). The process never ends, is always *going on*; the construction-reconstruction has always to be renewed; machines, cinema included, are there for that – and their ideological operation is not only in the images but in the suture.

The film poses an image, not immediate or neutral,[19] but posed, framed and centred. Perspective-system images bind the spectator in place, the suturing central position that is the sense of the image, that sets its scene (in place, the spectator *completes* the image as its subject). Film too, but it also moves in all sort of ways and directions, flows with energies, is potentially a veritable festival of affects. Placed, that movement is all the value of film in its development and exploitation: reproduction of life and the engagement of the spectator in the process of that reproduction as articulation of coherence. What moves in film, finally, is the spectator, immobile in front of the screen. Film is the regulation of that movement, the individual as subject held in a shifting and placing of desire, energy, contradiction, in a perpetual retotalization of the imaginary (the set scene of image and subject). This is the investment of film in narrativization; and crucially for a coherent space, the unity of place for vision.

Once again, however, the investment is in the process. Space comes in place through procedures such as look and point-of-view structures, and the spectator with it as subject in its realization. A reverse shot folds over the shot it joins and is joined in turn by the I reverse it positions; a shot of a person looking is succeeded by a shot of the object looked at which is succeeded in turn by a shot of the person looking to confirm the object as seen; and so on, in a number of multiple imbrications. *Fields* are made, *moving* fields, and the process includes not just the completions but the definitions of absence for completion. The suturing operation is in the process, the give and take of absence and presence, the play of negativity and negation, flow and bind. Narrativization, with its continuity, closes, and is that movement of closure that shifts the spectator as subject in its terms: the spectator is the point of the film's spatial relations – the turn, say, of shot to reverse shot their subject-passage (point-of-view organization, moreover, doubles over that passage in its third/first person layerings). Narrativization is scene and movement, movement and scene, the reconstruction of the subject in the pleasure of that balance (with genres as specific instances of equilibrium) – *for* homogeneity, containment. What is foreclosed in the process is not its production – often signified as such, from genre instances down to this or that 'impossible' shot – but the terms of the unity of that production (narration on narrated, enunciation on enounced), the other scene of its vision of the subject, the outside – heterogeneity, contradiction, history – of its coherent address.

Rear Window's Unity: Freedom through Constraint

John Fawell

Rear Window is Hitchcock's most unified film. Like *Rope* and *Lifeboat*, *Rear Window* limits itself to a single set. But it extends the experimentation of these films further because not only does *Rear Window* limit itself to one set but, for a large part of the film, to a single perspective, that of the protagonist, L. B. Jefferies, the photographer, played by Jimmy Stewart. Though the entire film is not told through Jefferies' point of view there is no other Hitchcock film in which we log so much time from a single perspective. Not only does Hitchcock limit himself to a single set, and for much of the time to a single perspective, but also that single perspective is fixed in one spot. Hitchcock hit upon the idea of having L. B. Jefferies wheelchair-bound, therefore restricting our primary point of view even further. *Rear Window* is Hitchcock's most claustrophobic film, set in one place, from one principal point of view, and from one principal fixed position. This film represents his most radical experiment in operating within self-imposed restrictions, in making something cinematic out of an almost stage-like world.

Hitchcock dedicated a large portion of his interviews to explaining the fruitfulness of establishing constraints on a film, both in the film's set and its camera perspective. He faults films that take plays, for example, and "open them up," setting them in woods and valleys, the real world to which the stage has no access. Hitchcock felt that such an approach dissipated the dramatic unity and integrity of the play. Cinema was not, he felt, a question of fields and trees. For Hitchcock, cinema is montage, pieces of film dramatically and significantly spliced together. One could, he repeatedly emphasized, make a film in a phone booth. By severely limiting the set in filmmaking, the director is forced to use the film's elements more fully, creatively, and the film will have a greater sense of unity.

As John Belton notes in "The Space of *Rear Window*," the film "plays with the differences between theatrical and cinematic film space, relying on set design and certain kinds of camera movements to establish a concrete, unified, theatrical space and on editing, framing, and camera movement to construct a more abstract, psychological, cinematic film space."[1] The stage is theatrical; the filming of the stage, "pure cinema," as Hitchcock liked to call it. The result of Hitchcock's experiment with a radically fixed perspective is the picture he always referred to as his most cinematic. It is a film that does not interest itself in the beauty revealed in the filmed work but in the mystery and beauty of montage. Hitchcock seems to be making a statement in *Rear Window* that cinema is a kind of sleight of hand, that with montage you can make a purse out of a sow' ear, or something cinematic out of the stagiest of sets, that the important thing about film is not the reality being filmed but the way that reality is filmed.

The Marvelously Plausible Set

There is only one set in this film, the hugest Paramount had even seen at the time,[2] and our gaze never leaves this set just as our body almost never leaves Jeff's apartment. The set is wildly implausible. The windows across the courtyard are much larger than they would be in real life and charged with far more electricity than they would be normally. Hitchcock frankly acknowledges the artificiality of the set when Charles Thomas Samuels asked him why he used a set rather than a real apartment house. "We had thirty-one apartments across that courtyard, twelve completely furnished. We never could have gotten them properly lit in a real location."[3] The sky is an expressionist ode to the orange-y polluted sky of a city but rarely convinces the viewer that it is a realistic backdrop. Beyond the alleyway that leads out of the apartment complex towards the cafe aero, the street is used as an intersection for so many dramatic moments that it is as if Hitchcock is saying to his audience, in the spirit theater, that this one spot will represent all that might go on in the outer world.

Hitchcock was strongly influenced by the time he spent in Germany as a young director and his visits to F. W. Murnau's sets. He was impressed with Murnau's experiments in distorted sets and perspective. Hitchcock described himself as an abstract expressionist, citing Klee as his favorite painter, and waged a perpetual war against "dullards" who were unduly concerned with plausibility, which he told Truffaut "was the easiest part so why bother."[4] Like an expressionist painting, the set is implausible in terms of distance and proportion, but leaps out at the viewer with its vivid color and large bold design.

And yet Hitchcock's expressionism, at least by the time of *Rear Window*, is a quiet one. Despite its artifice, there is a realism and plausibility to the set as well. Perhaps the most impressive quality of Hitchcock's set is that it could be so obviously artificial and yet so satisfying at the same time. Hitchcock seems to have had a very precise sense in *Rear Window* (he did not always) of just how far he could test his audience's sense of plausibility. Logically, we know that neighbors living in this kind of complex would not have such huge windows, leave them so widely open (the hothouse setting contributes to the plausibility here), or cavort before those windows so freely, but there are just enough concessions in the film to such things as muffled voices, obscured vision, interferences of shades, that we accept Hitchcock's premise anyway. The set of *Rear Window* does not make sense in real space and time but gains plausibility on the screen.

With this set, Hitchcock built a self-enclosed world that we never leave. Jeff only exits his apartment once, when he is thrown out. The camera only ventures outside of his window a few times, and then only for a short while, and we never leave this set. Tom Doyle, Lisa, Stella, Thorwald (and, of course, Mrs. Thorwald) leave, but we stay with Jeff. And even those characters who temporarily leave the set are unable to leave the situation. A lot of characters in this film would like to get out of this apartment complex permanently. Jeff wants desperately to escape looming marriage and get back on assignment. Lars Thorwald wants to get out of town and beat his murder rap. Even Stella, who smells trouble in the air, is anxious to finish her job and be on her way. Doyle would like Jeff to consult the yellow pages the next time he needs a detective. But all of these characters are there at the end of the film. None escape.

Hitchcock's set is, as usual, hermetically sealed off. When our eyes stray for background information what we get is Hitchcock's carefully arranged outer fringes: the orange sky, the two girls and small family briefly glimpsed from time to time on the fourth floor, the woman with the parrot who chats with the Sculptress: characters who are incidental to the film but whose movements are carefully placed to create a realistic backdrop and an occasional ironic commentary. Our one exit from the apartment complex, our one view to the outside world, is the carefully orchestrated alley where Lisa, Stella, Thorwald, Doyle, and Miss Lonelyhearts will take their cues at various times. The alley leads across the street to a cafe where we glimpse a couple of tables, one waiting for Miss Lonely-hearts and her ill-fated night on the town.

Hitchcock's set is so carefully arranged that the one time a character (Miss Lonelyhearts) decides to leave the complex for a night out, the place she is going to represents the one spot in the city we can glimpse from Jeff's window. "As in the theater," Belton notes:

> there is no space beyond the parameters of the set. The exception which proves the rule is the narrow section of the "outside world" which is seen through the alleyway next to the sculptress's apartment: Though it suggests access to an "elsewhere," through which we can see traffic and anonymous pedestrians, it is as confined a space as that of the courtyard. Indeed, Miss Lonelyhearts' entry into that outside space—she goes to a bar across the street where she picks up a young man—reveals its essentially confining nature; it provides no escape for her but returns her to an even more desperate loneliness.[5]

Belton's observation that Miss Lonelyhearts tries to escape the set only to return more trapped than ever is ingenious. But there is a happier way to look at this scene. There is something satisfying in Miss Lonelyhearts plunking herself down in one of the two tables we can see from Jeff's apartment. Of course, it is unlikely that we would have this kind of visual continuity in real life, but we are grateful to Hitchcock for hitting upon a means for arriving at that continuity on the screen. This idea is typical of Hitchcock: at once distinctly implausible and at the same time satisfying, since as viewers we do not really want to leave our cozy set, yet we do want to see what happens to Miss Lonelyhearts.

Here, Hitchcock calculates correctly how much we are willing to suspend our belief. We are grateful that he has allowed us to stay in with Jeff and go out with Miss Lonelyhearts.

Hitchcock had no problem with giving priority to unity over plausibility as long as it did not tax the audience too much. That is why he seems so confused when Truffaut faults him for the implausibility of the plot in *I Confess*, wherein the murderer of the lawyer confesses his killing to the priest who had been blackmailed by the lawyer. Here, Hitchcock chose not to concede the point to Truffaut, as he did so often in the interview: "Let's just say it comes under the heading of an old-fashioned plot," Hitchcock says and then testily turns on French cinema for sorely lacking this kind of ingenious story. "And, while we're on the subject, I should like to ask you a question. Why has it become old-fashioned to tell a story, to use a plot? I believe that there are no more plots in the recent French films."[6] Hitchcock's point is that what makes a story engaging so often is its unlikeliness, the marvel of coincidence.

Brill, too, in his study of Hitchcock as the author of romances, notes that the plots of romance "rather than being rationalized or made plausible emphasize lucky coincidence and exhibit a high degree of conventionality and artificiality." Hitchcock's films are characteristic of romantic narratives, Brill points out, in their use of three forms of antirealism: "conspicuous, artificiality, reference to their own fictionality, and the frequent use of marvelous plot elements."[7]

Hitchcock, however, defended the marvelous aspects of his films, not as a romanticist, but as an artist whose vision was sufficiently strong to warrant a more active imaginative response from his audience than customary. He regretted Americans' demand for realistic art. He argued to Bogdanovich that, in the mid-thirties, "the audience would accept more, the films of the period were full of fantasy, and one didn't have to worry much about logic or truth. When I came to America, the first thing I had to learn was that the audiences were more questioning. I'll put it another way. Less avantgarde."[8] The last comment is revealing, showing, as his identification with Klee does, that he did not always consider himself the great commercial showman, though he may have often displayed himself as such, but as an artist whose vision in its purest form was abstract enough to tax, rather than cater to, his audience.

Truffaut's comments about the set of *Frenzy* in his later edition of his interview with Hitchcock might apply equally to *Rear Window* and its clockwork-like set. In *Frenzy*, he discovers that "nightmarish, stifling Hitchcockian universe in which the characters know each other—the killer, the innocent man, the victims, the witness; that world boiled down to the essential, where each conversation in a shop or in a bar happens to deal with the killings; a world made up of coincidences so systematically organized that they crosscut each other vertically and horizontally. *Frenzy* is the image of a crossword puzzle on the leitmotif of murder."[9]

Rear Window could also be described as a world "boiled down to its essence." When Hitchcock pans counterclockwise around the entire complex, we contain the entire world of the film. We are at the opposite end of the spectrum from those un-Aristotelian films where backdrops change with the drop of a hat and characters age from generation to generation. Hitchcock had a fastidious mind when it came to the unities. He abhorred aging on film. He did not like films with international casts speaking English on foreign soil. He filmed the courtroom scenes in *Dial M for Murder* in such a way that they seem a swirling dream because, as he told Truffaut, "this way was more intimate, you see, so that the unity of emotion was maintained. If I had had a courtroom built, people would have started to cough restlessly, thinking, 'now they're starting a different picture.'"[10]

Double and Triple Bottoming

Hitchcock reinforced the unity of his set by keeping its materials few. He was fond of quoting Chekhov that if a gun is hanging over the hearth in act one of a play, it should go off by act three. In other words, make use of and fully exploit the material you have introduced into your play. As he never tired of pointing out to interviewers, Hitchcock followed this dictum religiously. One of the reasons he liked to limit his sets is that it forced him to work and rework the few items that found their way into that set and thus strengthen the sense of unity in his film. Once he has introduced a notable object, he tends to stick with it, not to introduce too many others, to use and reuse that object until he has wound it so tightly into his story that the object has been invested with multiple significances. He does this with setting as well. San Francisco is the proper background for a film about vertigo. If Mount Rushmore appears in your background, make sure Cary Grant is hanging from one of the faces by the end of your film. Like the French New Wave directors, Hitchcock held the picturesque backdrop in disdain. His interviews are filled with comments that manifest his frustration with useless sets and backdrops no matter how elegant or picturesque they are. He was frustrated with the fluffy attractiveness of *Suspicion's* set, which might strike an observer as an above-average Hollywood set. But for Hitchcock, the visual background's worth was proportionate to the use he could make of it. When Charles Thomas Samuels tries to get him to see the beauty of *The Bicycle Thief's* locations and background, which are open and which the viewer can explore freely, Hitchcock does not take the point. "I go further than a film like *The Bicycle Thief*, which shows a man and a boy walking in front of a panorama. I believe that your backgrounds must be involved in the story."[11] Hitchcock believed in making use of what found its way into his screen, not letting things lie there uselessly (as he saw it) to be noticed by his viewers and thereby detract from the determined thesis of his scene. So he uses the objects in his films and assigns them significance by making them part of the plot, the irony, the romance, the purpose of his film.

In *Rear Window*, for example, Hitchcock keeps working meanings out of Jeff's profession as a photographer. It was Jeff's job that landed him in his cast and in this mess, to which the pictures of the auto accident that disabled Jeff and that are scattered about his apartment attest. Jeff's profession seems tied to what the film reveals as his weaknesses—an inability to settle down, a desire to view the world from a distance, through a lens, rather than commit himself fully to one person or place. Who better to fall prey to the lures of voyeurism than a photographer, and a traveling one at that, one who not only wants to view the world but never settle into it.

It is almost comical—certainly implausible—just how many uses he finds for Jeff's camera throughout the film, but it is also a telling example of Hitchcock's mania for unity. Jeff uses it to peep on the Thorwalds when he becomes more obsessed with the case, thus strengthening the idea that Jeff's voyeurism is an extension of his career as a photographer. Jeff uses the camera to help break the case, comparing Thorwald's garden below with how it was in a picture he took weeks before to deduce that Thorwald has buried something in his garden. He readies his camera to flash warnings to Lisa when she is rummaging through the Thorwalds' apartment. And he uses the camera to defend himself when Thorwald comes to murder him, just as he has used the camera to defend himself from the world his entire life. Countless critics, knowing the lascivious turn in Hitchcock's humor, have seen visual puns in the image of Jeff's huge telephoto lens in his lap, especially given how many jokes there are about his weak sexuality and how many suggestions there are that he uses photography as a means of compensating for this. As Anthony Mazzella puts it, "The impotent L. B. Jefferies acquires power through his camera: the lens he uses for spying frequently rests on his lap and becomes the potency he lacks."[12] Hitchcock does not just make Jeff a photographer and leave it at that. He uses and reuses the machinery of Jeff's trade until his profession is intricately tied to character and action in the film.

Similarly, Hitchcock has a great deal of fun on the subject of jewelry. Lars Thorwald is a jewelry salesman, so Hitchcock contrives the means by which Lars will be implicated and caught for his wife's murder through mistakes he makes in handling her jewelry. He is undone by the very thing about which he is supposedly most professional. Lars is, at times, a very sympathetic villain, but there is something satisfying in his getting caught because he was fingering his wife's jewelry a little too voraciously, ogling her personal adornments with a cold professional eye.

Building the plot around jewelry also fits nicely with the story of Lisa, who Jeff feels is too superficial and fashion-conscious to handle the tough life he leads as a traveling photographer. Ironically, it is exactly because of her flair for fashion, jewelry, and handbags that Lisa cracks the case. Lisa envisions what she would be like if she were Mrs. Thorwald, deduces she, herself, would never have left her wedding ring and favorite handbag at home were she leaving for an extended vacation (we have seen how important marriage is to Lisa), sneaks into the Thorwalds' apartment and gets the ring.

There is also a great deal of meaning packed into the wedding ring in this film. Lisa wants to marry Jeff, and ironically, the key piece of evidence she and Jeff seek is a wedding ring. When Lisa gets the ring on her finger and wiggles her finger for Jeff to see from his window, she seems to be not only pointing out that she has found the evidence but to be proposing as well, a clever marriage of plot and character development that tickled Truffaut. Moreover, as she wiggles her finger with the wedding ring, Jeff is not the only one staring at the finger. So is Lars Thorwald, and at this moment Hitchcock is not only parading his key bit of evidence and urging Jeff towards marriage, but also saying something about the inviolability of the marriage vows. Thorwald had thought to do away with his marriage, but the ring will not die. (One thinks here of the troubled look Lars wore earlier when he examined the ring while talking to his mistress on the phone.) Mrs. Thorwald, who Hitchcock specifically cast as a Lisa look-alike, is resurrected, the ghost of marriage past. It is also interesting that Jeff and Lars meet for the first time over the wedding ring. While Jeff stares at it, so does Lars until, following the path from Lisa's finger to Jeff's window, his eyes meet those of Jeff. Jeff and Lars, who most critics see as a dark double of Jeff, are united over the ring, like a nervous couple at an altar. The ring ingeniously unites Jeff and Lisa and also unites Jeff and Lisa with their darker halves, Mr. and Mrs. Thorwald.

Hitchcock uses the same visual patterns over and over just as he reuses the physical objects in the set. Jeff lies sleeping with a broken leg at the beginning of the film and lies sleeping at the end with two broken legs. When the camera pans around the courtyard at six different times during the film, it does so on the same track and from the same direction, breaking up the action almost like so many chapter divisions. The first pan around the courtyard begins by following a cat up the staircase outside Jeff's apartment; a useful shot, it turns out later, in establishing the path Lisa and Stella follow when they go digging in Thorwald's garden. At the outset of the film, Hitchcock cuts from the shot of the thermometer, which establishes the hothouse atmosphere of the film, to our first view of the Composer, who is suffering not only from the heat but from a midlife crisis (if we are to deduce anything by the way he angrily switches off a radio that blares a commercial aimed at male menopause). At the end of the film, Hitchcock returns to the thermometer, establishing that the heat wave (along with all the moral crises of the film) has passed. Again, he cuts to the Composer, who is again listening to music, but much more happily this time. He and Miss Lonelyhearts are listening to his new hit record. The midlife crisis has given way to career, success. Early in the film, Lisa arrives at Jeff's apartment and, in a swirl of charming enthusiasms, takes a tour of his apartment, turning on his three lamps, stopping at each to strike a pose and announce one of her three names, "Lisa . . . Carol . . . Fremont." Later in the film, she will repeat the same pattern, turning on the three lamps, and stopping each time as she does, but this time her clothes and demeanor are more grave. She turns on the lamps as she weighs the mystery of the murder, stopping at each lamp to consider the clues.

Stefan Sharff refers to these scenes in which Hitchcock repeats earlier constructions and movements as "recalls." These recalls, he says, "are perhaps innocuous, not big happenings and, most likely, the perceptive motors are subliminal, yet they leave the viewer with a peculiar sense of fulfillment, a bit of a thrill."[13] Hitchcock, like Bresson, liked to "double and triple bottom to things."[14] He gives his films weight and gravity by deepening our familiarity with the film's materials and patterns. When we watch a Hitchcock film, we are on steady, firm ground.

Aural Intrusions

Another primary way in which Hitchcock contributes to the unity of *Rear Window* is through his meticulously laid sound track. Elisabeth Weiss has noted that Hitchcock's sound tracks were particularly creative in those films (*Lifeboat*, *Rope*, *Dial M for Murder*, and *Rear Window*) where he experimented with highly restricted space: "Having established such stringent visual limitations, Hitchcock uses sound in a highly creative way, often depending on it to establish tension."[15] In other films, Weiss notes Hitchcock "creates tension between what is in a frame and what is out of the frame. In the single set films, he creates tension between onset and offset space."[16] The ingenuity of Hitchcock's sound track in *Rear Window*, perhaps the best of any of his sound tracks, is probably owing to the strict limitations he imposed upon himself in the film. By forcing himself to respect unity of space as much as he did, by limiting his visual scope, he found himself more dependent on sound and consequently used sound more creatively. Moreover, the sound that he used, all incidental to the set, only served to further deepen the sense of place.

The sound track of *Rear Window* is comprised almost entirely of incidental sounds. The music we hear in the film issues from Jeff's apartment complex. Hitchcock cheats a little in the jazz theme that opens the film and seems, like any normal opening theme, to exist outside the action of the film. But as the film progresses, Hitchcock makes the music thinner and tinnier and finally reveals its source as the Composer's radio.

Hitchcock's sound track intensifies the unity of his films in several ways. First of all, obviously, by never allowing sounds to enter into the film from outside the world depicted in the film, he maintains his seal over his universe. It is true to itself, self-contained. Secondly, by only using sounds from the world of the apartment complex, he is able to keep using and reusing his material at hand, to stick, as was his wont, to a limited material close at hand. He is able aurally as well as visually to keep weaving the other apartment dwellers into Jeff and Lisa's life and to intensify the relationships between everyone in the courtyard.

Weiss notes that Hitchcock's use of sound and music "helps integrate the sense of space in the courtyard." This integration, Weiss further argues, "counteracts the effect of the film's editing and mise-en-scène, both of which tend to isolate the neighbors from one another."[17] Jeff's neighbors rarely interact or even see one another. When they do, it is usually a hostile collision, like that between the Sculptress and Lars Thorwald, or the dog owner's angry speech to the neighbors. But aurally, they cannot help but be connected. Their music and noises waft into each other's apartments, and to the peeping Jeff's apartment also. The effect is that their busy conscious selves take no note of one another, but on another, more unconscious level, communicated aurally, they are acutely aware of and involved with one another. The sound track weaves their lives together.

So the Composer's romantic song, "Lisa," spread throughout the entire film as it is, weaves together several stories. It seems to express Lisa's romantic ideals, but it also adds a sad counterpoint to the Thorwalds' marital squabbles and reaches out to Miss Lonelyhearts during her contemplation of suicide. An anonymous record player from somewhere in the complex spins out saccharin love songs, such as "To See You Is to Love You" and "Waiting for My True Love to Appear," that comment touchingly and ironically on Miss Lonelyhearts's pathetic pantomimes of romance. A crowd of revelers at the Composer's apartment belt out a boozy version of "Mona Lisa" that offers a sad undertone to Miss Lonelyhearts's struggle with an aggressive young man in her apartment. A recording of a lugubrious organ version of Rodgers and Hart's waltz, "Lover," issuing from some neighbor's late-night gramophone mixed with silence, the sound of distant fog horns from the bay, and of rain falling down the gutter serves as the ironic backdrop for Lars Thorwald's turgid bit-by-bit removal of his wife's body from the premises. A distant recording of hootenanny music contrasts sharply with Jeff's isolated panic when he realizes that Thorwald has just put down the receiver and is headed over to his apartment. A carnival piano rendition of "That's Amore" accompanies the arrival of the Newlyweds. An opera singer practicing her scales offers humorous counterpoint to Jeff's quest to reach over his stiff cast to the itch on his big toe.

Hitchcock does several things with sound in these scenes. Sometimes he uses sound or music to deepen an intended effect. The carnival version of "That's Amore" matches the scenes of innocent love we see with the Newlyweds' arrival. At other times he uses sound or music as ironic counterpoint, using music that seems opposed to the visual in order to add irony to the scene or complicate our reaction. The romantic idealism of the songs that we hear as we watch Miss Lonelyhearts, for example, contrasts sadly with the pathetic nature of her real-life situation. Weiss refers to Hitchcock's fondness for "asynchronous sound" noting that "less than one-tenth of the time that we are looking at Jeff's neighbors does the dominant sound emanate from the particular window under surveillance." By using sounds that are "contrapuntal to the visuals," by separating sound and image, Hitchcock is able to achieve, as Weiss summarizes it, "variety, denseness, tension, and . . . irony."[18] By separating sound and image, Hitchcock complicates and deepens scenes in *Rear Window*. He also taxes the readers' senses to their utmost. Hitchcock speaks often of the redundancy of offering the viewer a sound that matches what they are seeing. "It's essential to separate clearly the dialogue from the visual elements," he told Truffaut.[19] To Richard Schickel, he speaks of having the "dialogue counterpoint to the visual," and of dialogue "properly interspersed or overlaid."[20] To fully exercise the viewers, he gives them the vision of one thing and the sound of another. That is a true economy of expression and full use of the viewer's senses. It also makes for more active viewers, struggling as they are to incorporate what they see and what they hear, which are not, as they are in most directors' films, the same thing. Weiss also notes that Hitchcock hardly ever used sound "redundantly but rather as an additional resource,"[21] appealing to our eye in one place and our ear in another and thus more fully using his set and our senses and imaginative powers.

Robert Bresson, who bears many striking similarities to Hitchcock as a filmmaker, particularly in his meticulous use of sound, emphasized that sights and sounds have very different effects on the viewers' minds. Sounds, he felt, made the deeper impression. Sight he felt to be a more superficial sensation. "When a sound can replace an image," Bresson wrote, "cut the image or neutralize it. The ear goes more towards the within, the eye towards the outer."[22] Hitchcock, too, had a strong sense of gravity or power of sound. He often depended on what Weiss refers to as "aural intrusions," sounds from offscreen, to convey his moments of deepest terror. So the murder in *Rear Window* takes place offscreen somewhere, communicated only by a scream that is swallowed quickly in silence. The woman's discovery of her dog's body comes to us in an offscreen scream. Lars Thorwald's arrival in Jeff's apartment comes in aural increments: the click on the phone as the receiver is hung up, the jarring slam of the elevator doors as the elevator begins its ascent, the exaggerated sound of the footsteps in the hallway, the click of the hall light going off, the amplified sound of the door opening. Even in moments of lighter shock, for example, those scenes where Stella discovers Jeff (and us) peeping, Hitchcock has her voice precede her image. Hitchcock seemed aware, as Bresson noted, that sounds penetrate more deeply and consequently were a more efficient means of conveying terror.

The Rhythm of Sound

So Hitchcock's sound track contributes to the unity of the film by aurally tying together the neighbors even when they are visually separated from one another, by introducing the sound of one apartment into the image of another. Another way in which Hitchcock's sound track contributes to the unity in his film is by lending his scenes balance and proportion. Many scenes are choreographed, visually, to the sound track. For example, Jeff reaches that itch just as the opera singer reaches the top of her scales. Virtually all of Miss Lonelyhearts's scenes represent music videos of sorts. But the most haunting rhythms in the film are often those that mix music with other sounds from the neighborhood, what Naremore refers to as the "near symphony of effects and diegetic music."[23] Hitchcock gave careful consideration to the smallest sounds in his films. Theresa Wright noted during the filming of *Shadow of a Doubt* that "if an actor was strumming his fingers it was not just an idle strumming, it had a beat, a musical pattern to it—it was like a sound refrain, whether someone was walking or rustling a paper or tearing an envelope or whistling, whether it was a flutter of birds or an outside sound, it was carefully orchestrated by him. He really scored the sound effects the way a musician writes for instruments."[24]

Like Bresson, Hitchcock had an appreciation for the quality of an isolated sound. He often told interviewers that to describe a sound effect effectively one had to imagine its equivalent in dialogue. Hitchcock liked to approach his sounds imaginatively, sometimes giving them personalities, envisioning them as small characters in his films. For example, the distant, mournful sound of a ship's horn sounds out now and then in *Rear Window*, usually at quiet and poignant moments when we are watching the windows across the way, suggesting nothing so much as the sad exhale of a distant god watching the pathetic struggles of humans.

Hitchcock would isolate sounds that had for him a strong appeal and then weave them, as Bresson and Tati did, into a kind of *musique concret*. "Reorganize the unorganized noises of a street, a railroad station, an airport. . . . Play them back one by one in silence and adjust the blend," wrote Bresson. "Noise of a door opening and shutting, noise of footsteps, etc., for the sake of rhythm."[25] Similarly, Hitchcock spoke of aiming for, in *Juno and the Paycock*, "a medley of noises: the machine guns that were firing down the street; the tinny note of a cheap gramophone playing in the room; the chatter of other people in the room; the tread-tread tramp-tramp of a funeral procession going by."[26]

Rear Window represents one of his most striking "medley" of sounds. Snatches of conversation, foghorns, car horns, sirens, the sounds of children playing in the street, the whistle of the dog owner, and the whistle of someone who favors Strauss's waltzes combine with the Composer's tinkling of "Lisa," the stray pop tunes, and other varieties of music that issue from radios and gramophones to create an aural cubist work of art, a Godard-like collision of musical and aural fragments and suggestions. Hitchcock's lovely fluid pans around the courtyard in *Rear Window* are often appreciated for their visual sweep, set detail, and cunning timing but less so for the rhythm of sounds that accompanies and punctuates them: the sound of the Composer striking his piano keys, for example, in the second pan, which gives way to the woman whistling for her dog and the dog's bark, which is punctuated by the sound of a distant car pulling away before the whistle for the dog segues into a whistled waltz that floats pleasantly in the night air. What Spoto says of *The Birds*, one of Hitchcock's experiments in music-less sound, applies equally to *Rear Window*: "every noise and effect was orchestrated, every sound filtered and altered to support the feeling Hitchcock wanted in each scene."[27] Weiss, too, notes that whereas most directors tend to work on the three categories of their sound track (music, dialogue, sound effects) separately, Hitchcock "did not conceive of them as separate entities. One distinctive element of his aural style is a continuity in his use of language, music, and sound effects that reflects his ability to conceive of their combined impact before he actually hears them together."[28]

Hitchcock's respect for sound was so great that he often found the significance of his dialogue not in what is said but in the relationship of what is said to other sounds on the sound track. "Dialogue" he told Truffaut during the discussion of *Rear Window*, "should simply be a sound among other sounds, just something that comes out of the mouths of people."[29] *Rear Window* in particular, with its distant conversation, gave Hitchcock the opportunity to use dialogue as a sound rather than to convey an idea. We often cannot make out the words, only the tenor of conversations in the apartments across the way: the bitterness of the Thorwalds' fight, the admonitions of Miss Torso and Miss Lonelyhearts as they fend off aggressive suitors in their apartments. We cannot make out the exact words being said, but we get a feel for the tone, which, interspersed with the Composer's piano and other sounds of the courtyard, assume a musical rather than a verbal significance, a significance that is often all the more poignant for having been communicated through distant sounds rather than exact words. It is the aural equivalent of Hitchcock's visual plan. Just as a distant perspective on the neighbors makes them seem small and trapped and vulnerable, so the sound of marital discord or Miss Lonelyhearts's tears, only partially audible and striking out in an enveloping silence, is sadder and more touching.

Woolrich's hero Hal Jefferies, in the short story "Rear Window" on which the film is based, noted this sad quality in the sounds emanating from his neighbors' apartments.

> Here and there a wall played back, like a sounding board, a snatch of radio program coming in too loud. If you listened carefully, you could hear an occasional clink of dishes mixed in, faint, far off. The chains of little habits that were their lives unreeled themselves. They were all bound in them tighter than the tightest strait-jacket any jailer ever devised, though they all thought themselves free.[30]

This passage goes a long way toward explaining why Hitchcock was drawn to Woolrich's story. As mentioned earlier, Woolrich had been described as a literary Hitchcock, and Woolrich's biographer repeatedly refers to him as Hitchcock's "spiritual brother." One can easily imagine Hitchcock's shock of recognition in reading this passage that interprets sound so similarly to the way he did. It seems very likely that this passage influenced Hitchcock's treatment of sound in *Rear Window*. Woolrich expresses here what the intent of Hitchcock's sounds in *Rear Window* will be: to convey, as his distant images did, the faraway sound of human loneliness and entrapment.

The Rhythm of Sound: One Sequence

Perhaps the best example of the meticulous nature of Hitchcock's sound track, the beauty and complexity of his rhythms, is the sequence of scenes that carry us through Miss Lonelyhearts's charade with a fantasy lover, Miss Torso's juggling of wolves, and the Thorwalds' fight over Lars's telephone call to his mistress. The sequence is memorable enough by way of its elaborate visual layout and meticulously choreographed tracking shots. But the rhythms of the sound track throughout the sequence are also rich, emotional, and complex.

The sequence begins as Jeff and Lisa finish a conversation in which Lisa has tried to convince Jeff to "come home," to settle in New York. The conversation has been light and comical but has ended on a serious note. "I can see you looking handsome and successful in a blue flannel suit," says Lisa, who wants Jeff to open a photography studio in Manhattan. "Now, let's stop talking nonsense, shall we," Jeff responds cruelly and in such a way as to make it clear the discussion is over. As the conversation takes this darker tone, we hear the orchestral introduction to Bing Crosby's "To See You Is to Love You" (played on some neighbor's gramophone) that introduces, and will serve as the background for, Miss Lonelyhearts's pantomime. But at this point, the melancholy strains of the orchestra have nothing to do with Miss Lonelyhearts. They seem here to underline Lisa's sadness in her relationship with Jeff.

This is a favorite technique of Hitchcock's and one he uses often in the film (the Newlyweds' arrival is another example). Hitchcock is at once summarizing one scene and introducing another, using music to overlap his scenes and hide from the viewer the seam that binds them. Only when Lisa has left the room to make dinner do we, and Jeff, turn our gaze on Miss Lonelyhearts, who begins her pantomime not with the music but with the music's words. The music provides an elegant bridge between scenes and also strengthens the connection between Miss Lonelyhearts and Lisa that Hitchcock will spend so much time developing since the music seems to express both of their loneliness.

Hitchcock continues to choreograph his images to the song. The music of "To See You Is to Love You" begins with, and marks, the sad resolution of Jeff and Lisa's conversation. The words of the song are timed to begin with Miss Lonelyhearts's scene, which also is timed to last just as long as the song's lyrics do. Miss Lonelyhearts crumbles in despair to the last touching line of the song, "and I'll see you every night," and as the song returns to its instrumental orchestration, we return to Jeff and Lisa.

In the conversation that follows, Jeff continues to be cruel to Lisa, first missing the obvious parallels that Lisa makes between herself and Miss Lonelyhearts and then insultingly suggesting that Lisa is more like Miss Torso, the neighborhood party girl, to whose window they now turn their attention. The later instrumental portion of "To See You Is to Love You" continues to serve-as a backdrop to Jeff and Lisa's conversation and to the images of Miss Torso "juggling wolves." The song, which has taken us through both

Miss Lonelyhearts's and Miss Torso's romantic sagas and two conversations between Jeff and Lisa, is timed to wind down as Jeff and Lisa's conversation does. Lisa tells Jeff that Miss Torso does not love any of the prosperous men she is entertaining. When Jeff asks how she knows, she responds, "you said it resembled my apartment, didn't you," by which she means to say that she too is surrounded by handsome prosperous men, but she only loves Jeff. That Lisa gets the last word is reinforced by the fact that Hitchcock shuts down the music as she shuts down the conversation. "To See You Is to Love You" begins the descent of its final notes as Lisa turns her back to Jeff. There remains only a bit of stray instrumentation, which Hitchcock uses as background for Jeff taking a quick look at the Newlyweds' window. The final notes of the song punctuate Jeff's look of nervous humor as he contemplates what is going on behind that window.

Finally, then, "To See You Is to Love You" finishes, having served Hitchcock ably. It began at the end of one argument and finished at the end of another. In between, it provided a melancholy background to Miss Lonelyhearts's and Miss Torso's sagas and in the very final notes offered ironic counterpoint to the Newlyweds' window. Now silence reigns, and yet one would not say that the line of rhythm that Hitchcock uses to connect several scenes here does. With the silence, Hitchcock moves Jeff's gaze to the Thorwalds' apartment. It is notable how often Hitchcock quiets his sound track when we gaze through the Thorwalds' window. Hitchcock was aware of the power of sound and the way it could, if overused, dissipate drama. "Another thing to avoid," he wrote, "is using dramatic sound in a scene which is already charged with as much drama as it can hold. It does not increase the drama—it lessens it."[31] He recognized that the Thorwald apartment, the heart of the film's mystery and suspense, was of maximum interest to the viewer and therefore required the minimum use of sound.

After the elaborate "To See, You Is to Love You" music video he has just given us, he retreats to a silence carefully punctuated by neighborhood sounds. "Silence," Hitchcock said, "is often very effective and its effect is heightened by the proper handling of the music before and after."[32] We do feel the silence more acutely in this scene because of the music that has preceded it but also because of the carefully chosen neighborhood sounds that punctuate it. The sound track here is no less haunting for its lack of music. Hitchcock achieves here what Bresson refers to as a "silence obtained by a pianissimo of noises," a silence that itself seems musical and weighted with significance by virtue of its interplay with sounds. The distant sound of the Thorwalds' voices, only snatches of which we can discern ("you'll never get away with it" she tells him) are interspersed with the sounds of a distant siren that approaches and fades and the distant mournful sound of a ship's horn in the harbor.

The small scene in the Thorwald apartment has its own rhythm, first scored as it is by its series of distant, melancholy sounds, secondly in the way it finishes just as Hitchcock strikes up the music again. When Thorwald's wife catches him on the phone, he follows her like a dumb beast into her room where perhaps something he says or his generally foolish look of surprise and confusion make her break down into convulsive laughter. Hitchcock chooses this particular moment of hysteria to both end the scene and start up the music again, as the Composer in the apartment nearby begins to play "Lisa" once again. The effect is a classic Hitchcock contrast: the hysterical dissolution of marriage scored to the rich melody of romance. The result of this contrast is a feeling of sadness and pity for the Thorwalds and for what happens in marriage, a perfect instance of how Hitchcock often has strong things to say but usually chooses to say them in sounds and images, not words. In fact, if Hitchcock was most explicit in paralleling the Composer's music to Lisa, who often comments on and swoons to the music, he also uses the music at specific moments to score the tragedy of the Thorwalds' situation. The same music that serves to communicate Lisa's unfulfilled love is meant to convey Mrs. Thorwald's tragedy of a love gone bad. It is no coincidence that the richest, most heartfelt version of Lisa's theme takes place when Lisa and Mrs. Thorwald's worlds conjoin, the night Lisa struggles with Lars in Mrs. Thorwald's bedroom.

The Thorwalds' scene finishes with Mrs. Thorwald's laughter, but the music continues, serving as a backdrop to installment number three of Jeff and Lisa's ongoing squabble in Jeff's apartment. Lisa, after enduring two or three more insults from Jeff regarding the subject of marriage, sets the gourmet dinner she has prepared down before him, saying "well, at least you can't complain about the dinner." "Lisa," Jeff says with mock fatigue (this time getting the last word himself), "it's perfect," a sarcastic allusion to a previous conversation with Stella in which he described Lisa as "too perfect." Hitchcock gives us a shot of Lisa's pained reaction, and as he does so the Composer's song, rendered in one of the slower, gloomier pacings, finishes in sad, halting chords. The fade-out, followed by a scene much later in the evening, marks this conclusively as the point where Hitchcock meant to finish this sequence of scenes. The sequence has encompassed two songs and an intervening piece of *musique concret* and has scored significant and extended scenes in Miss Lonelyhearts's, Miss Torso's, and the Thorwalds' apartments, as well as three installments of Jeff and Lisa's fight. The sound track here has lent the scenes cohesion, and it has decorated them subtly and with some complexity: beginning, halting, resuming, finishing at key moments, punching certain lines of dialogue and dancing counterpoint with others. Hitchcock's sound track was a key ingredient in *Rear Window's* strong sense of structure.

The Conservative Background

Perhaps Hitchcock's most subtle contribution to the unity of *Rear Window* is in his careful approach to each shot. In *Rear Window*, as much as in any of his films, Hitchcock avoids stylistic extremes. Leitch notes an inconsistency in Truffaut's interview with Hitchcock where both Truffaut and Hitchcock agree that Hitchcock's style has become increasingly invisible and unobtrusive, and yet both spend most of their times glorying in Hitchcock's most "self-advertising" bits of style.[33] Perhaps Hitchcock's generally quiet technique serves as the background for his sharply expressive moments. *Rear Window* is hardly without unusual and expressive visual schemes. But Truffaut's praise for Hitchcock's increasingly invisible style seems on target when we consider *Rear Window*, a film in which the elaborate set seems to have relieved Hitchcock of the necessity for many elaborate shots.

In their discussion of Hitchcock imitator Lee Thompson, Truffaut and Hitchcock both agree about the absurdity of shots from extravagant points of view, for example, a shot of a man rummaging inside a refrigerator from inside the refrigerator or of a couple before a fireplace from behind the fire. Even in a scene where Hitchcock shoots from a distorted perspective, for example, the scene in *Notorious* in which Ingrid Bergman wakes from a drunken stupor to see Cary Grant in the convex image of a glass, he shoots from the perspective of character. The scene is designed to make us feel what it is like to see a mysterious figure from the perspective of someone who has a hangover. The shot is even more justified when we realize that Alicia is waking permanently from her drunken habits into a new, drink-free way of life. Hitchcock's camera does not find itself in odd places, like the back of a refrigerator, arbitrarily.

The camera in *Rear Window* is for the most part, like Jeff, fixed, not prone to extravagant movements. There are those six lovely pans around the courtyard, but such fluidity of movement is exercised very cautiously and given to us in almost musical increments and always from the same perspective and in the same directions. Only when the camera leaves Jeff's apartment and window altogether, during the scenes where the dog's body is discovered and Jeff is thrown out the window, does the camera compromise its stateliness. In these scenes, the radical departure from point of view and the extreme drama of the scenes warrant the excited montage of which they are comprised.

Nowhere is the conservative nature of Hitchcock's approach to his shots more apparent than in the sequences that intersperse shots of the apartments across the courtyard with reaction shots of Jeff. Hitchcock is careful in these shots in many ways. First, he is careful to constantly come back to Jeff so that Jeff can, through his reactions, help us understand what we have seen and what it means. Hitchcock, like Tati, liked subtle visual puns and often remarked that some of his best visual jokes were lost on his audience. There is a nice one early on in the film when the couple on the fire escape wake up and Hitchcock surprises us with the wife's presence, her head popping up absurdly at her husband's feet. But unlike Tati, Hitchcock was not willing to make his audience work too hard at discovering these jokes. We do not get lost in his long takes or distant visual schemes. When it gets too hard or when he has any doubt that we understand, he uses Jeff to clear things up for us. Montage comes to our rescue.

Also, Hitchcock measures his approach to the apartments across the way very carefully. As the film begins, we are restricted to distant shots, Jeff having not yet used the equipment that will help him zoom in for closer views. But as Jeff gets more preoccupied with the apartments, he breaks out his binoculars, which allow a closer, middle range view and then the telephoto lens, which allows us something approximating a close-up. Hitchcock is careful to approach the apartments slowly within scenes, first from a distance and then from a middle or closer distance. And he is careful to build up an intimacy with the apartments over the course of the film. At first, we are restricted in our view of them, but as we get to know them better, our views get closer.

Hitchcock is just as careful in his reaction shots of Jeff, usually filming Jeff in an above-the-waist middle-range shot but coming in for close-ups at key moments, for example, when he hears Mrs. Thorwald's scream or sees Lars Thorwald cleaning his knives, or when he squirms uncomfortably with the knowledge of what is transpiring behind the Newlyweds' window. In these shots, Hitchcock's camera, never afraid of the most massive close-ups, comes in suffocatingly tight, and Stewart's eyes roll about with the expressiveness of a scared animal or a silent screen actor. His eyes provide the movement upon which the shot focuses.

This is, of course, a central doctrine of Hitchcock's aesthetic: the shot should be determined by, or match, the emotions at hand. The fact that he repeated this doctrine ad nauseam does not detract from its importance in his art. "I am against virtuosity for its own sake," he told Truffaut. "Technique should enrich the action. One does not set the camera at a certain angle just because the cameraman happens to be enthusiastic about that spot. The only thing that matters is whether the installation of the camera at a given angle is going to give the scene its maximum impact. The beauty of image and movement, the rhythm and the effects—everything must be subordinated to the purpose."[34]

Hitchcock's shots within the apartment are as carefully or conservatively approached as his ones out the window. Most of the shots are John Ford-like in their natural balance, their dependence on balances of twos and threes. There is some composition in depth, but Leitch is absolutely right, at least in this film, that Hitchcock's "use of deep focus which emphasizes relationships between characters and their backgrounds rather than relationships among characters within the frame is consistently more like Wyler's than Welles'."[35] Stella, in those scenes where Hitchcock comically contrasts her busy efficiency with Jeff's blowhard inertia, at one point gets Jeff out of her industrious way by sticking him in a recessed area of the apartment that frames—and disempowers—him rather nicely. The composition, which Hitchcock directed back into the center of the frame, neatly highlights Jeff's physical weakness and marginality. But there is none of Orson Welles's baroque splendor in scenes like this. Rather, the walls, windows, and lamp frame the figure in the recess with a Ford-like classical balance.

Most of the scenes in the apartment are filmed from a medium distance and not with extreme angles. When they are expressive, it is with a quiet elegance that seems to match the fashionable lines of Lisa's and Doyle's clothes. Hitchcock arranges many compositions around the interesting vertical and horizontal angles Jeff provides, seated as he is with his leg projecting straight out ahead of him. For example, Jeff is arranged on one side of his window, his leg underlining the window's horizontal line while Doyle is on the other, the elegant lines of his suit accentuating the right vertical line of the window.

Many of Hitchcock's compositions in the apartment are nicely aligned with the dialogue. In the scene where Lisa, Jeff, and Doyle discuss Mrs. Thorwald's trunk, Doyle breaks one elegant composition of three to form an even more clever one. Lisa has just asked him if he confiscated Mrs. Thorwald's trunk at the railroad station, to which Doyle responds that he "sent it on its merry and legal way." As he says this, he plops himself down on Jeff's couch. But as he does, Hitchcock's camera moves to the right, creating an open space that anticipates Jeff's arrival in the composition from the right. Jeff arrives on cue, his movement simultaneous with his dialogue ("Why, when a woman is taking a simple short trip, does she take everything she owns?"). Doyle then cues Lisa's entry into the scene by saying, "Let's let the female psychology department handle that, shall we," and Lisa slides into her appointed spot, between the two battling men, her dialogue, like Jeff's, choreographed to her movement. Lisa replies, "I'd say it looks like she wasn't coming back," the drama of her interpretation reinforced by the visual drama of her arrival (see plate 1). This kind of mise-en-scène represents a quiet, elegant dance of sorts, attractive in its own right but also useful in giving the words that are rhythmically aligned with it different shades of significance. Hitchcock would quietly step up the drama of his mise-en-scène when he wanted to accentuate the drama of his dialogue.

There is a kind of seamlessness to the filming in the apartment. We will return from a visit across the way to a final reaction shot of Jeff, but in this one the left side of the screen will be empty, with the door in the background. Then Lisa or Doyle will walk through the door. This instead of an abrupt cut from the apartments across the way to an objective shot of the door, the doorbell ringing, Lisa running to the door, and so forth. Hitchcock likes to overlap the beginning of one scene and the ending of another, as in the scene where the beginnings of the tune "To See You Is to Love You" playing across the way somewhere act as a poignant finish to Jeff and Lisa's argument *and* an introduction to the visual pantomime with Miss Lonelyhearts that is going to constitute the next scene, or the scene in which Miss Lonelyhearts seats herself at the café across the street just as Lars Thorwald crosses the street on the way back to his apartment, thus effecting a smooth transition from Miss Lonely-hearts's story to Thorwald's in a single frame (see plate 2).

These are the kinds of scenes Hitchcock had in mind when he said that "it takes so long, and so much work, to achieve simplicity. " They are the kinds of scenes

Sharff has in mind when he says that the layout of *Rear Window* is "reminiscent of an architect's plans" with "stresses . . . figured out ahead of time, then harmonized with scores of correlates, never losing control of the overall aesthetic thrust."[36] As Sharff notes, it would have been easier to complete the transition from Miss Lonelyhearts to Lars Thorwald through a fade-out, "yet the elegance of the language would contract and the play of fate, the hint of an intimate connection of things, would be curtailed."[37] Hitchcock's seamless transitions witness an elegant aesthetic but even more importantly hint at the "intimate connection of things," strive to take the measure of fate.

Moments of Style

There are, of course, moments where the drama requires more intense cinematography, and this points to another signal aspect of Hitchcock's choice in shots. One important ingredient in his aesthetic mix is that emotion should match the shot. Another is that emotional shots should be infrequent. Hitchcock was chary in his use of close-ups and far shots. He used them when necessary and appropriate. "Don't put a great big close-up there because it's loud as brass, and you mustn't use a loud note unless it's absolutely necessary," he told Samuels.[38]

So when the shots become more expressive in the apartment there is usually a reason. For example, after Doyle has convinced Lisa and Jeff that no murder has taken place and that they are "ghouls" for wishing one to have, Hitchcock films the majority of Lisa and Jeff's subsequent conversation on "rear window ethics" with both of their faces turned from the camera. By giving us their voice without visual recourse to their faces, Hitchcock quietly conveys their shame. They are literally too ashamed to show their faces to the audience. There is a private confessional quality to their conversation. This was a staple of Hitchcock's film technique. He would often film actors from the back when the scene was dramatic enough that the dialogue would be sufficiently powerful on its own and only dissipated by visual reinforcement.

Hitchcock's camera also gets more expressive at certain times, for example, in the scenes where Lisa or Doyle dramatically moves towards Jeff's window, considering whether or not to believe him. In these shots, there is a kind of collision between actor and camera as Lisa or Doyle approaches the window and the camera zooms up at them from the window. It is a dramatic bit of camera work, meant to introduce a couple of the script's more dramatic lines. "Lars Thorwald is no more a murderer than you or I," says Doyle. "Tell me everything you've seen and what you think it means," says Lisa. Hitchcock's shot selection is sensitive and highly tuned to the inflections of his dialogue. We are anxious in these scenes that Jeff gets Lisa or Doyle to side with him, and we wait for their decision. Hitchcock senses our anxiousness and rewards it with a scene in which both the script and the mise-en-scène are appropriately dramatic.

Another moment in which Hitchcock departs from his conservative approach to composition within Jeff's apartment is when Jeff writes the note to Thorwald. The shot begins from far above, a ceiling-high (or higher) point of view, framing Stella, Lisa, and Jeff, who are crowded around the desk dramatically, then pans in (echoing the key shot in *Notorious*) for a close-up of the note. The dramatic angle, movement of the camera, and pose of the actors all stress that this is, for Hitchcock, a key moment. What makes it key is that this represents the first time that Jeff is breaking down the protective wall of total anonymity that separates him from Lars Thorwald. He is going to make contact with the man we have been all too happy to keep at a distance. Hitchcock's mise-en-scène in this scene recognizes the frisson of fear the audience feels at this point and capitalizes on that fear by filming the scene more dramatically.

Of course, the most obvious exceptions to the generally quiet technique of *Rear Window* are the two climactic scenes—the shots surrounding the death of the dog and the fight between Lars and Jeff—both of which Hitchcock films in a wildly expressive montage reminiscent of Sergey Eisenstein. Both are scenes of violence that, like the letter writing scene, involve the threat of Thorwald. And both scenes represent stern challenges to Jeff's voyeurism, the first in the angry speech of the dog owner, the second in Jeff's confrontation with Thorwald himself. The more distant Jeff is from the windows across the way, the more safely ensconced in a protected voyeurism, the quieter and more secure the shot selection. But the more the safety of Jeff's secrecy is threatened, the wilder the shot selection becomes. Hitchcock's shot selection is determined in direct accordance to the intensity of Jeff's feelings.

These moments of stylistic élan, however, are infrequent. Most of the film is characterized by a carefully monitored movement toward and away from the apartments across the courtyard, a restrained montage between shots of the neighbors' apartments and reaction shots of Jeff, and quiet, elegant mise-en-scène constructed around the movements of the four characters in Jeff's apartment. *Rear Window*'s set was busy and visually striking enough that Hitchcock could express himself with the most conservative of shots and achieve, as Truffaut said of *Notorious*, "a maximum of stylization and a maximum of simplicity."[39]

Part II

Film Guides

The Bicycle Thief *(1949)*

(Italian) 90 minutes

Directed by Vittorio De Sica

Cast:
Lamberto Maggiorani: Antonio Ricci
Lianella Carell: Maria Ricci
Enzo Staiola: as the son, Bruno

Appearing on almost every film critic's list of the top ten films of all time, *The Bicycle Thief* has consistently earned the admiration of viewers for its honesty, realism, and profound simplicity. Pauline Kael calls it "deceptively simple," because it is more complex than it first appears and because the humble plot and characters produce a much more powerful effect than one might expect (67). It's the simplicity and focus of the film that make it so great.

The Bicycle Thief is considered one of the best examples of the *neo-realist movement in film*. This movement began with the ideas of Umberto Barbaro, an Italian film critic who wrote in the early 1940s that filmmakers had a responsibility to show the painful realities of day-to-day life instead of producing frothy comedies and escapist musicals. His words inspired many young filmmakers from 1944–1952 to produce what came to be known as neo-realist films. These films often focused on the widespread poverty and hunger in Italy at the time. As Edward Murray in *Ten Film Classics* writes, "with Mussolini and Fascism gone, and Italy battered by poverty and disillusionment, the neo-realists proposed that the cinema present an authentic view of the times—and that it cope with social problems" (33). The neo-realists wanted to show social problems but did not try to solve them; their job, they felt, was to move their audiences by the realistic portrayal of the problems, and then the audience could seek solutions.

To heighten the realism of their films, neo-realist directors, including De Sica, usually used non-actors in the main roles (Ricci was actually a workman, Bruno was a courier, and neither became actors). Directors in this movement also tended to film in natural lighting using black and white photography, creating a documentary-like effect.

De Sica, like most neo-realist directors, wanted to show the drama of everyday life, the pathos and intensity of what may seem like minor events to an outsider. One shouldn't need to be presented with extraordinary events to be moved, he felt. He made films that focused on the basic humanity of a few characters and tried to get his audience to feel compassion for them.

Works Cited

Pauline, Kael. *5001 Nights at the Movies*. NY: Macmillan, 1991.

Murray, Edward. *Ten Film Classics: A Reviewing*. New York: Frederick Ungar, 1978.

Questions

1. How does De Sica take a simple story about a stolen bicycle and make it *dramatic*?

2. How does De Sica make you feel for Ricci, Maria, Bruno—even the thief?

3. Analyze scenes in which De Sica criticizes large institutions such as the government, the police, and the church. What is similar about these institutions in De Sica's view?

4. Why does De Sica include the restaurant scene with Bruno and his father? What purpose does it serve?

5. Does Ricci remind you of any famous figure of Western culture in the scene when the men who have caught him stealing hit him and scorn him?
What does this similarity suggest about him and the society in which he lives?

6. Describe the final minute of the film image by image. No words are spoken, but much is conveyed. What is Ricci thinking and feeling? What is Bruno thinking and feeling? What does Bruno's final gesture suggest to us about him, their family, their future? In what ways is the ending happy, sad, and realistic at the same time?

Casablanca *(1942)*

Directed by Michael Curtiz

Cast:
Humphrey Bogart: Rick Blaine
Ingrid Bergman: Ilsa Lund
Paul Heinreid: Victor Laszlo
Claude Rains: Capt. Renault
Peter Lorre: Ugarte
Sydney Greenstreet: Senor Ferrari
Dooley Wilson: Sam

Academy Awards for Best Film, Best Director, Best Screenplay

Every week during the 1940s, two-thirds of all Americans went to the movies. They paid, on the average, thirty-five cents per admission. For that price, the audience saw a newsreel of current events, a cartoon, and a main feature. Five major film studios (MGM, Warner Brothers, Fox, RKO, and Paramount) produced most of the films and formed the basis of "the studio system," which peaked in the 1940s. These companies not only made films, they also owned national chains of theaters that showed their films. Actors and actresses signed contracts with a specific film company and were obligated to act in that company's films—unless the company made a special arrangement with another company. The companies could calculate the amount of money a film would make based on the number of theaters they owned, the theaters' income, and the actors who were in the film. So, decisions about casting and directing were based on business principles rather than artistic considerations. The studio system resulted in major successes and in equally substantial failures (Gianetti and Eyman 199–200).

Casablanca, a product of the studio system, turned out to be one of Warner Brothers' success stories. The film is named for its location, a city and port on the Atlantic coast of Morocco during World War II. The French Vichy government, which collaborated with the Nazis during the war, controlled the city. (The Free French government supported the French Underground and joined forces with the Allies.) *Casablanca* was produced and released during the darkest days of World War II; it struck a responsive chord with its audience. How would the characters and plot appeal to Americans during the war? How does the film transcend its time period?

Film scholars consider *Casablanca* a "well made film." Define what a well-made film means to you and show how *Casablanca* meets your criteria. What, if any, aspects of the film do not meet your requirements?

By the 1940s, American films were known for their emphasis on narrative form. Discuss the narrative structure of the film using specific moments to support your observations. What conventions used in the film have parallels in drama and literature? What is the "double plot line" of *Casablanca*? How do you respond to the interaction of the two plots?

Humphrey Bogart (1899–1957) began his film career with Warner Brothers where he played loners and outsiders including gangsters, detectives, alcoholics, and psychotics. When and how does Bogart's portrayal of Rick complicate stereotypical expectations of a hero? How does Rick fit ideals of American manhood? Consider Rick's *Café Americain*. How does it live up to its name, or is it a metaphor for something else?

Ingrid Bergman (1915–1982), in the role of Ilsa, gained a popular following that continues today. What is your reaction to Ilsa as a film heroine? What contradictory qualities in her do you find? How do those qualities influence your response to her and to the film? How does Bergman's acting contribute to your interpretation of her character?

Character roles, and actors adept at playing them, were a mainstay of the studio system. *Casablanca* is peopled with some of the most memorable ones. Choose one of the "minor characters" and discuss his contribution to the film.

This film was made when the United States had mobilized for warfare. Eventually Hollywood studios would make explicitly propagandistic films. Do you consider *Casablanca* to be propaganda? Why or why not?

Works Cited

Gianetti, Louis and Scott Eyman. *Flashback: A Brief History of Film*, 4ᵗʰ ed. Upper Saddle River, NJ: Prentice Hall, 2001.

Maltin, Leonard. *Leonard Maltin's Movie and Video Guide*. New York: Signet, 1995.

Chinatown *(1974)*

"Let me tell you something Walsh, this business takes a certain amount of finesse."

131 minutes

Produced by: Robert Evans for Paramount
Directed by: Roman Polanski
Screenplay by: Robert Towne (AA)
Cinematography by: John A. Alonzo
Music by: Jerry Goldsmith

Setting: Late 1930s Los Angeles

Cast:

Jack Nicholson: J. J. (Jake) Gittes	**Faye Dunaway: Evelyn Mulwray**
John Huston: Noah Cross	**Perry Lopez: Lt. Escobar**
John Hillerman: Yelburton	**Diane Ladd: Ida Sessions**
Darrel Zwerling: Hollis Mulwray	**Belinda Palmer: Katherine**
Roman Polanski: Thug with the knife	**Burt Young: Curly**

"Is this a business or an obsession with you?"

Jake Gittes

We are tied quite tightly to Jake's point of view. We are never privy to more information than Jake has. We discover clues just when and just how he does. We follow him as he tries to sort out the truth from a growing tangle of deceptive appearances. Since his search becomes our search, we are bound to feel sympathetic towards him. Furthermore, Jake is a compelling character. At first we enjoy his sang-froid and wise guy sense of humor even if the manner in which he makes his "honest living" seems less than savory. Before long, we see a sort of self-made, self-imposed set of ethics come to the surface in Jake, just as they had emerged in his more hard-boiled prototypes of the forties' films. Eventually, Jake appears not only moral, but heroic. Despite threats and increasingly dangerous scrapes that would deter the ordinary "bedroom dick," he remains nosy; he persists in exposing the sources of Los Angeles's moral aridity. Finally, despite his apparently wide experience in uncovering unfaithful spouses in compromising positions, we learn that he himself still believes in some sort of faithfulness. Once before in Chinatown and eventually with Mrs. Mulwray, like a Bogart character, he remains faithful even though to do so involves risk and sacrifice.

What motivates Jake to pursue the truth so resolutely? When do you first begin to like Jake? To admire him? What is your opinion of him in the barber shop scene? Is he merely blustering in self-defense? Or does he really see himself as doing no wrong? Do you have a sense that he grows as a character? How self-aware does Jake seem? Is he more of a doer or a thinker?

Time

Polanski's film works and plays with the staples of two popular and overlapping American film genres: the detective film and film noir. The film directly addresses three, probably four, different time periods. The film is set in the late thirties. (Towne seems to have drawn upon some real-life incidents of 1937 Los Angeles as the inspiration for his story.) One of the film's strengths and no doubt one of the reasons for its popular appeal is its thorough attention to period details. The production values—clothes, hairdos, cars, houses, furnishings, music—are a consistent source of pleasure.

The film also speaks directly to the American mood of the mid-seventies. *Chinatown* followed closely upon the scandals of the Nixon administration (most notably the Watergate scandal) and the end of the American catastrophe in Vietnam. Americans were forced to confront the ugly fact that important and powerful leaders, even the President of the United States, had repeatedly lied to them and misinformed them about important issues. The line, "Forget it, it's Chinatown," struck a chord with audiences on more than one level.

The film evokes 1940s detective movies and film noirs. The complicated plot and emerging sense of paranoia are typical of these films. Perhaps no story-line since *The Maltese Falcon* (1941) has had more twists and turns.[1] Jake Gittes clearly follows in the footsteps of previous fictional and filmic hard-boiled detectives such as Raymond Chandler's Phillip Marlowe (e.g., *Murder, my Sweet* [1944]). Polanski chose not to try to recreate slavishly the look of the forties' film noirs. Most obviously *Chinatown* is not in black and white; rather, its predominant hues seem to be yellow and brown. But occasional visual allusions to these older films appear, including the retro style of the opening credit sequence and several scenes featuring Venetian blinds. Whether or not any forties' characters *chewed* on blinds, as Curly begins to do, is another matter.

Finally, the audience's experience of the film, its opinions of it, and the things that interest it the most will change over the course of time. The fourth time period important to the film, as with all films, is the ever-changing time-present of the viewer.

Endnote

[1] Polanski's choice of John Huston to play the megalomaniac Noah Cross creates interesting resonance, for Huston directed that film.

Questions

"No question from you is innocent, Mr. Gittes."

Can you not only answer these questions but also reconstruct how and when you come to know the answers?

1. How many people hire Jake? What do they hire him for? Are all of his employers "genuine"; that is, are they really hiring him for the reasons that they give him? In each case when are your suspicions aroused? When allayed?

2. Did Hollis Mulwray have an affair? If so with whom? How many people suspected him of having an affair?

3. How much has Lt. Escobar known all along? Is he one step ahead of Jake or one step behind? Is he trying to cover up or discover by whom the murders were committed? What does the last Chinatown sequence of the movie reveal?

4. Most good detective stories have red herrings, or false clues. *Chinatown* doesn't seem to present us with any false physical evidence, but, like Jake, we are apt to entertain some mistaken notions. Recollect some of the false conclusions you began to formulate during the film.

Critical Questions

5. One of the hallmarks of film noir is the blurring of distinctions between good guys and bad guys. Are these distinctions blurred in *Chinatown*, or is the movie too "easy" in the end, presenting us with a world of obvious good guys and clear-cut villains? Compare the film to older film noirs that you've seen. What do you think about such blurring of distinctions in general? Wonderfully complex? Sinister? Paranoid? The way things really are? Just entertainment?

6. Does the introduction of the incest theme weaken the film or make it deeper and more interesting? Is it consistent with other important parts of the film or does it seem tacked-on, perhaps sensationalistic?

Theme/Motif

7. Trace the importance of water in the movie. Not only is it the primary source of conflict, the primary locus of the mystery to be solved, it is also significant at several other levels: visual, metaphorical, thematic.

8. Did you notice how offices are people's private domains, maybe the seats of power, and Jake worms his way into them, annoys and disrupts until he can gain access to them? Yet there are some instances when his office is not exactly "his own" either. Think about these instances.

Citizen Kane *(1941)*

119 minutes

Cast:

Orson Welles: Charles Foster Kane	**Joseph Cotton: Jedediah Leland**
Dorothy Comingore: Susan Alexander	**Agnes Moorehead: Mrs. Mary Kane**
Ruth Warrick: Emily Norton Kane	**Everett Sloane: Bernstein**

Orson Welles (1915–1985) was only 24 years old when he co-wrote, directed, produced, and performed as the lead character in *Citizen Kane*. Welles had made his reputation in theatrical productions on Broadway and in radio—he directed the famous *War of the Worlds* broadcast of a Martian invasion of Earth in 1938. As the subject of his first film, Welles chose the thinly veiled life of William Randolph Hearst, a newspaper tycoon, whose story was well known to Americans in the early 1940s. Hearst was still alive when *Citizen Kane* was released, and he tried to use his influence to have the film stopped. While he did not succeed in that, he did cool its reception, and *Citizen Kane* was not the major box office draw the RKO company had hoped for. It was nominated for six Oscars, but only received one for Best Screenplay, which was written by Herman J. Mankiewicz and Welles. It was not until the 1950s that the genius of the film began to be fully recognized.

Narrative: Story versus Plot

The story of *Citizen Kane* is the life of Charles Foster Kane. One of the most interesting elements of the film is the plot; that is, the order in which the events of Kane's life are told—sometimes more than once. As you watch the film, try to keep track of how the plot is related to the events of the life. There are five flashbacks narrated by people who knew Kane (one dead, four alive), and the newsreel at the beginning of the film that gives an overview of Kane's life (and helps the viewer to fit together the pieces of what is to come). The film opens and closes in "real time." We see Kane's final dying moment when he utters the word "Rosebud," and the final sorting of Kane's possessions at the end of the film. Both of these "real time" sequences are framed by the "No Trespassing" sign that hangs outside the estate.

Flashbacks

Newsreel
Thatcher (banker who becomes Kane's guardian)
Bernstein (Kane's manager who now runs what is left of his empire)
Jedediah Leland (Kane's college friend and admirer)
Susan Alexander (Kane's mistress and second wife)
Raymond (Kane's butler in his final years)

Although the reporter Thompson seeks the meaning of "Rosebud" as the key to Kane's life, is it really the all-encompassing key? Or, is what Thompson says at the end more correct: "I don't think a single word can explain a man's life." Does "Rosebud" explain anything?

Style

The style of *Citizen Kane*—the way it looks—is part of what makes it so memorable. One important element is the way Welles uses the full capacity of each frame. Cinematographer Gregg Toland is credited with developing the special lenses and techniques needed for the **deep focus**, which allows objects in the front and rear of a frame to be equally in focus. An important example of the use of **deep focus** is a scene in

Thatcher's flashback in which we see the young Kane playing in the snow. The camera backs through the window of his home where his mother is preparing to sign the documents that will make Thatcher Charlie's guardian, thus giving him the advantage of life in the big city, but at the cost of his family. While the adults seal his fate, the frame's deep focus allows us to see the child innocently playing in the snow.

Welles is especially interested in using distance to map out relationships; he once said that he wanted a viewer to be able to look at a film and understand the relationship between the characters without any dialogue. Pay attention to how the distance shifts between characters—the famous breakfast montage between Kane and his first wife is a great example. As the years go by, they grow farther apart both emotionally and literally as their breakfast table elongates.

Camera angles are also an important and distinctive feature of *Citizens Kane's* style. Welles and Toland actually dug holes beneath the floors of some sets to have the camera angle as low as possible. This means that some characters loom large, and the ceiling above them can be seen. The effect is often claustrophobic. For instance, the youthful power and arrogance of young Kane and his friends when they take over *The Inquirer* is reinforced by how they loom over the camera and fill the frame, right up to the ceiling. We look up at powerful figures, and down at weak ones.

Lighting in *Citizen Kane* is dramatic, perhaps more what would be expected in the theater than in a film. Welles drew on earlier German Expressionist lighting techniques, and clearly broke with Hollywood norms when he set up scenes so that the speaker in a shot might be in darkness, while background characters remain in light.

Finally, Welles made his reputation in radio, so it is not surprising that sound innovations would be one of his primary contributions to modern film. Listen for "overlapping" sound, in which a voice, dialogue, or other sounds carry over from one scene into another. In this film, the jump may be dramatic, as in the "Merry Christmas. . . . and Happy New Year" sequence that leaps from Thatcher greeting a young Kane to about fifteen years later. One sequence begins with Kane's applause for Susan singing in her parlor, then overlaps into a campaign supporter's speech for Kane and finally into Kane's own speech in his race for governor. As with visual distance, Welles also manipulated our sense of distance with sound, as in the long shot that trails up from Susan's pitiful opera performance to two workers offering their opinion on the catwalk above. Her voice fades out, which creates the illusion that they are far above her and the stage.

Point to Ponder: *Citizen Kane's* original working title was simply *American*. Does the life of Charles Foster Kane sum up the ideal of an American (or of a "citizen")? If not, what might be the point in choosing (or contemplating) such titles? Can the life of Kane reflect on the lives of other Americans?

Other Welles Films: *The Magnificent Ambersons* starring Agnes Moorehead and Joseph Cotten (1942), *The Lady from Shanghai* starring Welles' then-wife Rita Hayworth (1948), *Macbeth* (1948), *Othello* (1952), *Touch of Evil* (1958), and *The Trial* (1963). You can see both Welles and Joseph Cotton in the great spy drama *The Third Man*, directed by Carol Reed, 1949 (see guide below).

The Color of Paradise (1999)

(in Farsi, "Rang-e khoda")

Country: Iran

Directed and written by: Majid Majidi

Cast:
Hossein Mahjoub: Father
Mohsen Ramezani: Mohammad
Salameh Feyzi: Grandma
Farahnaz Safari: Big Sister
Elham Sharifi Little Sister

Majid Majidi's *The Color of Paradise* offers a multi-sensory depiction of the natural world. *The New York Times* called it an "explicitly religious movie," which evokes the "relationship between man and nature and man and God with a near ecstatic sensuousness along with an awed awareness of nature's destructive power." The camera takes us through fields of flowers and misty forests, across streams and into craggy backwoods country, making sure that we hear, see, and even imagine the texture of the rugged Iranian landscape in all sorts of weather. The soundtrack, itself a player in the drama, registers the shifting chorus of birds (especially woodpeckers), insects, wind, rain, footfalls, and human voices. The film focuses on the uncertain fate of the blind 8-year-old Mohammad, whose widowed father resists caring for him. While the film foregrounds Mohammad's disability, it also accentuates his acute receptivity and sensory attunement to the environment.

Works Cited

Holden, Stephen. Rev. of *The Color of Paradise*. *New York Times* 25 September 1999: E25.

Questions

1. How does Majidi introduce us into Mohammad's world? Describe the film's opening (unseen) scene.

2. What character qualities make Mohammad such an extraordinary young boy? Does Mohammad's blindness provide him with a greater capacity for some kind of "inner sight?"

3. How does Majidi enable us to read the father's thoughts? Characterize the father and his relationship toward family members. In which scenes are we encouraged to develop sympathy for the father?

4. According to a reviewer in the *New York Times*, "Although the film sympathizes with the father, who is impoverished, desperately hard-working and eager to marry a young woman from a strict Islamic family, it ultimately takes the grandmother's side by suggesting that the father's reluctance to care for Mohammad is a sin that is certain to be punished" (Holden E25).

5. What acts of compassion link the grandmother and Mohammed? Where in the film do we see them sharing a certain kind of sensibility? How does the camera help to reveal their connectedness?

6. What role does education play in the film? Why does Mohammad want so desperately to go to the school his sisters attend?

7. What kind of prominence is religious feeling and thinking given in the film? Consider the scene with the blind carpenter, when Mohammed says: "Our teacher says God loves the blind more because they can't see but I told him if it was so, he would not make us blind so we can't see him." The teacher answers, "God is not visible. He is everywhere because you can feel him. You see him through your fingertips."

Also, in one scene, Mohammad's father says to his devout mother: "Why doesn't that great God of yours help me out of this misery? Why should I be grateful to him? For the things I don't have, for the miseries, for a blind child, for the wife I have lost?" Discuss the difference between Mohammad's father and his grandmother in terms of their outlook on life.

8. How is *The Color of Paradise* a fable about the lucidity of children and the desperation of adults?

9. Which shots (and what noises from the soundtrack) were the most memorable to you? Why?

10. Discuss the use of recurrent images in the film (hands, fingers). Mohammed learns to read Braille in school and then employs this skill to read the face of the pebbles on the bottom of the stream, to read the texture of grain; he also uses his hands to touch the faces of those he loves (except, notably his father's). Mohammed's touch is so sensitive that after he strokes his sister's face he says that she has gotten older; with his fingers he also explores the soft terrain of his grandmother's hands.

11. When Mohammed moves his fingers over certain (usually natural) surfaces, what is he whispering? Why is he repeating the letters of the alphabet?

12. How do camera angles and framing reveal Mohammed's isolation?

13. Describe and analyze in detail the closing scene (yet another journey) and its symbolic value. How is the final miracle presented?

14. Why is there a recurrent, eerie animal cry in the forest? What does it signify at such moments? Does the sound precipitate some kind of action or thinking?

15. How would you categorize this film? A fable? A "disability" film?

Double Indemnity *(1944)*

"Let's Ride"

Directed by Billy Wilder
Screenplay by Billy Wilder and Raymond Chandler
From the novel by James M. Cain. B&W. A Paramount Picture.

106 minutes

Cast:
Fred MacMurray: Walter Neff
Barbara Stanwyck: Phyllis Dietrichson
Edward G. Robinson: Barton Keyes
Porter Hall: Mr. Jackson
Jean Heather: Lola Dietrichson
Tom Powers: Mr. Dietrichson

Double Indemnity is one of Hollywood's classic *film noirs*. A film noir, which literally translates as dark or black film, depicts a world darkened by deception, crime, lust and greed. Like other *genre* categories, such as the western, the musical, and the horror film, film noir has conventions that are both stylistic and thematic. Visually, film noirs are darker and compositionally more abstract than the typical Hollywood movie. Shadows, fog, rain, and night define the atmosphere; angular points of view and oblique perspectives define the camera's vantage. Thematically, film noirs are considerably more pessimistic and deterministic that the common rung of American movies; they bespeak alienation, despair, and a tragic sense of life. Drawing upon *Double Indemnity*, catalog the stylistic and thematic conventions of the film noir.

From roughly 1930 to 1956, an extensive Production Code "rulebook" held Hollywood cinema to strict accountability in matters of taste and morality. Overseen by straight-laced censor Joseph Breen, the Production Code Administration (PCA) assured that on the surface at least Hollywood movies upheld a traditional, Judeo-Christian "moral universe." To challenge that moral universe, filmmakers working under the restrictions of the Production Code resorted to covert strategies, employing suggestion, implication, and innuendo. Catalog moments in *Double Indemnity* where the filmmakers seem to be breaking the spirit, if not the letter, of the PCA laws. Note, for example, the extended "automotive metaphor" in the initial dialogue between Neff and Phyllis ("There's a speed limit in this state, Mr. Neff.") Also: how does the viewer know Neff and Phyllis have consummated their affair?

Because film is a collaborative art, it is often difficult to properly assign credit or blame. *Double Indemnity* is a particularly troublesome case as it was adapted from the novel by "hardboiled" writer James M. Cain (*The Postman Always Rings Twice, Mildred Pierce*), scripted largely by detective fiction writer Raymond Chandler (*The Big Sleep, Farewell, My Lovely*), and co-scripted and directed by Billy Wilder (*Sunset Boulevard, Some Like It Hot*). Generally, the director has final responsibility for purely visual elements (editing, lighting, framing) and the screenwriter for elements such as plot and dialogue. In this sense, is *Double Indemnity* more a director's or a screenwriter's movie? In other words, who is the film's true *auteur*?

The chief characters in *Double Indemnity* play with and against familiar stereotypes. In what ways is Walter Neff the flip side of the American businessman—his lust for money just a slight twist on the American success ethic? What makes him sympathetic? Phyllis is the classic femme fatale—the woman who lures men to destruction by appealing to their lust and/or greed. Does she transcend this stereotype?

Keyes and Neff have a mutually solicitous and caring relationship. Note the gestures (sharing a match) and the catchphrases ("I love you, too") that bind the two men together. What significance, if any, might you attach to this thinly veiled homoeroticism?

"It suddenly came over me that everything would go wrong," says Neff. In what ways does this sensibility, in dramatic interaction with the "flashback" narrative, contribute to the film's "tragic" sense?

Dr. Strangelove, or How I Learned to Stop Worrying and Love the Bomb *(1964)*

Cast:
Peter Sellers: Group Captain Lionel Mandrake;
President Muffley: Dr. Strangelove
George C. Scott: General Buck Turgidson
Sterling Hayden: General Jack D. Ripper
Keenan Wynn: Colonel Bat Guano
Slim Pickens: Major T.J. "King" Kong
Peter Bull: Ambassador de Sadesky
Tracy Reed: Miss Scott
James Earl Jones: Lieutenant Lothar Zogg

Kubrick said of his 1964 film, "After all, what could be more absurd than the very idea of two megapowers willing to wipe out all human life because of an accident, spiced up by political differences that will seem as meaningless to people a hundred years from now as the theological conflicts of the Middle Ages appear to us today?" (qtd. in Kagan 111).

He had been struck by how apathetic people had become now that nuclear war was a genuine possibility. Kubrick had been reading journals like the *Bulletin of the Atomic Scientists* for about 6 years before beginning this project. He worked on adapting the novel *Red Alert* (a serious story about nuclear catastrophe) by Peter George on his own. As he worked, he discovered that the ideas he came up with that seemed the best were those that were funny and ludicrous. The satiric writer Terry Southern as well as Peter George co-authored the final script with Kubrick.

This nightmare comedy was received with overwhelming praise with varieties of protest—many thought it a brilliant, stylized, and unsparing treatment of the nuclear crisis; others felt that it justified and confirmed people's fears.

Consider how this film is a moral tale about Man vs. The Machine—how many ways do you see machinery or mechanization affecting/controlling the lives of the human characters? With the exception of one minor character, all the others are men. How would you do a reading of this film that emphasizes the fetishization of technology and its allure/threat for the male characters? How does the film develop a sense of the eroticism of machines? (Kubrick's next film after this one was *2001: A Space Odyssey* in which the main character is HAL the computer.)

Satire

Satire is the art of denigrating a subject by making it ridiculous and evoking toward it attitudes of scorn and amusement. Satire uses laughter as a weapon against the "butt" of its joke—it derides an individual, a type of person, a class, a social institution, a political organization, or the entire human race.

Mel Brooks' movies, the *Airplane*, and *Mighty Ducks* films are all parodies—they use the formulaic conventions, characters, and plot lines of classic Hollywood films, disaster films, and so forth and show us a ridiculous underside. *Dr. Strangelove* is a satire—note how Kubrick uses the satirical art to affect us. How does he play with certain stereotypic characters, actions, settings, and dialogue to create his joke? What kind of cliched phrases—"the American people," for instance—do the politicians and military men toss around as they discuss the possible end of the world?

How does *Dr. Strangelove* draw on film conventions—camera work, etc.—to shape the film, to build suspense and to make us laugh? Analyze the *mise-en-scene*; the film moves among three different settings. Describe the camera action in each, and the music, lighting, placement of characters, and so forth.

Pay attention to the film's frame—what happens in that opening scene? What does the voiceover explain? What do we see? Compare that to the film's closing sequence.

Names are very important in this film. Why, for instance, is the Soviet leader called Dmitri Kissoff? (Look up some of the names in the dictionary—"mandrake," for instance, or "turgidson.")

Works Cited

Kagan, Norman. *The Cinema of Stanley Kubrick*. NY: Continuum, 2000.

The Gold Rush *(1925)*

Written and Directed by Charlie Chaplin.

82 minutes

Cast:
Charlie Chaplin: The Lone Prospector (Little Tramp)
Georgia Hale: Georgia
Mack Swain: Big Jim McKay
Malcolm Waite: Jack Cameron
Tom Murray: Black Larson
Henry Bergman: Hank Curtis

Considered one of the greatest comic masterpieces of all time, *The Gold Rush* was the film for which Charlie Chaplin most wanted to be remembered. On August 16, 1925 the *New York Times* wrote that "it is by all means Chaplin's supreme effort, as back of the ludicrous touches there is truth, a glimpse into the disappointments of Chaplin's early life" (when he was a struggling actor). *The Gold Rush* was the first film Chaplin starred in for United Artists, which he had co-founded six years earlier with D. W. Griffith and husband-and-wife team Douglas Fairbanks and Mary Pickford. Several sources influenced Chaplin's interest in the subject matter. The idea first occurred to him as he was having breakfast with Fairbanks and Pickford, who showed him pictures of the Klondike gold rush on a stereopticon. But he already had an interest in tales of snow-bound travelers and cannibalism; he'd been fascinated by the story of the Donner expedition of 1846, who had become trapped in a snowstorm in the Rockies and had resorted to eating the less fortunate members of the party. You may want to discuss how Chaplin takes potentially grisly material like eating people, freezing to death, and falling off a cliff and makes it funny. Why would such material inspire him to make a *comedy*? What does *The Gold Rush* suggest about the relationship between comedy and tragedy? (It is worth noting that Chaplin originally wanted to be a great tragic actor, but comic parts were more available.)

The Gold Rush was filmed in the remote Sierra Nevadas and required hundreds of extras, making it one of the most expensive films of its time (more than $900,000—

about the price of some commercials today). Chaplin was a perfectionist as a director, constantly reshooting scenes until they met his standards. Consider the flawless grace and choreography of the following scenes:

a. When Big Jim McKay and Black Larson struggle over the rifle and Chaplin scurries around the cabin, futilely trying to avoid being at the end of the barrel. What makes this scene more humorous than suspenseful? (In this scene and several others Chaplin emphasizes similarities between his character and the dog. Why? What is the effect of this comparison?)

b. The dance hall scene in which Chaplin hitches up his trousers with his cane and then ties them up with a rope attached to a dog. Note how he manages to be perfectly graceful and dignified (until he's pulled over) while simultaneously being perfectly absurd. Discuss the relationship between grace, dignity, and absurdity in Chaplin's character.

c. The literal "cliffhanger" scene in which the cabin teeters on the edge of a precipice. How does Chaplin prolong the irony and suspense of this scene? Why does it take so long for The Little Tramp and McKay to discover what is wrong? How does this cliffhanger scene compare to others you've seen (perhaps in Hitchcock or action films)?

d. The famous "Oceana Roll" scene in which Chaplin does a dance with two forks and two dinner rolls. (Fatty Arbuckle had performed a similar scene in *The Cook* in 1918 but not with such élan.)

e. The boot-eating scene, which is not as highly choreographed as the others but is equally famous for the steadfast earnestness of Chaplin as he carves up his boiled boot for dinner. What makes this scene more funny than revolting or pathetic? Analyze Chaplin's gestures and expressions here. (The boot was made of licorice—20 pairs were made to cover the takes that might be needed. The licorice apparently made actor Mack Swain quite ill, and his revulsion when Chaplin offers to cook up the other boot was not feigned.)

General Issues and Questions for Discussion

1. Describe elements of Chaplin's physical comedy. What is comical about his appearance, movements, expressions, gestures? Discuss the effect of his clothes, body shape, walk, etc. What do they suggest about his history? Compare Chaplin's physique and manner to the other men in the film—particularly McKay, Larson, and Jack Cameron. What is the effect of seeing Chaplin paired with these men?

2. Why is Chaplin's Little Tramp character so universally and timelessly appealing? What are some of the ironies of his character? Film theorist Andre Bazin asserts that "Charlie [and the character he represents] is a mythical figure who rises above every adventure in which he becomes involved. . . . For hundreds of millions of people on this planet he is a hero like Ulysses or Roland in other civilizations—but with the difference that we know the heroes of old through literary works" (144). What else distinguishes the tramp from heroes of the past? Why do you think Chaplin called the character "a satire of humanity"? Can you think of characters in more recent films that fall in the Little Tramp tradition?

3. Analyze the effect of the musical score. Does it enhance or detract from the comedy? Did you recognize any familiar melodies? Can you detect any irony in the contrast between the melodies and the scenes they accompany?

4. Discuss Chaplin's use of dramatic lighting and close-ups. Do you remember any scenes where the lighting or a close-up was particularly effective?

Works Cited

Bazin, André. *What is Cinema?* Transl. by Hugh Gray. Berkeley: U of California P, 1967.

Hero *(2002)*

Directed by Zhang Yimou
Cinematography by Christopher Doyle

Cast:
Jet Li: Nameless
Tony Leung Chiu Wai: Broken Sword
Maggie Cheung: Flying Snow
Zhang Ziyi: Moon
Daoming Chen: King of Qin
Donnie Yen: Sky

The martial arts epic *Hero* premiered in Hong Kong in 2002 as *Ying xiong*, and went on to become the second-most-successful film ever in China, next to *Titanic*. The most expensive Chinese film ever made, *Hero* stars the Hong Kong superstar Jet Li and is directed by Zhang Yimou, known for such great films as *Ju Dou* (1990), *Raise the Red Lantern* (1991), and *The Story of Qiu Ju* (1992).

The film concerns Ying Zheng (259–210 B.C.), the cruel king whose ruthless conquests established him as Qin Shi Huangdi (First Emperor of the Qin dynasty) and unified China for the first time after more than two centuries of disorder known as the Warring States Period. The story begins when a warrior called Nameless (Jet Li) is admitted into the presence of the king in order to explain how he hunted down and vanquished the king's three deadliest foes: assassins named Sky, Snow, and Broken Sword. The film borrows its structure from Akira Kurosawa's *Rashomon* (it's also influenced visually by the master's *Ran and Throne of Blood*) inasmuch as four differing versions of Nameless's story are recounted. Each version is dominated visually by a different color: first red, then blue, white, and green (the real-time beginning and end of the film are primarily black). Name other ways in which the four versions differ.

Although the story purports to take place in third century B.C. China, the setting is really the realm of legend and fable. Nameless and the assassins are only human in the sense that they are not immortal; otherwise, they are essentially demigods. Each of these characters can fly, hover, run across lakes, effortlessly deflect thousands of arrows, and singlehandedly fight off what is perhaps the most gigantic and fearsome army ever depicted in any film.

As a Chinese filmmaker, Zhang has always had to deal with the threat of censorship by China's communist government even though he has repeatedly said that he has no interest in politics. Yet the ending of *Hero* is quite controversial. Does the film as a whole seem to question or support the idea of totalitarianism and conquest for the sake of order and stability?

It Happened One Night *(1934)*

105 minutes

Directed by Frank Capra

Cast:
Clark Gable
Claudette Colbert
Walter Connolly
Roscoe Karns Alan Hale
Ward Bond

Critical Reception

This was the first film to win all five major Oscars: Best Picture, Best Actor, Best Actress, Best Director, and Best Screenplay. (Note scenes that highlight the quality of the acting, directing, and screenplay.) Leonard Maltin praises the film as a "legendary romantic comedy [that] doesn't age a bit. Still as enchanting as ever" (667). Do you agree with his comment that the film doesn't age a bit?

Pauline Kael states that "the film . . . caught on with the public and made audiences happy in a way that only a few films in each era do; in the mid 30s, the Colbert and the Gable of this film became America's idealized view of themselves—breezy, likable, sexy, gallant, and maybe just a little harebrained."

Director Frank Capra (most famous for his films, *Mr. Smith Goes To Washington*, and *It's a Wonderful Life*) has often been criticized for producing light-weight, maudlin movies. Does this film strike you as overly sentimental? Why or why not? What attributes could you point to in defending it against this charge? Capra has also been considered a maker of movies with a message. Do you think this film has a "message?" If so, what is it?

Genres

This film has the characteristics of several film genres: road film, romantic comedy, and screwball comedy:

Screwball comedy: A type of comedy prevalent in the 1930s typified by frenetic action, wisecracks, and sexual relationships as an important plot element. Usually about middle and upper-class characters and therefore often involving opulent sets and costumes as visual elements. It's a highly verbal form, as opposed to slapstick comedy.

Road films: Road films, as the name suggests, involve a lot of travel, usually by car, bus, or foot. The physical journey usually parallels an emotional/ spiritual journey and often involves the development or dissolution of a relationship.

Romantic comedies: These films follow the development of a relationship that often begins with discord. The couple usually face many hurdles (involving comical and absurd situations and misunderstandings) before they inevitably get together in the end.

Examine how this film uses and transcends these genres.

Works Cited

Kael, Pauline. *Pauline Kael Reviews A-Z*. www.geocities.com/paulinekael/reviews/6/29/09.

Maltin, Leonard. *Leonard Maltin's 1997 Movie & Video Guide*. New York: Plume/ Penguin,1997.

Ju Dou *(1989)*

(In Mandarin, with English subtitles)

Directed by: Zhang Yimou (pronounced jchung ee MOW)
Written by: Liu Heng (based upon a contemporary short story, "Fu Xi, Fu Xi")

Cast:
Gong Li: Ju Dou
Li Baotian: Yang Tianqing
Li Wei: Yang Jinshan
Zhang Yi: Yang Tianbai (infant)
Zheng Jian: Yang Tianbai (youth)

Oscar Nominee for Best Foreign Film

Set in a remote northwest Chinese village of the 1920s, *Ju Dou* (pronounced joo DOE) is the story of a young woman who has been sold as a bride to Yang Jinshan, an elderly owner of a dye factory. Jinshan has already tortured to death two previous wives for failing to produce an heir; this despite the fact that it is he who is impotent. Unable to overcome his impotence, he beats his new wife, all within hearing of his adopted nephew, Yang Tianqing. Motivated more by her need to protect herself from her despotic husband than her need for passion, Ju Duo begins a love affair with Tianqing. Soon they produce a son, whom the elderly Jinshan is willing to acknowledge as his own. When the old man suffers an accident that paralyzes him, the two lovers flaunt their affair as revenge against him. But theirs is not the final revenge. As the baby boy matures, he calls the old man *father* and comes to be jealous of his mother and hateful toward her lover. In a twist of fate, the son, caught in an Oedipal struggle, gains the final revenge against the illicit lovers.

In addition to appreciating its strictly formal properties, viewers will no doubt find equally compelling psychological and political interpretations of the narrative. Not a few critics have seen the film's parallel to *The Postman Always Rings Twice*, with its love triangle that ultimately destroys everyone. Others have noted the similarity to Eugene O'Neill's *Desire Under the Elms*. While Gong Li doesn't achieve the malevolence of Barbara Stanwyck in *Double Indemnity* or Lana Turner in *Postman*, she is certainly the initiator of the affair. Note especially the scene in which she looks through the peephole that Tianqing has used to observe her. Cinematically, this seems a conscious imitation of the well-known scene of voyeurism by Norman Bates in *Psycho*, but unlike Hitchcock, who maintains Marion as an unknowing sexual object, Zhang here confers upon Ju Duo an agency whereby she becomes a conscious object of Tianqing's desire. She sees herself through the peephole as he might see her, and then she seeks to become alluring, initiating by her self-presentation the affair she hopes will save her.

The examination of *Ju Dou* in Freudian terms with the double triangle that only resolves itself in tragedy might also be fruitful. The adopted nephew who displaces his "father" when he succeeds in his affair with Ju Dou is repeated when his own son displaces him by calling the old man "father" and ultimately destroys the relationship between his mother and her lover. Consider the parallels with high tragedy: flaws of *hubris*, passions gone wild, twists of fate, revenge, and the tragic resolution.

Many critics have noted the political allegory in the film. Director Zhang Yimou is one of the "Fifth Generation" of filmmakers. Two others have become known in the West as well—Tian Zhuangzhuang, director of *Horse Thief* and *The Blue Kite*, and Chen Kiage, director of the recently released *Farewell My Concubine*. The first to attend the Beijing Film Academy since its reopening in 1978 in the wake of the Cultural Revolution, these directors all suffered bitter experiences during that event. Their continuing criticism of both the past and the present in China has resulted in the censorship of their films. All of Zhang's films tend to treat the subject of sexual oppression, realized by the fine acting of his companion and artistic partner Gong Li: *Red Sorghum* (1987), *Ju Dou* (1989), *Raise the Red Lantern* (1991), and *The Story of Qiu Ju* (1992). Consider how the film might be seen as a political allegory of the repressive old ways but the equally repressive new guard after Mao. In this interpretation, the elderly despot and the similarly repressive son are paired. Note that the woman is at the center of the allegory, in that she is the necessary "vessel" for the continuation of the generations. How might sexual oppression be seen as a metaphor for broader social control?

That Zhang began his career as a cinematographer will come as no surprise, as you witness the brilliant photography in this film. Consider how the themes of passion and revenge are established through the swaths of white and then newly dyed cloth. Note the changes in Ju Dou's clothing—from white to red and back to white—which parallel the events in the narrative. Note, as well, the motif of the village photographed with the swaths hanging in the distance—the village, in its neutral tones, seems ominous against the brilliant colors of red and yellow (or from another perspective, perhaps, the brilliant colors threaten the security and stability of the village). The film becomes a cultural artifact, illustrating how individual will (agency) is limited by social constraints. What is Zhang's ultimate vision about history and agency as it is translated into the lives of individuals?

The Kid *(1921)*

Written and directed by Charlie Chaplin. Music by Chaplin.

Cast:
Charlie Chaplin: The Tramp
Jackie Coogan: The Kid
Also starring: Edna Purviance, Chuck Reisner, and Lita Grey
Other classic feature-length comedies by Chaplin:

The Gold Rush (1925), City Lights (1931), Modern Times (1936)

Like the Kid in the film, Charlie Chaplin was a penniless orphan as a young child and danced on street corners in London with his brother for spare change. At age eight, he joined a child dance troupe and began taking child roles in London plays. When he was 23, Chaplin toured the United States with a stage troupe and was discovered by producer/director Mack Sennett, who had him star in 35 short films in one year (1914) for his production company Keystone.

By the end of the year, Chaplin was a wealthy man and an established presence in the filmmaking world. Through his initial 35 films, Chaplin evolved the character of The Tramp, an "invincible vagabond, [a] resilient little fellow with an eye for beauty and a pretense of elegance who [stands] up heroically and pathetically against overwhelming odds and somehow triumph[s]" (Katz 225).

He perfected the character in 1915 in *The Tramp*. By the 1920s, this figure was universally recognized as a *cinematic icon* and still is today. Discuss these questions about this iconic figure of the Tramp and Chaplin's brilliant creation and portrayal of him:

- Why is he so appealing? What is so comical about him? Is it his personality/character (i.e., *who he is*) or merely the things he *does*? Both? Does most of Chaplin's humor derive from his encounters with various obstacles in his life, the things that Fate or Chance throw into his path, or does it derive from his creative efforts to overcome these obstacles, no matter what happens to him?

- What makes him sympathetic and even at times admirable?

- What differentiates him from other generic vagabond characters that you may have seen in other movies? Does he completely present himself as a "bum" or "hobo?" Explain, especially in relation to why you think that American audiences throughout the history of cinema have identified so strongly with such a character.

- Describe the many contradictions in both his personality and his physical characteristics. Why would Chaplin deliberately make his signature character so paradoxical? Why would audiences relate to such a paradoxical or self-contradictory figure?

Chaplin went on to work for such film studios/companies as Mutual and Essanay, but he always retained tight control over his filmmaking and artistry. Eventually he helped to form the United Artists studio with fellow silent movie actors Douglas Fairbanks and Mary Pickford, and fellow movie director D. W. Griffith.

The Kid was Chaplin's first feature-length film and marked the beginning of his tendency to mix *comedy* with *pathos*, a quality that arouses feelings of sympathy, pity, or compassion. The comedy in *The Kid* is more rooted in character and serious situations than in the mindless slapstick of many other silent comedies.

Other Questions

1. Consider the most comic moments— how are they enhanced by the presence of pathos in the film? And how is the pathos enhanced by the comedy? Give specific examples. What would the film be like without the comedy or without the pathos?

2. Discuss the character of the Kid. Jackie Coogan became a star with this role and stayed a star throughout his childhood. His career slumped when he became an adult, however, and by the mid-1930s he was virtually unknown. He had a comeback as Uncle Fester in the original *Addams Family* TV show. What makes the Kid so appealing? Is there anything complex about his character? What do he and the Tramp do for a living? In which ways are the Kid and the Tramp similar and different?

3. Analyze the dream sequence at the end of the film. Why is it there? Is there anything symbolic in it? Does it add to the emotional effect of the film or to your understanding of character? What kind of "heaven" does the Tramp eventually find? And how does this sequence help to integrate the two different cinematic traditions established by the Lumière brothers (realism) and Georges Méliès (creationism/fantasy-making)?

4. Chaplin continued making silent films long after sound films (i.e., films with synchronized verbal dialogue) became popular (e.g., his *City Lights* [1931] and *Modern Times* [1936] were both silents when most other pictures were "talkies"). Discuss why a director would *choose* silents over talkies. What can silent films do that talkies can't?

Works Cited

Katz, Ephraim. *The Film Encyclopedia*. NY: Putnam, 1979.

The Lady Eve *(1941)*

Directed by: Preston Sturges (born Preston Biden)

Cast:
Barbara Stanwyck: Jean/Eve Harrington
Henry Fonda: Charles Pike

Also with:
Charles Coburn, William Demarest, Eugene Pallette, and Melville Cooper

Preston Sturges is widely considered one of the great Hollywood director/screenwriters of the late 1930s and 1940s and the "foremost satirist of his time" (Sarris 113). The son of wealthy socialites, Sturges was educated in France, Germany, and Switzerland as well as in American private schools. Aristocratic settings and characters came naturally to him, then, when he turned to writing plays and later to writing and directing screenplays. His first play on Broadway was *Strictly Dishonorable* (1929–1930 season), notable for its urbane, sophisticated dialogue, a quality that can also be seen in his very literate scripts for *The Lady Eve, The Great McGinty, Christmas in July,* and *Sullivan's Travels.* In discussing the film, consider scenes that highlight Sturges's screenwriting talents. Which dialogue exchanges seem particularly lively, rhythmic, and memorable. Why? How does Sturges work both with and against the Eve story in Genesis? Do you find his use of this reference overbearing or effective? Did you notice any double-entendres?

The Lady Eve falls into the genre of *screwball comedy*. Screwball comedies are a type of film, developed in the 1930s, that depends on "fast, witty dialogue and a battle of the sexes in which male and female roles [are] often reversed." High society characters and situations are mixed with "low," slapstick comedy in these films (Ellis 140). Classic examples are *It Happened One Night, Ball of Fire, The Awful Truth, His Girl Friday.* In his use of slapstick (physical) comedy, Sturges demonstrates his indebtedness to Chaplin and Keaton. Consider specific moments that indicate this indebtedness. Which are the most effective? Why? Does Sturges use the running gag of Fonda falling as more than just slapstick comedy? How do these "falling" gags tie into larger thematic issues in the film?

Although Sturges is more famous for his literate scripts than he is for his cinematic qualities, the pacing and editing of his films distinguish his work as well. Discuss scenes or scene sequences in which the pacing seems particularly brisk and the editing particularly noteworthy. His opulent sets also deserve notice. Does the mise-en-scene of any particular scene stand out for you? How so?

The *New York Times* called *The Lady Eve* the best film of 1941, yet critics faulted Sturges for being "unwilling to develop the implications of his serious ideas" (Sarris 113). What are the "serious ideas" at stake in this film, if any? Do you think they are, or should be, developed?

Sturges's films often cast an ironic light on the American Dream, showing how "the lowliest boob could rise to the top with the right degree of luck, bluff, and fraud" (Sarris 113). Discuss how this theme emerges in *The Lady Eve.* Does the film mock the American Dream, or does it simply cast it in a humorous light?

Finally, consider the masterful acting of Stanwyck, Fonda, and the character actors. How does Stanwyck manage to make her character appealing even when she's being ruthlessly deceitful and manipulative? How does Fonda make his character appealing even when he's such a dupe? Sturges liked to feature character actors in his films, and he maintained his own stock company of regulars such as Demarest, Pallette, and Coburn. Discuss the effectiveness of these peripheral characters. How might Sturges's repeated use of these character actors add to their appeal/effect?

The Lady Eve was remade in 1956 with Mitzi Gaynor, George Gobel, and David Niven (dir. by Norman Taurog). If you get a chance to view it, you'll see the difference between a really well-made film and a grade-C remake.

Works Cited and Consulted

Ellis, Jack C. *A History of Film*, 4th ed. Boston: Allyn and Bacon, 1995.

Katz, Ephraim. *The Film Encyclopedia*. New York: Putnam, 1979.

Mast, Gerald and Marshall Cohen, eds. *Film Theory and Criticism*, 3rd ed. New York: Oxford UP, 1985.

Sarris, Andrew. *The American Cinema*. Chicago: University of Chicago Press, 1985.

M *(1931)*

110 minutes, black and white, in German, with subtitles

Directed by: Fritz Lang (Other Lang films include: *Metropolis, Scarlet Street, You Only Live Once*)

Script written by: Thea von Harbou and Fritz Lang, based on the story of serial killer Peter Kuerten from Dusseldorf, executed July 2, 1932.

Cast:
Peter Lorre: Hans Beckert
Ellen Widmann: Frau Beckmann
Inge Landgut: Elsie Beckmann
Otto Wernicke: Inspector Karl Lohmann
Theodor Loos: Inspector Groeber
Gustaf Gründgens: Schränker
Georg John: Blind man

Plot: Police and criminals in a German city hunt for a serial child murderer.

Style

Banned in Germany from 1933–1945, this early talky is considered by many to be director Fritz Lang's masterpiece. In it he blends the styles of expressionism and realism. Expressionism is a style that exaggerates or distorts physical appearances (in film, primarily through light and shadow) to reflect subjective, emotional realities. Discuss scenes that seem expressionistic; for instance, consider how Lang first shows us the killer—as a shadow only. Discuss why this is effective and expressive. Do any other scenes strike you as particularly expressionistic? What about the high angle shots (ones taken with the camera far above the characters, such as the first scene and the one of men fighting about the murder around a table)? What emotional effect does the high angle produce? How does it make characters look? But realism plays a role here, too. Realism is a style that tries to capture the outward appearance of everyday reality. For instance, Lang's depiction of police detective procedures seems almost like a documentary. Why do you think Lang was so intent on capturing the details of police proceedings? Why does he contrast them so closely with the tactics of the criminals in the long montage that cuts between both groups as they plan their strategies? What is he suggesting about both groups by placing them side by side? To enhance the realism of his film, Lang hired real criminals to play criminals, and 24 of them were arrested before the end of filming.

Lang, a master of silent films, demonstrates his skill at telling a story with visuals instead of words, although he makes excellent use of sound as well in this film. Examine examples of both. For instance, he conveys the murder of Elsie Beckmann through several distinct and chilling shots: Elsie's empty chair, the empty laundry room, her ball rolling to a stop, her balloon caught in power lines. In these four quick shots, Lang indicates Elsie's murder without showing any violence or using any words. Analyze why this sequence is so effective, how it differs from scenes of violence in contemporary films, and why one might argue that Lang's approach is preferable. Lang's use of the murderer's whistling demonstrates his creative use of sound. The song that Beckert whistles is "In the Hall of the Mountain King" from Edvard Grieg's *Peer Gynt Suite*. Analyze how the whistling enhances the intensity and suspense of several scenes. (Lang himself apparently dubbed the whistling.) Note who nabs Beckert first and why. How does this character, the one who first pinpoints the murderer, function symbolically?

Ethical Concerns

The penultimate scene, the criminal court, is still disturbing 70-some years later in its emotional, moral, and psychological ambiguities. Peter Lorre's performance here is riveting (and it's particularly impressive as he was thrown down those concrete stairs more than a dozen times before his "defense" speech). Analyze his defense. Does his pathology make him sympathetic to you? Does his sickness make the criminals' call for killing him seem terribly unjust? What do you think of the insanity plea? What do the mothers say? Who do you sympathize with in this scene? Why? Who does Lang seem to sympathize with? The final scene takes place at a real court. Why does Lang end the film before the verdict is read? (Note: the original ending showed the verdict—see facts that follow.) What does he seem to be saying about justice? Who gets the last word?

Critical Responses

The critical response to *M* has been outstanding over the decades, although some initial reviewers found it shocking. Gabriele Tergit in 1931 referred to it as "sadistic" and accused Lang of the "swiftest opportunism" since the murderer on whom it was based had just been in court. Stanley Kauffmann states that "it is more engaging of the eye, more incisive in its irony, more firm in its grasp of social complications than most films that come along today"(3). Almar Haflidason, reviewing the restored version on DVD for the BBC, calls the film "dark and uncompromising" and writes that "Fritz Lang's *M* disturbs even today, and serves as a highly effective benchmark against which other serial killer films should be judged." Leonard Maltin considers it "riveting and frighteningly contemporary; [and] cinematically dazzling" (789). Lang himself felt it was his finest film and stated in 1931 "if this film . . . helps to point an admonishing and warning finger at the unknown lurking threat . . . emanating from the constant presence among us of compulsively and criminally inclined individuals . . . and if the film also helps perhaps even to avert this danger, then it will have served its highest purpose" (11).

Random facts, courtesy of IMDb "the Earth's Biggest Movie Database" http://www.imdb.com/title/tt0022100/):"Peter Lorre was Jewish and fled Germany in fear of Nazi persecution shortly after the movie's release. Fritz Lang, who was half Jewish, fled two years later." The film was "chosen by the Association of German Cinémathèques as the most important German film of all times." As for the ending, "the film shown at the premiere (11 May 1931, 110 minutes) had an alternate ending: it shows the full trial of the murderer. This ending was later replaced by a woman sobbing, 'Man muß eben noch besser auf die Kinder achtgeben. IHR...' (You must look out for your children even harder. YOU...)"

Works Cited

Haflidason, Almar. Review of *M* (*Ultimate Edition DVD*). www.bbc.co.uk/films/2003/10/06/m_1931_dvd_review.shtml. 6/30/09.

IMDb. http://www.imdb.com/title/tt0022100. 5 September 2007.

Kauffmann, Stanley. "The Mark of *M*." Booklet on *M* from Criterion Collection DVD, 2004.

Lang, Fritz. "My Film *M*: A Factual Report." Criterion, 2004.

Maltin, Leonard. *Movie and Video Guide*. NY: Penguin, 1994.

Tergit, Gabriele. "Fritz Lang's *M*: Filmed Sadism." Criterion, 2004.

The Manchurian Candidate *(1962)*

Directed by: John Frankenheimer
Screenplay by: George Axelrod, from a novel by Richard Condon

Cast:
Frank Sinatra: Bennett Marco
Laurence Harvey: Raymond Shaw
Janet Leigh: Eugenie Rose Chaney
Angela Lansbury: Mrs. Iselin
Henry Silva: Chunjin
James Gregory: Sen. John Yerkes Iselin

The Manchurian Candidate deserves recognition for its own merits as a suspenseful political thriller, but it has become a film legend because of its bizarre history. Its plot about the assassination of a presidential candidate eerily mirrored the assassination of President John F. Kennedy a year after the film's release. The painful coincidence, as well as the film's terrifying evocation of growing Cold War paranoia, led to it being withdrawn from theaters. Frank Sinatra, who plays Bennett Marco, bought the rights to the film and kept it shelved for 25 years, partly out of respect to JFK, partly because of a profit-sharing dispute with United Artists. Oddly, it was Kennedy, urged on by his friend Sinatra, who had originally encouraged Arthur Krim, President of United Artists, to produce the film. Krim was concerned about the provocative subject matter, but Kennedy assured him he didn't mind.

Director Frankenheimer creates a paranoid atmosphere that persists throughout this taut thriller. It both evokes and satirizes Cold War fears about communist takeovers and brainwashing. How do the "enemies" in the film manipulate Cold War fears to their advantage? How do they justify Cold War paranoia?

Other Questions

1. Describe how playing cards function as a plot device. How do they also work symbolically? Where does the film's plot surprise you? How does the film build up to these surprises?

2. Analyze the character of Mrs. Iselin. What makes her so terrifying? What makes Angela Lansbury's performance so effective? What makes Bennett Marco's character interesting? Describe and analyze one scene in which Sinatra's performance in this role is particularly memorable.

Camera Angles, Editing and Mise-en-Scene Questions

1. How does Frankenheimer use unusual camera angles and movements to create suspense and paranoia? Can you think of any shot in particular that struck you as memorable and effective?

2. Consider in particular the dream scene that reveals how the platoon have been brainwashed. Analyze the 360 degree tracking shot that Frankenheimer uses in this scene to reveal simultaneously what the platoon is seeing and what is actually happening to them. What is the effect of this shot on the viewer? Why move in a full circle? Analyze how the scene pairs banality and terror; does the contrast enhance or lessen the terror?

3. The film is full of patriotic symbols (flags, eagles, etc.), in foreground and background shots. What is the effect of these symbols? Analyze how Frankenheimer ironically juxtaposes shots of patriotic symbols with shots of people or more mundane objects. What does he accomplish with this kind of editing?

Midnight Cowboy *(1969)*

Directed by: John Schlesinger

Cast:
Dustin Hoffman: Enrico "Ratso" Rizzo
Jon Voight: Joe Buck
Brenda Vaccaro: Shirley
John McGiver: Mr. O'Daniel
Ruth White: Sally Buck
Sylvia Miles: Cass
Barnard Hughes: Towny

The 1960s are regarded as a period in which significant challenges to tradition were issued. Whether or not May 1968 and the "Summer of Love" were as important to cultural change as those documentaries that PBS uses to sell itself to aging boomers claim, it is undoubtedly the case that some significant and influential changes were afoot. The Civil Rights Movement is an obvious example. Assassinations of political figures and the loss of the remaining vestiges of American innocence in Vietnam are other factors. In the arts, the relative freedom of the decade allowed a degree of experimentation that usually resulted in films that failed miserably, but sometimes in ones that succeeded brilliantly. Despite the ostensible liberation from conventional sexual mores in the 1960s and the relative s(t)olid reputation of its creators (Schlesinger came to this film only a few years after Julie Christie earned an Oscar for her role in his 1965 *Darling*), *Midnight Cowboy* earned the distinction of being the first major studio production to win an X rating from the MPAA. Three Oscars (Best Screenplay for Waldo Salt, Best Director for JS, and Best Picture) later, the organization yielded, dropping the rating to an R. Tame by today's standards, the party scenes and frank (homo)sexuality of the film affronted many reviewers.

In many ways, this film is the tale of the death of the 1960s. Drugs, sex, and "dropping out" all fail to produce little more than misery (recall that Schlesinger, an Englishman, was shocked by NYC attitude and allegedly had never tried marijuana before working on this film). When the trappings of its period are overlooked, however, *Midnight Cowboy* may be seen as offering an astonishingly sophisticated mélange of traditional material (the "buddy" film, the travel narrative, country vs. city, North vs. South, etc.) while simultaneously offering noteworthy formal and thematic challenges to its own filmic ancestors.

Perhaps the most significant of these challenges is the repudiation of an American archetype that was particularly dear to American filmgoers: the cowboy. Joe Buck conveniently unites the gum-chewing, starry-eyed idealism, earthy "wisdom," and wide-open spaces of cowboy mythology in a character whose believability would falter if Voight were not so talented. The Texan sights and sounds of the film's start quickly disappear, and the unsavory reality of the town from which Joe hails is revealed in a series of disturbing flashbacks, but his honky-tonk clothes and seemingly unimpeachable naïveté prevent viewers from forgetting what he represents. If Joe's geographic, moral, and psychological displacement were not enough to suggest the irrelevance and essentially fabricated nature of the mythic Old West, Schlesinger and crew offer several direct attacks on Westerns. First, as Joe walks near the restaurant in which he worked as a dishwasher (consider the ways he tries—and often fails—to clean up for others throughout the film . . . there's no escaping your past), he passes an abandoned movie house. The few letters dangling from the marquee reveal that it last screened a John Wayne film. Wayne's name will return in the film (and it is hard to believe his campy Westerns were anything more than sexual fetishism), but the persistent popularity of the man would haunt *Midnight Cowboy* well after production ended. Wayne beat out both Hoffman and Voight for the Academy Award for Best Actor. Other references to the cowboy and/or Western abound, including a torn poster of Paul Newman as Hud that hangs in Joe's first NYC room. It is only when Joe finally throws away his cowboy duds at the film's close that the myth is put to rest, and that his reliance on the image of himself (constantly tested in front of mirrors) as a cowboy and his image of the cowboy as sexual athlete are dissolved. Such events make it clear that it is not only cinema's visions of the Old West that are dismissed. It may also be worth reflecting on the other media, aside from film, explored in this film (Joe's radio is an important prop; television is a problematic presence throughout his life; even while wrapping himself in newspapers, Ratso pauses to read a story; there are billboards, comics, MONY, etc.).

If it is clear that any idealist view of Joe's Texas is undermined by *Midnight Cowboy*, it is the scenes with Ratso in New York that drive home the extent of the film's realist agenda. While Joe's outward appearance reveals that he is a rube rather than a hustler, Ratso's appearance makes him look like anything but a mark. At the same time, he has been sold an orange company's vision of Florida, a vision that he has built into what is perhaps the movie's biggest lie. Curiously, it is Ratso's conventional dream that reveals the most about his character. Surrounded by the excesses of New York, his ambitions are rather simple and his morals and spirituality remarkably conventional. The point is driven home clearly in the Warhol-esque party scene (Schlesinger's conversation with other films continues even here; careful viewers will recognize Paul Morrissey, who was responsible for many of the films attributed to Warhol, as well as other Factory "superstars" and personalities). Ratso may instinctively steal food and rifle through coats in search of wallets, but he just as easily condemns the eccentric behavior, drug consumption, and excessive sexuality of the partygoers. His street-smarts unite the city for Joe, as the film moves from the lower East Side to late-1960s Times Square, to Fifth Avenue.

More interesting than all of these thematic issues may be the film's several departures from the linear narrative on which most Hollywood film relies. Joe has flashbacks. He and Ratso both have fantasies about the future. Sometimes montage is used to unite the memories shown in flashbacks with visions of the future and events in the present, as during the expressionistic sequence demonstrating Joe's angry pursuit of Ratso after the Mr. O'Daniel episode. The erratic cutting and cinematography during the party sequence heighten a sense of disorientation. Changes in lighting, filtering, and film stock reinforce the different temporal and psychological settings: Ratso's Florida is overexposed and blinding, New York is often filtered a sickly blue-green, while Joe's past is shot in a variety of ways, including a pseudo-Super-8 format reminiscent of family films before video cameras and the sometimes monochromatic sequences of his last night with "Crazy" Annie (trivia: Annie is played by the daughter of the film's writer).

Finally, Hoffman and Voight offer us a new "odd couple," and the brilliance of the acting they and others offer cannot be overlooked. The film hinges on a handful of moments and lines that only these characters could hand us: Joe walks down the sidewalk, towering above the surrounding crowd; Ratso yells, "I'm walkin' here"; Joe discards his cowboy clothes; Joe closes Ratso's eyes, and we see the hotels of a Florida beach town reflected in the bus's windows.

Questions

1. What do you make of the very distinctive music? What about the lyrics to "Everybody's Talking" (a hit at the time), the background music to the sex scene between Joe and the woman from the party?

2. What do you think of this late 1960s portrayal of homosexuality? How is it different from the portrayal of homosexuality today? What does Joe Buck seem to feel about homosexuals?

3. What do you make of Ratso's fantasies of Florida? What do they represent for him? Is the sequence different from the rest of the film in terms of cinematography and the use of color?

4. Is Joe Buck a typical hustler? How is he different from what you'd expect? What is Ratso's occupation?

5. What can we say about the friendship between Joe Buck and Ratso? What holds it together? Why are they friends at all?

6. John Wayne's name appears on the movie marquee in the opening sequence. What is the relationship between this film and a typical Western? Does Joe possess the characteristics of a real cowboy? What do you make of the opening shot of the cattle and the drive-in movie screen?

7. What is the view of the film regarding Texas? Is it a commentary on the nature of the country?

8. What is the film's view of New York? Is it a commentary on the nature of the city?

9. During the cold New York winter, why don't Joe and Ratso just get a job?

10. What do you make of the party sequence? Does it add to your appreciation of the film? How is it filmed to create the overall impression of strangeness?

11. What is Joe's background? What can we say about his relationship to his mother and grandmother? What happens to him and Crazy Mary? Why use black and white photography during these scenes?

12. What is happening in the strange encounter with the man with the plastic Jesus? Why is he particularly abhorrent to Joe?

13. Why does Joe discard his cowboy outfit at the end?

14. Is there anything admirable about Joe and Ratso? Are they essentially good people? How does Ratso try to maintain his dignity?

15. Despite (because of) being rated X, this film won the Academy award for best picture. What are the strongest elements of this film? What will you tend to remember?

16. Why does Joe Buck want to become a hustler anyway?

17. What is significant about the names of the two main characters?

18. Why set the film in New York rather than a place like Dallas or Miami? Are there any memorable shots of the city?

19. What is gained by the use of flashbacks in this film? How would the film be different without them?

20. Who is the more realistic of the two protagonists? Is he realistic in all respects?

21. Does the film have any long shots that you can remember? What is the effect of these shots?

22. Why are there particular ads in this film? What do you make of MONY?

Miller's Crossing (1990)

Directed by Joel Coen
Written by Joel and Ethan Coen

Other films by Coen Brothers: *Blood Simple, Raising Arizona, Barton Fink, Hudsucker Proxy, Fargo, The Big Lebowski, Oh Brother Where Art Thou, The Man Who Wasn't There, Intolerable Cruelty, The Ladykillers*

Cast:
Gabriel Byrne: Tom Reagan
John Turturro: Bernie Bernbaum
Marcia Gay Harden: Verna
Jon Polito: Caspar
Albert Finney: Leo

Some Questions to Consider about Miller's Crossing

1. What do you make of the image, early in the film, of the hat blowing down the road? Tom says he dreamed of this image—do you remember Verna's response to

his dream? Why does Tom say that "there is nothing more ridiculous than a man chasing his hat"? What do you make of the film's quiet obsession with hats, both as symbols and recurrent visual motifs? Try to recall one of the many scenes that are shot or choreographed around a hat. And why is everyone always talking about giving each other "the high hat?"

2. Gangster films tend to be cynical but moral at the same time. They mock much of what we conventionally believe in but salvage a few important virtues. What are those virtues in this film? What does Tommy believe in despite his cynicism?

3. Where does this film display the conventional trappings of the gangster film? Where does it deviate from them?

4. How do the Coen brothers handle violence? What's unusual, for example, in the way they shoot the discovery of Rugg Daniels' corpse in the alley or the scene in which Tommy is beaten up after he refuses to join Caspar's gang or the execution of the Dane? Where are violent scenes played for laughs? Why is the scene in which Leo survives an assassination attempt one of the most famous in the film?

5. What do you make of Caspar? Why is he portrayed as a family man of sorts? What do you make of the scenes with his son? How is Caspar strangely sympathetic at times? What do you make of his ponderings over "ethics," "character," and "honesty"? Are these strange preoccupations for a vicious gangster?

6. What would you say are the distinguishing characteristics of the Coen brothers' visual style? Where do they use composition in depth? Strange or oblique angles? Where does the film seem cartoonish in the way it sets up its shots? What scenes are particularly expressive, visually?

7. What do you make of Tommy's relationship with Verna? Does he love her? Does he care more for her or for Leo? Does Tom want to get back with Verna as Verna insists he does? Why, then, does he sacrifice his relationship with her by killing her brother?

8. What is Tom's relationship with Leo? Why is he so loyal to him? Why doesn't Tom join up again with Leo at the end of the film since he's gone to so much trouble for Leo up to that point?

9. Why does Tom kill Bernie? Why does he say "what heart?" just before he fires the shot? Has Tom lost his heart somewhere along the way in this film?

10. What do you make of Bernie Bernbaum? Why does he turn on Tom after Tom spares his life? What is the relationship between Bernie and his sister Verna? Why does Bernie ridicule her when she expresses such empathy for him? What of his allusion to incestuous overtures on her part?

11. What do you make of the dialogue in this film? It's pretty smart repartee. What are some of the snappier bits of dialogue in the film? How is the dialogue in scenes with Tom and Verna particularly rich? What's a "twist," a "grifter?" Did gangsters really talk like that? Why do they in movies?

12. What do you make of the homosexual strands in the plot? Do you understand how the relationships between the Dane, Mink, and Bernie contribute to the story? Does this seem like a unique twist to a gangster film?

13. Question for the pathologically observant (and those of you who have seen *Rear Window*): What name is featured on the boxing advertisement in the boxer's apartment.?

My Life as a Dog *(1987)*

"Ingemar didn't let us down."   "It could have been worse."

Directed by Lasse Hallstrom.
Screenplay by Hallstrom, Reidar Jonsson, Brasse Brannstrom, Per Berglund.
Based on Reidar Jonsson's novel. Swedish, with subtitles.

Svensk Filmindustri, Color, 101 minutes

Cast:
Ingemar: Anton Glanzelius
Uncle Gunnar: Tomas von Bromssen
Mother: Anki Liden
Sage: Melinda Kinnaman
Aunt Ulla: Kicki Rundren
Berit: Ingi-mari Carlsson

The film is set in 1958, Ingemar's difficult and discombobulated 13th year. Two events of that year are given special weight: the Russian launch of the dog Laika into space and the first heavyweight championship fight between Ingemar Johansson and Floyd Patterson, which Johansson won.

Lasse Halstrom's father was an amateur filmmaker and Hallstrom made his first movie (a 10-minute thriller) at the age of 10. He shot his first professional film while in high school (about a pop music group). While many of his early films are autobiographical, *My Life as a Dog*, he says, has nothing to do with his own youth. But he captures the vulnerability of being a child with rare sensitivity, and critics have placed the film among the classic treatments of childhood. Notice how Ingemar reacts when his mother is taken away on a stretcher—how different this is from his older brother's reaction—his silences, his covering his ears to distort his mother's angry cries. Much of Ingemar's behavior, most obviously his imitation of a dog, is a kind of code for feelings, feelings mostly about loss—of his mother, his dog Sickan, his home, the absence of his father, his humiliations and painful coming-of-age in the village of Smaland, which seems populated exclusively by eccentrics.

Initiation generally entails a change in status and awareness following some ordeal. How well does this pattern apply to the film? Does the film aim at a depiction of Ingemar's growth or rather at showing us the trying events of just one year, the year in which he led "a dog's life"? What do you think of Ingemar's philosophy of "It's important to have things to compare with" and "It's important to keep a certain distance"? Do these statements really show detachment and coolness of feeling? To whom are these statements addressed?

Consider some of the key images in the film. For instance, the first thing we see is an image that recurs: Ingemar doing a backflip and making his mother laugh by a lake. How is this visually different from other images? When does it take place? Why does it recur and when? Consider also the last image, the one Hallstrom chooses to leave us with. What does it suggest?

Hallstrom is good, not only at showing us the tension between behavior and feeling and between sentiment and sentimentalism, but also at spinning out motifs and running gags. Take, for instance, the love-battle between Ingemar and the tomboy Saga, who is going through changes of her own; Uncle Gunnar's fondness for his record of "I've Got a Lovely Bunch of Coconuts" (in Swedish); the long sequence of Ingemar's screwups and disasters; the two "spaceship" episodes. One of the most effective motifs is the image of the starry sky, piano music, and Ingemar's catalogue of "comparisons" of his own problems with bizarre news items: a tram accident, a man struck by a javelin, the motorcyclist who clears one too few buses, etc. His concern with the fate of Laika is given special weight. How is Laika connected to the loss of his mother and of Sickan? Consider the line: "I think I love Sickan as much as Mama." There are few occasions when Ingemar expresses feeling directly. What are they and what do they reveal? (e.g., "I didn't kill her!" or "Why didn't you want me, Mama?")

How are other events and images connected to the theme of Ingemar's condition: for example, the comic episode of Berit's sculpture ("the Ur-Mother, source of love, contact") or the fixation on female breasts (Berit's, Saga's, Arvidsson's ads, the bottles)? While sex is not high on Ingemar's priority list, there are whiffs of it all over Smaland: Arvidsson's taste for lingerie ads, Uncle Gunnar and Aunt Ulla, the grappling with Saga, the party scene, Ingemar's "curiosity" in the skylight scene. Are 12 year-old girls more interested in all this than 12 year-old boys? Why does Ingemar act like a dog when two girls fight over him?

Describe Ingemar's relationship to his mother, to Sickan, to his brother, to his aunt and uncle. Describe the contrast between the city and rural Smaland. In what specific ways does Hallstrom show us the village as a tight community, always coming together for events, and ultimately providing Ingemar with emotional sustenance? Contrast life with Gunnar and Ulla with his stay at the Sandbergs'.

Consider some of the filmic devices Hallstrom uses: flashback, slow motion, voice-over, close-up. What images did you find most memorable and why? As a way of telling a story, film has special capacities and limitations. What things does Hallstrom do *visually* that are distinctly filmic? For example, what effect does he achieve by using silence coupled to an image, say, of Ingemar guilelessly standing before his angry, tubercular mother? How is Ingemar always kept the focus of our attention?

The film depends on a balance between what is *sad* and what is *funny*. How is this balance presented to us? Is it just a matter of alternating or do the two moods ever coincide (e.g., in Ingemar's brother's sex-lecture and bottle demonstration—and notice the motif of the bottle here and elsewhere)? Why is music used so sparingly? When *is* it used? What is its effect?

Does Uncle Gunnar become a sort of new father for Ingemar? (Notice the tropical association of both coconuts and bananas.) Are there surrogate mothers? When does Ingemar become violent and why?

Finally, consider what the film does with time. Is it straightforward and linear, or does Hallstrom rearrange chronological order in some places? How is Smaland different in the winter than in the summer? What period of time does the film cover, and does this suggest something about the full meaning of the film's title? And what does "Keep a tight rope" mean? Who says it, and when? How is this *verbal* cue linked to a *visual* image?

Nosferatu: A Symphony of Horror *(1922)*

(German) 84 minutes

Directed by F. W. Murnau

Cast:
Max Shreck: Orlock
Gustav von Wangenheim: Hutter
Greta Schroeder: Ellen, Hutter's wife
Alexander Granach: Knock

Film Critics' Reviews

According to Pauline Kael: "Though ludicrous at time (every horror film seems to become absurd after the passage of years, and many before—yet the horror remains), this first important film of the vampire genre has more spectral atmosphere, more ingenuity, and more imaginative ghoulish ghastliness than any of its successors" (*Cinemania 96*).

According to Leonard Maltin: This "early film version of *Dracula* is brilliantly eerie, full of imaginative touches that none of the later films quite recaptured" (1013).

About the Director

F. W. Murnau (1888–1931), born Friedrich Wilhelm Plumpe, studied literature and art history at the University of Heidelberg (note the visual references to art masterpieces in *Nosferatu*), and then served as a combat pilot and a producer of propaganda films in World War I. Immediately after the war his career as an actor and director took off; he made 22 films between 1919 and 1931.

Influenced by films such as *The Cabinet of Dr. Caligari* (1919), Murnau utilized an expressionistic style in his most successful films, *Nosferatu* and *Sunrise*. Expressionism is an artistic style "borrowing from movements in painting and literature early in the twentieth century, that allows liberal use of technical devices and artistic distortion to evoke the emotional state of the characters, and in which the art of the medium is always obvious and carries the meaning of the film" (*Cinemania 96*). For many artists, expressionism "evoked the instability, disorientation and despair" of the post-World War I period. Note particular moments in the film when Murnau exaggerates light/shadow contrasts, accelerates the speed of the film, or prints from the negative to create certain atmospheric, emotional and thematic effects. Also note that Murnau, unlike most expressionist filmmakers, uses real locations instead of sets, which produces an eerie combination of realism and expressionism.

Murnau came to the United States in 1926, hoping that the cinematic resources of Hollywood would allow him to expand his art. But he struggled with the Hollywood studio system, wanting more artistic independence than studio executives would allow (*Cinemania 96*). His struggles, however, produced excellent results. *Sunrise*, his first film produced in the United States, has been hailed by numerous critics as "'the last high peak of German silent cinema'" and "the greatest film of all time" (Katz 840). Although widely differing in subject matter, both *Sunrise* and *Nosferatu* explore the theme of human weakness and redemption in a threatening world (*Cinemania 96*).

As with all great silent film directors, Murnau strove to tell a story visually not verbally. Note how much he conveys through visual imagery; like a good poem, *Nosferatu* shows instead of tells. We see not only the plot but also what people are thinking and feeling, and all the while Murnau uses almost no intertitles. Note scenes in the film in which Murnau details a complex series of actions and/or emotions via visual imagery alone.

Murnau's career was cut tragically short when he died in a car crash in 1931, but his films have continued to influence other great directors such as Orson Welles, Ingmar Bergman, and Werner Herzog, who directed a reverent remake of *Nosferatu* in 1979. Welles' and Bergman's films particularly pay tribute to Murnau's expressive use of light and shadow.

Themes and Interpretations

The striking light/dark contrasts in *Nosferatu* visually underscore major thematic contrasts in the film, such as the universal struggles of life and death, good and evil, self-sacrifice and greed, health and sickness, and spirit and matter. Describe scenes that vividly depict these struggles and note how the lighting, set, position of characters, etc. emphasize the thematic contrasts. Also note numerous images of feeding: Hutter heartily enjoying his dinner, in spite of Nosferatu's ghoulish presence; Nosferatu feeding on Hutter and Ellen; the carnivorous plants; the spider feeding on its prey. Is there a point behind the proliferation of these images?

Numerous political interpretations of *Nosferatu* have been suggested. Siegfried Kracauer has argued that the film foreshadows the rise of the Nazis, with Nosferatu symbolizing Hitler spreading his plague through Europe, although none of this had yet happened when Murnau made the film (77-79). A more direct and immediate political allegory would take into consideration the fact that the film was made just a few years after the end of World War I. Consider how Nosferatu, a Count who wants to expand his property, and who spreads death and disease across the countryside, could represent the powers that drove Germany into reckless imperialism, a world war, and ultimately defeat and devastation. A Marxist might argue that the Count represents the old aristocracy, refusing to die and sucking the life out of the middle class. A psychoanalytic interpretation might linger on Hutter's latent homosexuality—after all, why doesn't he leave the castle as soon as Nosferatu has sucked his thumb at the dinner table (and then his neck in bed at night?) A gender analysis might explore why Hutter seems so eager to go on a trip away from his wife, while his wife dreads the separation, and why must she sacrifice her life to save him? What do these facts suggest about traditional marriages? An interdisciplinary analysis might focus on how Murnau pays tribute to famous paintings in this film (e.g., Nosferatu looks a lot like Munch's famous screamer, several shots mirror masterpieces of the German Romantic painter Caspar Friedrich, and Rembrandt's *Anatomy Lesson* is reflected in the autopsy of the captain). See Lotte Eisner's *The Haunted Screen* for a more detailed analysis (Thom 2).

Works Cited

Cinemania 96. Microsoft, 1992–95.

Katz, Ephraim. *The Film Encyclopedia*. New York: Putnam, 1979.

Kracauer, Siegfried. *From Caligari to Hitler*. Princeton: Princeton UP, 1966.

Maltin, Leonard. *Leonard Maltin's 2001 Movie and Video Guide*. New York: Penguin, 2000.

Thom, Fred. "Nosferatu." *La Plume Noire: Trans-Cultural Collective of Film and Music Commentary*. www.plume-noire.com. July 31, 2002.

The Piano *(1993)*

127 minutes

Directed by Jane Campion
Cinematography by: Stuart Dryburgh

Cast:
Holly Hunter: Ada McGrath
Harvey Keitel: George Baines
Sam Neill: Alastair Stewart
Anna Paquin: Flora McGrath

The Piano caused quite a stir at the Cannes Film Festival when it was released. It was hailed as startlingly original, unlike any other movie. How does it differ from other movies (specifically love stories) you've seen? Vincent Canby of the *New York Times* calls *The Piano* "a post-Freudian period romance." What kind of Freudian reading does the film suggest? How is sex (and not "love") foregrounded? Does sexual desire turn into love? When and why?

How are the Baines/Ada "lessons" scripted to emphasize a kind of equality: a mutually agreed-upon exchange? Does the film dispense with that when the two dispense with the bargain? How is it continued in the piano key/severed finger equation?

Why can't Ada speak? How does her voicelessness matter to the men who love her? How does her muteness place her in a special category among the settlers? What does the piano mean to her?

Flora McGrath acts as voice for her mother, interpreting for her to the outside world. What kind of a relationship do they have? How does it change during the movie? Why does she move from rejecting her step-father at the outset of the film ("I'm not even going to look at him") to informing on her mother to him?

Does Flora's illegitimacy matter? What kind of stories does she tell about her father, and what do they reveal about her?

The Piano is historically accurate up to a point. New Zealand was indeed partly settled by Scots Presbyterians who purchased land from the native Maori people. What does the film say about the colonial condition? What are the Maori like, and how is their culture most different from the Scots? How does the "Bluebeard" shadow play work both to further the themes of the film and to show us something about cultural difference? George Baines has "gone native." What does that tell us about him? About Europeans? About the Maori?

How does the final surprising event of the film encapsulate its themes? How is it, "What a finish"?

Can you tell this movie was made by a woman? If so, how?

The film is set during a time when England was experiencing the Romantic Movement, a broadly influential rejection of Enlightenment rationality. Romantic philosophy (Kant, Coleridge, Goethe, Rousseau), poetry (Blake, Keats, Shelley, Byron, Wordsworth), fiction (Emily Bronte), and painting (Constable, Whistler, Friedrich) valued, as W.B. Yeats would have put it, "passion" over "precision," emotion over rationality, simplicity and innocence, as of children, over complexity and sophistication. Romantics searched for contact with the Sublime, a divine power sensed but not quantifiable, often found in Awesome Nature.

Campion has said that she felt, "a kind of kinship between the kind of Romance Emily Bronte portrayed in "Wuthering Heights" and this film. Hers is not the notion of Romance that we've come to use; it's very harsh and extreme, a Gothic exploration of the Romantic impulse" (qtd. in Urban 146). What do you think? Is Ada a Romantic?

Music, in its appeal to emotion and seeming evasion of rationalist analysis was the most highly privileged Romantic art. How is music tied to the release of powerful emotion in the film?

Caryn James's review of the film traces within much New Zealand and Australian literature and film a Gothic sensibility: disturbing, sinister, twisted, violent, and mysterious. She tells us how Australian novelist Thomas Keneally "traces his country's Gothic to European settlers, whose spirits and sense of God were distorted by their abrupt contact with the harsh Australian landscape." She quotes Keneally saying,

"There are many stories of settlers arriving in Western Australia with their pianos and being unable to move them. . . . It was a more sunburnt climate than Jane Campion's New Zealand, but the idea of [an] abandoned grand piano is very strong in the Antipodes. In the old world, the piano is where it belongs, in the living room. . . . In the New World, the piano is on the beach. The feeling was very powerful for a long time that there were not the proper civilizing elements here, that the environment was a deranging environment. There is a residue of feeling that the country is so harsh on the European soul, that it can easily tip the European soul into brutality. The God you talked about in Europe, the God you found in the landscape, isn't here. Some other bugger's here." (H13)

How are the land and its climate players in the drama? What are their effects on the Scots? How have the Europeans attempted to resist "derangement"?

Works Cited

Canby, Vincent. "Critic's Notebook: Early Cannes Favorite a Post-Freudian Romance." *New York Times* 18 May 1993. www.nytimes.com/1993/05/18/movies. 6/30/09.

James, Caryn. "A Distinctive Shade of Darkness." (Rev. of *The Piano*). *New York Times* 28 Nov. 1993 (v. 143, s2): H13.

Urban, Andrew L. "Piano's Good Companions." *Jane Campion: Interviews*. Ed. by Virginia Wright Wexman. Jackson: UP of Mississippi, 1999.

The Player *(1992)*

Directed by Robert Altman
Screenplay by Michael Tolkien

Cast:
Tim Robbins
Gretta Schacchi
Fred Ward
Whoopi Goldberg
Lyle Lovett
Brion James

Robert Altman is a rare thing in American film, an artsy, personal filmmaker who has managed just enough commercial success to keep churning out films year after year.

Some of Altman's 25 or so films since his first success in the late sixties: *M*A*S*H*, *Nashville*, *California Split*, *Thieves like Us*, *O.C. and Driggs*, *Three Women*, *McCabe and Mrs. Miller*, *Brewster McCloud*, *Come Back to the Five and Dime, Jimmy Dean*, *Tanner '88* (Altman's favorite). Some of these films, such as *M*A*S*H* and *The Player*, have been commercial successes; more have had limited commercial play or bombed entirely. Almost all have achieved a strong measure of critical success. His success with *Vincent* and *Theo*, *The Player*, and *Short Cuts* brought him back to the forefront of public attention where he was in the early seventies after the success of *M*A*S*H*.

Altman's films are quirky and personal, sometimes experimental. He's considered an actors' director and his love of spontaneity and his willingness to let his actors improvise has resulted in talky and strangely paced films that often tax the average filmgoer's patience. *The Player* is not this kind of film. *The Player* represents Altman's conscious attempt to make a tightly constructed, commercial Hollywood film. *The Player* has most of the elements that Griffin Mills, the hero of the film, says are essential to a successful Hollywood script: suspense, violence, laughter (enter Whoopi Goldberg), sex and nudity, and, of course, a happy ending. But Altman is very self-conscious in his use of these elements. He seems to mock them as he uses them. For example, *The Player* finishes with a happy ending, but such a ridiculously happy ending—replete with a pregnant, happy homemaker, a waving American flag and a superabundance of roses—that it's obviously a satire of happy endings. *The Player* gives us sex and nudity when Griffin and June visit the spa, but this spa, with its Latin rhythms and naked couples swimming in unison, is such a ludicrous fantasy that it seems to mock Hollywood's bland, puerile notion of sensual paradise. The spa scenes are shot with a kind of glossy, commercial lighting, more characteristic of a television commercial than an Altman film.

In short, in *The Player* Altman makes a classic Hollywood film and makes fun of it at the same time. The film operates on two levels, as a Hollywood film and as a critique or study of Hollywood films. This two-pronged approach is apparent from the first shot (an elegant long-take in which one character blathers on pretentiously about the beauty of long-take filmmaking) to the last when Altman wraps up his film with the same bit of insipid dialogue with which Griffin Mills wrapped up his film ("what kept you?" "traffic was a bitch.")

One of the great ironies and pleasures of *The Player* is that Altman skewers Hollywood with the help of Hollywood's elite. Probably no film before has been so packed with "star" cameos. Altman has always been more popular with actors than with producers and it has become, for actors, a badge of sophistication to get a cameo in one of his films. Ironically, this director that Hollywood so often refused to finance eventually became a kind of intellectual idol there. Among the famous faces one can spot in this film are Karen Black, James Coburn, Buck Henry, Cher, Terri Garr, Nick Nolte, Angelica Huston, John Cusack, Joel Gray, Martin Mull, Jack Lemmon, Sally Kellerman, Steve Allen, Jayne Meadows, Harry Belafonte, Sherry Belafonte, Sidney Pollack, Rod Steiger, Jeff Goldblum, Burt Reynolds, Andie MacDowell, Malcom McDowell, Susan Sarandon, Peter Falk, and of course Julia Roberts and Bruce Willis, the stars of the film Griffin Mills is producing in *The Player*. One of the running gags in the film is that no matter who is pitching a project, they will, invariably, in their desperation to sell the project, suggest Roberts and Willis in the leads.

As closely as *The Player* resembles a typical Hollywood film, it is still plainly something different also. There are a number of dissonant moments and enigmas more characteristic of Altman's arthouse flicks than a typical Hollywood film. For example, a great deal of mystery surrounds the icy artist, June Goodmunsdotter. First, what is the point of her strange name and why do people keep pronouncing and analyzing it? Why does she say she is from Iceland when she apparently isn't? Where is she from? What was the nature of her relationship with the dead writer, David Keohane? Why can't she grieve for him? Why is she so often associated with ice and icy blues and whites? What is the nature and purpose of her art, of which we get ample viewing? Why doesn't she care to market her work? Why doesn't she like books or movies? What does she mean when she says, "I like words and letters. It's sentences I'm not crazy about"? Why does Griffin describe her as a "pragmatic anarchist"? Does her "anarchism" or moral relativism contribute to Griffin's seeming guiltlessness over his crime?

Altman's satire moves quickly and there might be questions about his take on studio politics also. What's the point of the Boston banker's son who has come to Hollywood to play tennis, date starlets, and maybe produce? What role does he play in the shake-up at the studio? Why is Griffin's boss, Levinson, fired? Griffin's lawyer jokes that Levinson was fired because the banker's son "caught a case of the clap." What does he mean? How does Griffin end up on top at the studio?

And then there are just some very odd moments in the film. Why do the police laugh uproariously (and nightmarishly) at Griffin in the police station? Why is the detective's assistant (played by Lyle Lovett) forever swatting and catching flies? And why does he repeatedly chant "one of us, one of us" when everyone is laughing at Griffin? Why is the first shot at David Keohane's funeral that of a dead fish being fed upon by scavenger fish? Why does Altman film Griffin's and June's sex-scene to a soundtrack of abstract, jazz-like drum sounds and echoes? And why does Griffin choose that moment to confess his "responsibility" for Keohane's murder? Why does that scene segue into a disorienting close-up of June's knee emerging from her mudbath (a shot to which audiences often respond with groans of disgust until they find it is only a knee)?

Psycho *(1960)*

Directed by Alfred Hitchcock
Screenplay by Joseph Stefano
Paramount Pictures, from the novel by Robert Bloch

Cast:
Anthony Perkins: Norman Bates
Janet Leigh: Marion Crane
Vera Miles: Lila Crane
John Gavin: Sam Loomis
Martin Balsam: Milton Arbogast

Alfred Hitchcock (1899–1980) was British by birth, and began his career as a silent film title-writer in England. He directed his first films in Germany, where he encountered and was deeply influenced by German Expressionism, a style that emphasized subjectivity, dramatic lighting, and an interest in psychology. His first feature film, *The Lodger* (1926) was a suspense thriller about Jack the Ripper. Once his reputation was established in Europe, Hitchcock came to Hollywood. He made many commercially successful pictures that also were explorations in cinematic technique. *Psycho* demonstrates Hitchcock's continued interest in manipulation of his audience through the use of special effects and careful editing. *Psycho* was also accompanied by an extensive advertising campaign that promised viewers the shock of their lives, and politely suggested that the more sensitive or those with heart conditions should stay away for their own safety. Needless to say, this tactic generated huge audiences for the film.

Psycho represented an abrupt break with the Production Code, a set of rules established in 1934 to control the content of American films. This code forbade bad language, nudity, or even intimations of sex (ever wonder why so many married couples in films and TV slept in separate beds?) as well as brutality or criminal activities that went unpunished. *Psycho*, with its bizarre plot featuring grisly murders, mental illness, theft, and nudity (or at least hints of it), caused an uproar among critics.

The interest in *Psycho* goes beyond its content, however, to the way in which Hitchcock presents his material. In terms of plot, Hitchcock took a risk in killing off his main character about a third of the way into the film. Like other films that are centered on a mystery, the plot must work to keep the audience interested while not revealing too much too soon. As you watch, pay attention to how the story is kept going, but we are still not able to put the pieces together until the very end. What "red herrings" or false leads are we given? How satisfying do you find the final explanation?

Editing

Psycho's most famous scene is the murder in the shower, which is one of the finest examples of **montage**. In the 45-second sequence, 78 rapidly alternating shots are spliced together, which give the impression of a violent attack, yet we see the knife penetrating only once, and it is bloodless. How would this scene's impact have been different if it were filmed as a single shot?

Framing

Most modern films make use of **mobile framing**; that is, the camera moves during a shot, whether it pans from side to side, or, as is frequently the case in *Psycho*, it moves forward. This is the case in the opening long shot when the camera begins with the cityscape view and ends up sneaking under the barely open hotel window to reveal a hidden love affair. It is appropriate that in developing a plot about penetrating secrets, the camera itself moves forward, just as characters move deeper and deeper into Norman Bates' mansion until, at the very end, we are given a view into his twisted mind. When we peek into the hotel room and see Marion and Sam, are we any different than Norman when he peeks into Marion's room as she undresses?

Sound

Hitchcock originally wanted to use only natural sound in the shower scene, and no score at all for the film, but the composer Bernard Herrmann talked him into using violins played at a very high pitch, which created an unnatural shrieking sound. What is the effect of seeing a woman scream, but actually hearing screaming violins? Hitchcock also makes use of **displaced internal diegetic sound** (as opposed to **simple diegetic sound**, which comes from a source visible on the screen or implied by the action of the scene). The displacement is chronological: we hear a sound that came earlier than the image, such as Marion's memories when she's driving of what her boss said to her, or a sound that comes later than the image, when she imagines what her boss and sister will say on Monday when she has disappeared. We also have an example of **simple internal diegetic sound** when we hear Norman/Mother's thoughts at the end. How is sound used in this film to help keep the mystery going?

Black and White versus Color Film

Hitchcock made his first color film in *1948 (Rope)*, so he was making an artistic decision when he chose to film *Psycho* in black and white. Why do you think he might have done so? What aspects of the film would be different if it were in color? Of course one of the few changes in the remake of *Psycho* (1999) was filming in color. What is gained or lost with this change?

The *Psycho* remake raises the issue of Hitchcock's lasting contribution to film. Certainly many of his special effects are clunky and primitive to modem eyes. Is there anything more to a Hitchcock film than purely technical innovation and experimentation? If not, then why was the *Psycho* remake, which claimed to have reproduced every shot in the original, a flop? Do you see any difference between Hitchcock's films and other suspense or thriller movies that you've seen?

The most notable aspect of Hitchcock's horror is that it tends to arise from every-day circumstances: talking to a stranger on the train, a bored man with a broken leg watching his neighbors out the window, or a shy young man with a taxidermy hobby. Hitchcock took the well-ordered universe of Hollywood films and replaced it with a very dark and dangerous modern vision of the world.

Rear Window *(1954)*

Directed by: Alfred Hitchcock

Cast:
James Stewart: Jeff
Grace Kelly: Lisa
Thelma Ritter: Stella

Plot Summary

A professional photographer, Jeff (James Stewart) becomes temporarily disabled when he breaks his leg while on an assignment. His injury confines him to a wheelchair in his apartment for six weeks. To entertain himself, he watches his neighbors in the apartment complex and courtyard through his apartment's rear window. Tended daily by his nurse, Stella (Thelma Ritter), and visited regularly by his girlfriend, Lisa (Grace Kelly), he becomes obsessively drawn into the events unfolding outside his window. Jeff becomes convinced that one of his neighbors (Raymond Burr) has murdered his sick wife. Jeff calls on Stella and Lisa to help him gather enough evidence for the police to make an arrest, placing all of them in jeopardy.

Themes

Voyeurism

Hitchcock's films often revolve around characters who watch and who are being watched. They observe hidden, secret, and often forbidden acts. The plot of the film metaphorically enacts the role of the film's viewers. The audience watches what happens on screen in a darkened theater, making the viewers voyeurs as well. Explain how this film presents the voyeur theme.

The Wrong Man

Virtually all of Hitchcock's films contain the theme of an innocent man who is presumed guilty. Circumstantial evidence accumulates and the hero faces almost insurmountable odds to defend himself. Hitchcock's characterizations lent themselves to this theme. His heroes were not completely admirable; they often had a weakness or character flaw that made them vulnerable. Similarly, Hitchcock's antagonists often had some redeeming quality that mediated their villainy. How do these characterizations appear in *Rear Window*?

MacGuffins

Hitchcock frequently uses gimmicks in his films that provide false leads for solving the mystery at hand. The characters generally care about these objects while the audience realizes they are not significant. In *Psycho*, the robbery and stolen money seem to be the focal point of the story until the first murder takes place. Illegally imported diamonds are the macguffins in *Notorious*. What macguffin(s) do you find in *Rear Window*?

Worldview

Hitchcock sees the world as a place full of absurdity. No one is completely good or thoroughly evil. When "happy endings" occur, they are usually compromised or limited in some way. Authority figures (police, government officials) do not provide safety for the characters; they are weak and often unable to understand what is happening to the main characters. Francois Truffaut believed that Hitchcock's cynicism was a defense against his emotional vulnerability. The fears and anxieties Hitchcock experienced in his own life, he transmitted to audiences through his films.

Visual Effects and Influences

German Expressionism

Hitchcock went to Germany in the early 1920s. There he observed the techniques of German filmmakers who specialized in compositions that emphasized dramatic lighting, odd camera angles, and montage editing. Throughout his work, Hitchcock emphasized strong emotions and distortions of time and space. When do you find Hitchcock using lighting, camera angles, and edits to add emotional impact to the film?

Psychology

Hitchcock's imagery and themes lend themselves to psychoanalytic interpretations. The mothers in Hitchcock's films are overbearing ogres. The relationships between mothers and sons are neurotic. Freudian psychology identifies obsessive behavior and interprets it based on childhood experience; obsessions are common in Hitchcock films. Hitchcock's heroines are emotional, frequently overwhelmed by their environment. They can be victimized or at least controlled by the hero. How would you describe Stella and Lisa as characters in this film? How do you explain Jeff's compulsive behavior?

Suspense Genre

Hitchcock preferred not to prolong the mystery for his audience. Instead, he specialized in suspense. "I believe in giving the audience all the facts as early as possible," he explained (Giannetti & Eyman 281). By giving the audience information and then manipulating its anxieties in subsequent scenes, the viewers become more engaged and less sure of what will happen. When do you think Hitchcock effectively draws his viewers into the suspense of the plot? Because suspense is formulaic and often imitated, Hitchcock tried to find new approaches. One of his techniques was to shift moods in the middle of a scene or to create unusual combinations of emotions in the film as a whole. How would you describe the emotional tone of the film? Do you detect any unusual shifts? Does Hitchcock catch you "off guard" at any point? When? How?

Hitchcock Filmography (partial):

The 39 Steps, 1935	*To Catch a Thief*, 1956
Sabotage, 1936	*The Wrong Man*, 1957
The Lady Vanishes, 1938	*Vertigo*, 1958
Rebecca, 1940	*North by Northwest*, 1959
Shadow of a Doubt, 1943	*Psycho*, 1960
Notorious, 1946	*Frenzy*, 1972
Strangers on a Train, 1951	*Family Plot*, 1976
The Man Who Knew Too Much, 1955	

Works Cited

Giannetti, Louis & Scott Eyman. *Flashback: A Brief History of Film*, 4th ed. Upper Saddle River, NJ: Prentice Hall, 2001.
http://www.Geocities.com/Athens/Oracle/6494/rearwindow1.htm

The Searchers *(1956)*

Directed by: John Ford
Screenplay by: Frank Nugent
Music by: Max Steiner
Cinematography by: Winston Hoch
Based on novel of same title by Alan LeMay

Cast:
John Wayne: Ethan Edwards
Jeffrey Hunter: Martin Pawley
Ward Bond: Reverend Captain Samuel Clayton
Vera Miles: Laurie Jorgensen

It is 1868 in Texas when Ethan Edwards, the ex-Confederate soldier portrayed by iconic Western star John Wayne, returns to the home of his brother, Aaron, his sister-in-law, Martha, and their three children. It is a moving homecoming, as the family wonders where Ethan has been for the three years that have passed since the Civil War ended and where his gold has come from. He is uneasily welcomed back into the family structure. In the opening scenes, Ethan is revealed as the classic Westerner: a Southerner who fought in the Civil War on the losing side who has no choice but to become a Westerner. Edwards is a "good bad man," who has been on the wrong side of the law for some time, presumably as a gunfighter. He is an outsider, a loner with no lover or best friend.

Ethan is undoubtedly Ford's most complex and problematic hero. This has much to do with Ethan's commitment to avenging his loved ones' murders. This desire for retribution appears to be fueled most intensely by his hatred of "the red man" and by his fear that his niece Debbie (Natalie Wood) has been defiled by Chief Scar (Henry Brandon). We would not regard Ethan as morally ambiguous, perhaps, if he were simply a killer bent on revenge for justified purposes, but his thirst for vengeance is mixed with blatant racism. Ford (along with screenwriter Frank S. Nugent) makes this clear throughout the film. While revenge against Chief Scar for the murders of Ethan's loved ones may earn our sympathy, his urge to destroy his niece if she has been sexually defiled and assimilated by "the Other" tends to raise major questions about his morality. Such questions lend psychological depth and complexity to the character of

Ethan Edwards. The viewer already feels troubled, in fact, by the very possibility that a character played by *John Wayne* is even contemplating such an action.

Questions for Thought

Is it possible to call Ethan Edwards a "hero," given his obsession with revenge and, more controversially, his underlying racism? Is he truly heroic only in certain parts of the movie? Is he closer to being a villain than a hero in certain scenes? Explain.

Ford's movie blends many themes that can be found in much of Ford's work: the story of the **American Old West**; the importance of **duty, tradition, community,** and **ritual**; the role of the "**outsider**" or "**outcast**" at odds with (or in exile from) conventional society; the opposition between **chaos and order,** between **wilderness** and **civilization**; the **need for violence** to maintain security and peace; and the personal **sacrifice** made by **heroes**.

The film also uses the beauty and sublimity of **Monument Valley** to great effect, as do many of Ford's westerns, including his landmark classic *Stagecoach* (1939). In many cases Ford, who was influenced by American Romantic painters of the Old West like Frederic Remington and Charles Russell, allows **landscape** to play a role in his films that is as significant as the role of the leading actor. As one Ford scholar tells us: "A new magnitude enters cinema with Monument Valley . . . Not bigger physically, like the ocean or sky, but bigger in feeling . . . Space becomes subjective; ideas become space . . . It's not simply a valley, but a valley turned into melodrama, like a consciousness expanding as it stares at the world's immensity . . ." (Gallagher).

The landscape and the hero are inseparable. In the relentless sun of the desert valley, the toughness and intractability of the one infuses the other. Ethan's constant roaming among the majestic rocks, in a tireless search for his captured niece, is in furious response to all that he has lost. His quest becomes a search for his lost soul. It is as if Ethan's passage over the contours and through the dangers of the external landscape mirrors the process of internal self-transformation that his search really becomes.

Questions

1. In which ways has Ethan changed over the course of the film? Has he truly become "more human"? If so, how so? Which scenes help to measure this change?

Think about his characterization. Ethan Edwards is the knowing Westerner who grew up in the wilderness and understands the terrain, its dangers, and its inhabitants. He is an expert about his enemy, the Indians, and he is a man of violence who lives by the use of his gun. Ethan is also at one with the landscape; he is ever impatient to be in it, on the move to somewhere. So fearless is Ethan that he never hesitates in his pursuit. He is cunning and cruel as he shoots buffalo in trying to scare off the winter food supply, or when he shoots out the eyes of a dead warrior to make his spirit wander forever. The pursuer becomes as frightening as the pursued, and just as vengeful.

2. The movie includes some brief scenes of rather corny slapstick humor and some scenes in which characters reveal **bigoted attitudes towards Native Americans** as well as **women**. Given your experience of watching the film, do you think that the director and screenwriter were being sexist and bigoted in certain scenes? Or do you think that the filmmakers were intentionally creating stereotypical characters and attitudes to provoke reflection on this kind of bigotry?

In 2007, the America Film Institute ranked *The Searchers* as the #12 Greatest Movie of All Time. In 2008 it was ranked #1 on the American Film Institute's list of the

10 Greatest Western Films of All Time. This Western classic has influenced many contemporary American filmmakers including Martin Scorsese, Steven Spielberg, George Lucas, and John Milius.

On Director John Ford

Ford is the only filmmaker to have won six Academy Awards, including two earned for creating WWII documentaries for the US Navy. He is known primarily as a director of westerns, though he also directed family dramas, historical epics, and romances. Ford made 136 diverse films over his long career, many of them classics. The greatest of moviemakers—including Orson Welles, Akira Kurosawa, Ingmar Bergman, Sidney Lumet, and Martin Scorsese—have acknowledged their enormous debt to Ford. In general, Ford's style of filmmaking depends primarily on images rather than dialogue. Daryl F. Zanuck, the legendary Hollywood producer, concluded in 1972, toward the end of his long life and career, that John Ford was "the best director in the history of motion pictures" because "his placement of the camera almost had the effect of making even good dialogue unnecessary or secondary" (Gallagher).

Other Classic Films by Ford

Stagecoach
How Green Was My Valley
She Wore a Yellow Ribbon

Young Mr. Lincoln
Fort Apache
The Man Who Shot Liberty Valance

The Grapes of Wrath
The Quiet Man

Works Cited

Gallagher, Tag. "Ford Till '47," www.sensesofcinema.com, accessed 9/04.

The Seventh Seal (1957)

(Swedish)

Directed by Ingmar Bergman

B&W, 96 minutes

Cast:
Max von Sydow: Antonius Block (The Knight)
Gunnar Bjornstrand: Jons (The Squire)
Nils Poppe: Jof, or Joseph (one of the players)
Bibi Andersson: Mia, or Mary (another player, Jof's wife)
Bengt Ekerot: Death
Ake Fridell: Blacksmith Plog
Inga Gill: Lisa
Maud Hansson: Tyan, the witch
Gunnel Lindblom: Girl
Erik Strandmark: Skat

Bergman began his film career as a screenwriter (his first script was for *Torment*, 1944), but he quickly advanced to direction with films such as *Crisis* (1945), *Three Strange Loves* (1949), and *The Naked Night* (1953). But it was *The Seventh Seal* that really catapulted Bergman into international fame and critical acclaim. In 1958, filmmaker and critic Jean-Luc Godard proclaimed in the journal *Cahier du Cinema* that Bergman was "'the most original auteur of the modern European cinema'" (qtd. in Ellis 299). "Auteur" usually refers to a director whose stylistic signature is imprinted on all aspects of the film. The term fits Bergman well, since he exerts tight control over every element of his films. Bergman wrote his own screenplays, specified the framing of every shot, and supervised the placement of every sound on the soundtrack and how it should be juxtaposed with the visual images. He also worked with a stock company of actors and technicians, so he was surrounded by people accustomed to recreating his artistic vision. Bergman's unique stylistic signature can certainly be seen in *The Seventh Seal*, which deserves to be considered one of the most visually striking works in all film history. Describe the shots you find to be most dramatic and memorable. What characterizes these images in terms of lighting, mise-en-scene, imagery, and so forth?

The son of a minister, Bergman was preoccupied with religious questions throughout his career as a filmmaker. In *The Seventh Seal*, he directly confronts these questions through the disillusioned Knight, who returns from the Crusades to find his homeland riddled with plague, self-flagellating religious fanatics, witch burnings, and fear and despair in general. Confronted by Death, who has come to claim him, the Knight buys himself one extra day by challenging Death to a game of chess, undertaken in several stages. The Knight seems to want two things in the little time he has left: he wants knowledge about God, and he wants to accomplish "one significant action." In particular, he wants to know if there really is a God, and if there is, why he allows such suffering and if he offers anything beyond death. Consider the Knight's adventures and conversations over the course of his remaining day on earth. Does he gain any knowledge? Does he manage to achieve one significant action? Does Bergman at least suggest an answer to the Knight's theological/philosophical questions?

Cinemania offers a somewhat patronizing review of this film, calling it "an unsubtle but engaging religious allegory." The allegorical elements of the film are clear, it is true: Death is personified, the action takes place in one day, the questions of the protagonist are bold-faced and universal. But does that make the film as a whole unsubtle? Are there subtle ideas presented here, even in the midst of the black-and-white allegory?

Consider how the Knight's experiences in this one day can be representative of the span of an entire life. The opening image of the Knight and Squire sprawled on the beach just beyond the waves, suggests that they just emerged from the sea, a kind of birth image. Their return to the vast expanse of sea at the end brings their lives full circle. In between birth and death, they witness great suffering, cruelty, and ignorance, but also a few moments of loveliness, grace, and forgiveness. Through it all the Knight struggles with his questions about God, but he can find no definitive answers and must face death, like everyone else, with no guarantees. Through his depiction of the Knight's last day, what does Bergman seem to be saying about the essential elements of the human condition?

Jof, Mia, and their baby Michael provide an interesting parallel and contrast to the Knight and Squire. As with Block and Jons, we watch Jof, Mia, and their baby wake and spend the day and weather the fearful night. What role do Jof and Mia play in the film? Who/What might they represent? How are they filmed in terms of lighting? How/why do their paths cross with the Knight? What is it that they are able to do for him? What is it that he is able to do for them? The quiet and lovely center of the film is the scene in which the players share wild strawberries and milk with the Knight, at dusk, while the baby sleeps and Jof plays the lute. In terms of action, nothing much happens in this scene, yet it is utterly essential to the film. Why?

The film begins with voices singing "Dies Irae," which literally means Day of Wrath or Day of Judgment, and is sometimes used in Latin masses for the dead. Then we hear a quotation from the Bible, *Revelation* 8:1-2, 6: "And when he had opened the seventh seal, there was silence in heaven about the space of half an hour. 2 And I saw the seven angels which stood before God: and to them were given seven trumpets. . . . 6 And the seven angels which had the seven trumpets prepared themselves to sound." The book of *Revelation* was written by John as a visionary account of Judgment Day. What connections can you draw between the quotation and the film? Discuss the penultimate image of the film: the silhouetted dance of death across the hillside. This shot, one of the most famous in the film, was entirely unplanned and spontaneous. What does it suggest about the nature of death? What emotions does it inspire?

Works Cited

Cinemania. Microsoft, 1996.

Ellis, Jack C. *A History of Film*, 4th ed. Boston: Allyn and Bacon, 1995.

Stagecoach *(1939)*

Cast:
John Wayne: the Ringo Kid
Claire Trevor: Dallas
John Carradine: Hatfield
Thomas Mitchell: Dr. Josiah Boone
Andy Devine: Buck
George Bancroft: Sheriff Curly Willcox

Winner of two Oscars: Best Supporting Actor (Mitchell) and Best Music Score.

On the Film

The year 1939 was remarkable for American cinema. It was the year of *Gone with the Wind, The Wizard of Oz, Wuthering Heights, Mr. Smith Goes to Washington,* and several other Hollywood classics. But 1939 was also a remarkable year for director John Ford. Between October 1938 and November 1939, he made four films "that together stand as the greatest collective achievement in the history of cinema": *Stagecoach, Young Mr. Lincoln, Drums Along the Mohawk, and The Grapes of Wrath.* (Ford 134)

While *Stagecoach* was edged out of winning a Best Picture Oscar by *Gone with the Wind*, it had audiences initially mesmerized by its detailed **character development** (rare for a western up until that time) and then standing and cheering during its intense action sequence near the end, one of the greatest chase scenes ever filmed (owing much to Ford's masterful use of rapid-fire editing or **montage** and also to the feats of legendary stuntman **Yakima Canutt**).

Stagecoach blends many themes that can be found in much of Ford's work: the importance of duty, tradition, community, and ritual; the "outsider" or "outcast" at odds with (or in exile from) conventional society; the opposition between **chaos and order,** between wilderness and civilization; the need for **violence** to maintain security and peace; **class consciousness;** the exercise of **freedom** within fated conditions that are beyond human control; and the personal **sacrifice** required by **heroism.**

The film also uses the majestic beauty of **Monument Valley** to great effect, as do many of Ford's later westerns, including his classic *The Searchers* (1956) as well as his "Calvary Trilogy" (*Fort Apache, She Wore a Yellow Ribbon*, and *Rio Grande*). As Ford scholar Tag Gallagher tells us:

> A new magnitude enters cinema with Monument Valley in
> *Stagecoach*. Not bigger physically, like the ocean or sky,
> but bigger in feeling . . . Space becomes subjective; ideas
> become space. Ideas are real . . . It's not simply a valley,
> but a valley turned into melodrama, like a consciousness
> expanding as it stares at the world's immensity . . .
>
> (Gallagher, "Ford Till '47")

For Ford, landscape plays a role in his films as if it were an actor doing a scene. In *Stagecoach*, each passenger is on his or her way through dangerous territory and unintentionally makes "a pilgrimage of **self discovery** and **redemption**" (Gallagher, "Ford Till '47"). But each passenger's odyssey is expressed as much by the vast spaces and eternal formations of the environment as by the fleeting details of the characters' words and gestures and actions.

As for the influence of *Stagecoach*, Ford biographer Joseph McBride tells us: "When Kenneth Tynan asked **Orson Welles** in 1967 which directors he most admired, Welles gave an oft-quoted response: "The old masters. By which I mean John Ford, John Ford, and John Ford." In other interviews, Welles elaborated: "John Ford was my teacher. My own style has nothing to do with his, but *Stagecoach* was my movie textbook. I ran it over forty times . . . I wanted to learn how to make movies, and that's such a classically perfect one . . ." (McBride 299–300)

Jack Ford (born Sean Martin Feeney in Cape Elizabeth, Maine, in 1894) acted in and assisted with his brother Francis's silent films from 1914 to 1917. He also played a brief role as a Ku Klux Klansman in **D. W. Griffith's** landmark film *Birth of a Nation*. He then began directing his own movies, many of them silent westerns starring the cowboy star **Harry Carey**.

While having been influenced by film pioneer **D. W. Griffith** as well as by his brother, Ford was most influenced by the legendary expressionist director Friedrich Wilhelm (F. W.) Murnau, who came to Hollywood from Germany after making the silent classics Nosferatu (1922) and *The Last Laugh* (1924). It was Murnau's classic Sunrise (1927) that prompted Ford to imitate the **expressionist style** of this master filmmaker, setting him on his own path to becoming a highly innovative director. It was Murnau who taught Ford that filmmaking could be art.

Ford's first big success was 1924's silent film *The Iron Horse*, an "epic" about the construction of the transcontinental railroad. After *The Iron Horse* in 1924, Ford made 3 *Bad Men*. But during the 1930s, westerns were no longer very popular, and Ford did not make another one until Stagecoach in 1939, when he brought the genre back to respectability.

Ford also won Best Director Oscars for *The Informer* (1935), *The Grapes of Wrath* (1940), *How Green Was My Valley* (1941), *The Battle of Midway* (1942), *December 7th* (1943), and *The Quiet Man* (1952). He died in 1973. (See the guide for The Searchers for more information on director John Ford)

Works Cited

Ford, Dan. *Pappy: The Life of John Ford*. NY: Da Capo Press, 1998.

Gallagher, Tag. "Ford Till '47." 2004. On-line. www.sensesofcinema.com Accessed 9/04.

Gallagher, Tag. *John Ford: The Man and His Films*. Berkeley: Univ. of California Press, 1986.

McBride, Joseph. *Searching for John Ford: A Life*. NY: St. Martin's Press, 2001.

Sunrise: A Song of Two Humans *(1927)*

Directed by: F.W. Murnau
Written by Carl Mayer, from a story by Herman Sudermann
Cinematography by: Charles Rosher and Karl Struss
Asst. Director: Hermann Bing
Titles: H.H. Caldwell
Art Direction: Rochus Gliese
Special Effects by: Frank Williams
Music by: Hugo Riesenfeld.

Cast:
George O'Brien: The Man
Janet Gaynor: The Wife
Margaret Livingston: The Woman from the City/The Vamp
Bodil Rosing: The Maid
J. Farrel MacDonald: The Photographer
Ralph Sipperly: The Barber
Jane Winton: The Manicure Girl

Sunrise is the first American and Hollywood-backed film of German director Friedrich Wilhelm Murnau, who was born in 1888 and died in the United States at the age of 42 just a week before the premiere of his last film, *Tabu*. After a successful movie-making career in Germany, with films like *Nosferatu: A Symphony of Horror* (1922, the chilling and tricky vampire movie) and *Faust* (1926), Murnau moved to Hollywood. *Sunrise* was a tremendous success, if not with the public, then with the film industry. It won several awards at the first Oscar ceremony, including Best Actress for Gaynor. It shared the best picture Academy with *Wings* (directed by William Wellman).

Murnau is one of the greatest of German directors from that early period in German Cinema, which had its roots in a very specific kind of theatrical presentation and movement. The years 1919–1924 represent a period of tremendous national instability in Germany—economic, social, political—but film scholars say it's also the great period of German silent cinema, beginning with the horror thriller *The Cabinet of Dr. Caligari* (Robert Wiene, 1919). Before this time there had been a German film industry, and official recognition of the importance of a national film culture often resulted in financial support by the government. German cinema gained international repute because of its amazingly high quality—film directors, like Fritz Lang, Ernst Lubitsch, and Murnau were artists. Many, like those just mentioned, after great celebrity in their own country would go on to Hollywood but with varying degrees of success. In Hollywood, some, because of the studio system's authority, eventually lost their own creative control. Murnau, for instance, signed a 4-year contract in 1925 (*Sunrise* was part of that contract) that he eventually broke to make his last film, Tabu.

Murnau's background is in art history—you might want to remember that when you watch *Sunrise* and think of how the director's clear interest and training in analyzing visual compositions affects his cinematic choices and design. Murnau also was a student of Max Reinhardt, the great German theater director, who worked in Reinhardt's Deutsches Theater, which was extremely popular and important before and after WWI. Reinhardt himself would relocate to the United States after the Nazis began to assume power in Germany.

Reinhardt's style was one of extreme theatricality—known for dramatic effects of light and shadow in particular. This effect becomes one that appears in so much of the work of these German moviemakers who delve into the psychological workings of the individual. They often emphasize man as a victim of forces from his secret and dark fantasies, his impulses and instincts, or, even a victim of the supernatural and the horrific. This struggle is between those Bad and Nasty forces and the Good and Innocent. When you watch *Sunrise*, think carefully about how Murnau divides characters and places into these camps. Who represents what? How do costumes, gesture, sets, and so forth help develop the archetypal battle? What kinds of redemptions does the director offer his characters—or is it kind of a done deal with no hope? Compare the sophistication of Murnau's didacticism with Chaplin's in *The Kid*.

So, Murnau, like Lang and so forth, belong to the film movement we call German Expressionism. It emerged after WWI, some say as a response to the social and political trauma of the Great War and as a prelude to Germany's acquiescence to Hitler. Stylistically directors create an extremely expressionistic effect with the stark and extreme lighting, unusual images, dramatic use of camera angles, and peculiar set design. Its subject matter focuses on characters' subjective emotions rather than on realism and/or a realistic rendering of actual factual experience. German Expressionists like Murnau exploit camera work, set design, costume, everything as much as they can to explore feelings and hidden desires way more than other directors do.

Murnau was especially notable for his very imaginative use of images, camera tricks, negative film, maskings, superimposed images and so forth. As you watch *Sunrise*, pay very careful attention to how the camera works—for instance, the shot when The Wife and The Man are on the streetcar is one of the most famous in film history. It's truly beautiful—Murnau loved to use a moving camera to help disclose and develop his characters' states of mind, their vacillations and desires. Think carefully about how important this moment is in the actual story of the film—how does the shot work as a transitional device? What does it transition from or help the viewer, as well as the characters, move between?

Sunrise actually had an original soundtrack, music by Hugo Riesenfeld. And, in 1927 the silent film industry was in its final stages. Sound pictures were already appearing. Think of the film's title—it's *Sunrise: A Song of Two Humans*. *Nosferatu*'s subtitle is *A Symphony of Horror*. So consider that, the actual music aside, Murnau wants you to "hear" the lyricism, to "listen" to the poetry in his visual techniques. How does this movie seem to be a "song" about a man and a woman, or about human beings? Follow the film's structure as carefully as you can—how many times do things happen twice and what's the difference in their repetitions? For instance, what importance do the bulrushes play? How many times does The Man enter The Wife's bedroom? How else would you explain the film as a kind of melodic structure—think of specific cinematic tricks and techniques in *Sunrise* for your evidence.

Because German Expressionism relies so much on the deeply psychological and emotional effects to be gained from playing with light and shadow, it's key that you watch Murnau's manipulation of dark and light areas. For instance, how does Murnau emphasize his story and his characters' inner lives, their souls so to speak, with shadows—how are those shadows symbolic? When does Murnau emphasize glittering and dancing lights whether in the natural world or in the metropolitan life of the city? How does he use mirrors as another source of light? As a view into the soul? What do those mirrors reflect and how do the reflections add to the unfolding of the plot?

Some film scholars point out that one of Murnau's great themes in his films, or at least in his films not lost to time, is a man's redemption by the self-sacrifice of a woman who loves him. How does the plot, the sequence of events in *Sunrise* develop this theme? How does Murnau show The Man's extreme passivity? For instance, in the scene with Margaret Livingstone, the seductress from the big, bad city, who is in control and how does the camera show that power? When does he use a moving camera and when does he not and how do the different uses emphasize female dominance and/or male helplessness?

What is the symbolism of water and the couple's journey across this body of water? Again, think of how Murnau repeats an image or an action but repeats it with a difference.

Murnau asks us to associate the urban life with a certain type—that Vamp. And yet, the city has lots more than just what she represents. How do the places the couple visit, the kinds of entertainments they enjoy, and the situations they "escape" in the city represent a kind of redemptive or rejuvenating progress? Why won't Murnau and *Sunrise*'s story just let them return home easily—why do we need the sudden complication of the storm?

Women's hair is always important in any kind of artistic representation—think of Janet Gaynor's appearance and how it changes through the film. The Wife is part of a pastoral world Murnau shows that The Man wants to escape. How does the film show that rural world as innocent, pure, simple? Is it desirable? How does he link The Wife to this simpler place?

Works Consulted

Collier, Jo Leslie. *From Wagner to Murnau: the Transposition of Romanticism from Stage to Screen*. Ann Arbor and London: UMI Research P, 1988.

Eisner, Lotte H. *Murnau*. London: Secker & Warburg, 1973.

Sunset Boulevard *(1950)*

Directed by Billy Wilder
Paramount Pictures, 110 minutes

Cast:

Gloria Swanson: Norma Desmond	**Playing Themselves:**
William Holden: Joe Gillis	**Buster Keaton, Cecil B. de Mille,**
Erich von Stroheim: Max	**Hedda Hopper, H. B. Warner,**
Nancy Olson: Betty Schaeffer	**Anna Q. Nilsson**

Sunset Boulevard was released in 1950, a year in which the Hollywood film industry found itself adjusting to the challenges of postwar America and shifts in its entertainment choices. The first network television broadcasts took place in 1941, but because of the war, broadcasts were severely curtailed, and television posed little threat to films as American's preferred that form of entertainment. During the economic boom that followed the war, however, Americans began purchasing television sets, and networks increased the number of broadcasting hours. In 1949, one million TVs were in American homes, a number that jumped to 10 million just two years later. Movie attendance dropped by 20 million in just one year, from 90 million in 1948 to 70 million in 1949.

At this moment, when the film industry was questioning its own survival, Billy Wilder's *Sunset Boulevard* opened Hollywood's closet and let the public see the skeletons: the overblown egos and ambition, and the clash between those who made films for profit's sake, and those who believed in it as an art. The film presents the struggling forces within the industry personified by three main characters: Joe Gillis, the scriptwriter who lost his dreams of making it big and now merely wants to survive; Betty Schaeffer, "one of those message kids," who believes that films should be original and meaningful; and Norma Desmond, the aging silent film star whose delusional hope in a "return" (she hates the word "comeback"), and lifestyle of isolated extravagance recalls the extremes of Hollywood indulgence and the power (for good or ill) of the star system.

Through the opposing characters and characteristics of Norma Desmond and Betty Schaeffer, *Sunset Boulevard* raises a number of issues about women, particularly ambitious women, in Hollywood. Does the film perpetuate or question the idea that a woman should desire to be the object of desire, pleasing to the eye and needing male approval? It is made clear that Norma's ambition to return to the screen is pure delusion, but is this a criticism of Norma's egoism or of the cruelty of Hollywood and the restrictive way it constructs desirability? (Norma, we learn, is now 50). The film also suggests that it is age and status that make Norma ridiculous as she tries to attract Joe Gillis, while the case would be quite different if the older, richer character were a male pursuing a female. Does the film seek to diminish the power that should accrue from age, wealth, and status if the ones with power are women? Betty decides to succeed off-screen only after she is told she can't act even with a straightened nose. How is her femininity and ambition portrayed? Which female character is more memorable?

Sunset Boulevard could be considered a compressed history of American film, beginning with the glory days of silent films in the 1920s. As the decade progressed, films became increasingly elaborate spectacles, vehicles for the famous directors and stars who made them. Erich von Stroheim, who plays Norma's butler Max, was one of the greatest directors of this period; his films, such as the epic *Greed* (1924), originally 10 hours long, sought to push the silent film form as far as it could go. Von Stroheim's directing career came to an abrupt end in 1928 when the star of his film *Queen Kelly*, Gloria Swanson, and producer Joseph Kennedy (father of the future president) abandoned the project mid-way to begin a sound film, which they felt would be commercially more viable. Playing the roles of a former silent film director and the star he helped mold, von Stroheim and Swanson were reprising roles they had played in real life. Von Stroheim went on to have a very successful career as an actor. Cecile B. de Mille, who plays himself in *Sunset*, was one of the few directors who successfully made the transition from silent to sound films.

The portrayal of Norma Desmond's home, "the kind crazy movie people built in the crazy 20s," draws on Gothic elements popular in the horror films of the 1930s, when films such as *Frankenstein* (1931) and *Dracula* (1931) were made. What ingredients of Gothic horror are used in *Sunset*, and to what effect? Of course, the screwball comedy was also developed in the 1930s, and we might see the relationship between Norma and Joe as an example of the role reversal that genre often portrays. Does *Sunset* fit the screwball genre?

The 1940s saw the development of *film noir*, literally "black film," which got its name from the dark, cynical viewpoint and shady dealings of the characters portrayed in these films. Wilder's *Double Indemnity* (1944), starring Barbara Stanwyck, is one of the first and very best of this genre. How does *Sunset* make use of film noir characteristics? What do they add to the overall feeling of the film and its portrayal of the current state of Hollywood?

Billy Wilder (1906–2002) was born in Galicia, now part of Poland. He got started in film as a writer for the German UFA studio in the 1920s, but left in 1933, when the Nazis came to power and took over UFA. Wilder, a Jew, could no longer find work in Germany and came to Hollywood. He made films in many different genres, including the World war II satire *Stalag* 17 (1953), and two comedies starring Marilyn Monroe: *Seven Year Itch* (1955) and *Some Like It Hot* (1959). His *Sabrina* (1954), starring Audrey Hepburn was remade in 1995. *The Apartment* (1960), and *One, Two, Three* (1961), were sharp critiques of American corporate culture and values.

The Third Man *(1949)*

Directed by: Carol Reed
Story by: Graham Greene and Alexander Korda
Screenplay by: Graham Greene
Original Music by: Anton Karas

Cast:
Joseph Cotten: Holly Martins
Orson Welles: Harry Lime
Alida Valli: Anna Schmidt
Trevor Howard: Major Calloway

Famous Scenes

Note the conversation atop the ferris wheel, the climactic chase through the Vienna sewers, and the final "anti-romantic" shot of Holly and Anna, leading into the end credits.

Acting

Joseph Cotten is an underrated actor who performed in some of the greatest of film classics including *Citizen Kane* and *The Magnificent Ambersons* (both directed by Orson Welles, who plays Harry Lime here), *Shadow of a Doubt* (directed by Alfred Hitchcock), and of course Reed's *The Third Man*.

Director

Look for Carol Reed's expressionistic use of tilted camera angles, giving an added sense of psychological disorientation and suspense and paranoia (influenced by German Expressionism). Critics praise *The Third Man* for its evocative atmosphere that reflects the mysteries of the human character. Note scenes where the atmosphere seems to mirror the mood of the characters or the complexities of the situation. Reed also directed such British film classics as *Odd Man Out, The Fallen Idol, Our Man in Havana,* and the musical *Oliver!* (based on the novel *Oliver Twist* by Charles Dickens).

Screenplay and Dialogue (listen for Greene's remarkably clever dialogue)

Graham Greene allegedly developed the entire story after penning one single opening sentence: "I had paid my last farewell to Harry a week ago, when his coffin was lowered into the frozen February ground, so that it was with incredulity that I saw him pass by, without a sign of recognition, amongst a host of strangers in the Strand."

So much of Greene's dialogue is memorable, and there are dozens of brilliant lines, but perhaps the most famous lines in the film were allegedly improvised by Welles in the legendary scene at the top of the ferris wheel, where Harry tells Holly: "**Don't be so** gloomy. After all, it's not that awful. Like the fella says, in Italy for 30 years under the Borgias they had warfare, terror, murder, and bloodshed, but they produced Michelangelo, Leonardo da Vinci, and the Renaissance. In Switzerland they had brotherly love - they had 500 years of democracy and peace—and what did that produce? The cuckoo clock."

Critical Commentary

"Listening to *The Third Man*" by John Doe (excerpted from www.criterion.com):

"As *The Third Man*'s opening credits roll, the vibrating strings of Anton Karas's zither slide you into an angular, dreamlike state. The instrument has this particularly sideways and elusive quality that is both playful and dark, sometimes making you turn your head sideways as well. Like the story unfolding, it has a casual velocity, like winding down the shadowy cobblestoned streets of postwar Vienna."

"The One and Only . . ." by Luc Sante, film scholar (taken from www.criterion.com):

"*The Third Man* (1949) is one of that handful of motion pictures (*Rashomon*, *Casablanca, The Searchers*) that have become archetypes—not merely a movie that would go on to influence myriad other movies but a construct that would lodge itself deep in the unconscious of an enormous number of people, including people who've never even seen the picture. The first time you see it, your experience is dotted with tiny shocks of recognition—lines and scenes and moments whose echoes have already made their way to you from intermediary sources. If you have already seen it, even a dozen or more times, the experience is like hearing a favorite piece of music—you can, as it were, sing along . . . *The Third Man* presents such a nonstop visual experience that it is easy to miss what a small, seat-of-the-pants picture it essentially was . . . It is a singular object, a fluke, a well-oiled machine, a time-capsule item, a novelty hit. There has never been another movie quite like it."

Works Cited

Doe, John. "Listening to *The Third Man*." www.criterion.com. 6/30/09.

Sante, Luc. "*The Third Man:* The One and Only . . ." www.criterion.com. 6/30/09.

Trouble in Paradise *(1932)*

Directed by Ernst Lubitsch

Cast:
Miriam Hopkins: Lily
Kay Francis: Madame Mariette Colet
Herbert Marshall: Gaston Monescu
Charles Ruggles: The Major
Edward Everett Horton: Francois Filiba
C. Aubrey Smith: Adolph J. Giron
Robert Greig: Jacques

German-born director Ernest Lubitsch began his career as a bit actor in Max Reinhardt's legendary Deutsches Theater in Berlin. Just eight years later, Lubitsch began directing his own films to critical acclaim (*Madame Du Barry*, 1919, and *Anna Boleyn*, 1920). These films reached American audiences, encouraging him to make the move to Hollywood in 1922. Lubitsch was soon signed to a three-year contract with Warner

Brothers Studios, where he polished his stylized brand of silent comedy with *The Marriage Circle* (1924), *Lady Windermere's Fan* (1925), and *So This is Paris* (1926). Lubitsch made his transition to sound by signing with Paramount, which was widely recognized as "the most European" studio in Hollywood (Gianetti 128). Here Lubitsch explored the possibilities of the new medium by directing a series of musical comedies, *The Love Parade* (1929), *Monte Carlo* (1930), and *The Smiling Lieutenant* (1931). Lubitsch collaborated with screenwriters Samson Raphaelson and Grover Jones to write his first non-musical comedy, *Trouble in Paradise* (1932).

Trouble in Paradise was adapted from a Hungarian play by Aladar Laszlo, *The Honest Finder*, which itself is based on the 1907 *Memoirs* of the famous Hungarian swindler Georges Manolescu (changed to Gaston Monsecu in the film). Adaptation was nothing new to Lubitsch; in fact, he preferred rehabilitating obscure European plays for use on the screen. As Scott Eyman explains, "Psychologically, it made more sense to him to fix what was broken than to build from the ground up" (189).

The famous opening scene of this film is a perfect example of what critics came to call the "Lubitsch touch," a staple of Lubitsch's middle period. The romance and whimsy of Venice is thoroughly undercut by the mundane work of a trash collector. Ephraim Katz defines the **Lubitsch touch** as a style "characterized by a parsimonious compression of ideas and situations into single shots or brief scenes that provided an ironic key to the characters and to the meaning of the entire film" (724). For Lubitsch, the setting was not merely a backdrop for action, but instead functioned as "a metaphor for the characters who inhabit [it]" (Eyman 194). Like Venice, the characters of *Trouble in Paradise* revel in their stunning facades, even as the filth piles up, threatening the fantasy. ("*It doesn't matter what you say, it doesn't matter how you look; it's how you smell.*")

Trouble in Paradise was released a year and a half before strict enforcement of the Hays Code began, which would have made a film focused on sexual innuendo, partner-swapping, and glamorized larceny an impossibility. Lubitsch regarded these plot details as essential to the articulation of "the tenuous nature of romantic relationships, and . . . the necessity of variation and some gentle mutual deceit to stave off lethargy and boredom" (Eyman 193). *Trouble in Paradise* was not able to escape the reach of the Hays Code for long. In 1935, the film was taken out of circulation and was not reinstated until 1968.

How does *Trouble in Paradise* expand on the conventions of the screwball comedy? Would you characterize the film as escapist? Does the film ever acknowledge the socio-economic circumstances of the day? How are these concerns treated in terms of the overall plot?

Film critic and historian Scott Eyman describes the characterization in *Trouble in Paradise*: "The characters' heartlessness is part of their charm. They may lie, but never to each other; unlike Giron, they're not hypocrites" (193). What do you think Eyman means by this assessment? Who is the protagonist of the film? Why do you think Lubitsch chose this character as his focus? How does the film justify the misdeeds of the protagonist? What does this justification say about the state of society? Can *Trouble in Paradise* be regarded as a form of social satire? (What is the "trouble" and what is "paradise"?)

Does it surprise you that *Trouble in Paradise* was found in violation of the Hays Code? How are the relations between the sexes articulated? Who has the upper hand in these romantic relationships? How is the upper-hand established and maintained throughout the course of the film? Is criminality sexualized in the film? How does

Lubitsch articulate the relationship between sex and crime?

Works Cited

Eyman, Scott. *Ernst Lubitsch: Laughter in Paradise*. New York: Simon & Schuster, 1993.

Gianetti, Louis and Scott Eyman. *Flashback*: *A Brief History of Film*, 4th ed. Upper Saddle River, NJ: Prentice Hall, 2001.

Katz, Ephraim. *The Film Encyclopedia*, 4th ed. New York: Harper Collins, 2001.